A Publication of the Egon-Sohmen-Foundation

Springer
Berlin
Heidelberg
New York
Barcelona
Budapest
Hong Kong
London
Milan
Paris
Singapore
Tokyo

Publications of the Egon-Sohmen-Foundation

Herbert Giersch (Ed.)
Towards a Market Economy in Central and Eastern Europe
1991, IX, 169 pp. ISBN 3-540-53922-0
Out of print

Herbert Giersch (Ed.)
Money, Trade, and Competition
1992, X, 305 pp. ISBN 3-540-55125-5

Herbert Giersch (Ed.)
Economic Progress and Environmental Concerns
1993, X, 302 pp. ISBN 3-540-56466-7
Out of print

Herbert Giersch (Ed.)
Economic Aspects of International Migration
1994, X, 275 pp. ISBN 3-540-57606-1
Out of print

Herbert Giersch (Ed.)
Urban Agglomeration and Economic Growth
1995, VIII, 278 pp. ISBN 3-540-58690-3

Herbert Giersch (Ed.)
Fighting Europe's Unemployment in the 1990s
1996, XIV, 240 pp. ISBN 3-540-60833-8

Herbert Giersch (Ed.)
Reforming the Welfare State
1997, X, 331 pp. ISBN 3-540-61493-1

Herbert Giersch (Ed.)
Privatization at the End of the Century
1997, X, 367 pp. ISBN 3-540-63027-9

Herbert Giersch (Ed.)

for the Egon-Sohmen-Foundation

Merits and Limits of Markets

With 1 Figure
and 6 Tables

 Springer

Prof. Dr. Herbert Giersch
Past President
Kiel Institute of World Economics
Düsternbrooker Weg 120
D-24105 Kiel

*This book was produced with financial support
from the Egon-Sohmen-Foundation*

ISBN 3-540-64446-6 Springer-Verlag Berlin Heidelberg New York

Library of Congress Cataloging-in-Publication Data
Merits and limits of markets / Herbert Giersch (ed.)
p. cm. -- (A publication of the Egon-Sohmen-Foundation)
Papers from the 9th Symposium of the Egon-Sohmen-Foundation held
in 1997 in Stamford, Connecticut.
Includes bibliographical references.
ISBBN 3-540-64446-6 (alk. paper)
1. Capitalism--Congresses. 2. Markets--Congresses.
3. Competition--Congresses. 4. Privatization--Congresses
5. Individualism--Congresses.
I. Giersch, Herbert. II. Series: Publications of the Egon-Sohmen-Foundation.
HB501.M618 1998 □ 330.12'2--dc21

Hardcover design: Erich Kirchner, Heidelberg
SPIN 10655548   42/2202-543210 - Printed on acid-free paper

Preface

The 1997 Symposium of the Egon-Sohmen-Foundation, which gave rise to this book, took place in the United States, on the East Coast between New York and New Haven, more precisely in Stamford (Conn.). The original choice had been a place close to Yale University, where Egon Sohmen taught economics from 1958 to 1960, subsequent to his period at MIT. But the hotel in New Haven was closed down by a new owner—to pass through a process of creative destruction.

Change of ownership—on a large scale and as a transition from public to private hands—had been the topic of the preceding Egon-Sohmen-Symposium (in Budapest in 1996) published under the heading: *Privatization at the End of the Century* (Springer-Verlag, 1997). Yet mere change of ownership, some of us at the Foundation felt in subsequent months, was too narrow a focus to properly deal with the movement under consideration: a transition of ownership together with a general move towards a competitive market system characterized by global openness, uncertainty, decentralized risk-bearing, and the increasing importance of information and innovation.

Moreover, the transfer of ownership from public to private hands also needs to be viewed in a wider context, given the many activities and functions that governments here and there have chosen to perform. Surely, there is an ample supply of good literature in the field of "public choice" which helps us to understand why governments expand and behave as they do. Sometimes, I even feel overwhelmed by all the apparent evidence for historical determinism. But is there really so little room left for the power of ideas? Was and is the intellectual discourse in the social sciences and in philosophy not sufficiently fruitful and innovative as to account for—or only make us better understand—some of the new developments we have recently observed in the bipolar tension between the individual and society?

Such were the questions that came to mind when we looked back at the Budapest conference and forward to a possible symposium in 1997. Suggestions from various quarters were received and considered as elements of a program that would show some coherence and still cover the most exciting topics in the vast area that has been—or could be— left to private entrepreneurship in both established and newly emerging markets. A provisional title was formulated to focus our efforts in searching for possible authors and participants; it read "The Merits of Markets: Critical Issues of the Open Society." For the title of the book we chose a version that is shorter and sounds less presumptuous.

The first section of this book, entitled "Individualism in a Social Context," contains the papers dealing with fundamental issues of an open society, such as self-interest, welfarism, and the evolution of moral norms and institutions. Communitarianism was included in the hope that their leading proponents would find time to attend the symposium to forcefully argue with us about the movement's views on funda- mental issues of social and economic policy. Our hopes turned out to be too optimistic. Nevertheless, we found an encouraging solution at the late stage. It can help us to bridge what appears to be an inter- disciplinary gap.

The second section focuses on "The Frontiers of Markets." The markets selected for discussion cover the arts, education, health and legal services. In dealing with these markets the authors in this section attempt to locate the markets' frontiers along the continua between pri- vate property and state property, between competition and monopoly, and between self-reliance and subsidization. It appears that what has been traditionally deemed the frontier between "public" and "private" in the supply of goods and services is actually quite blurred and has become more than questionable in the course of time. During the con- ference, not all of the relevant issues could be raised, and quite a few of them remained without a satisfactory answer. This makes me believe that there is wide scope for the research ambitions of young econo- mists in the tradition of what the Germans call *Ordnungspolitik* and what in the future may form part of a new brand of institutionalism.

The third section deals with "Normative Issues of Global Trade." We felt that these had to be included in the symposium because com- petitive capitalism has gained ground with the liberalization of trade in a process popularly referred to as "globalization." The papers in this section cover international competition policy, trade in "bads," and social protectionism. While it often happens that interest in a symposium's agenda markedly declines towards the end of the meeting, this did not occur at this symposium, since the papers on the last topic gave rise to an increasingly lively debate.

I feel encouraged to express my hope that the experiment of bringing together scholars from various fields and even disciplines will be followed up by others and that noneconomists will benefit from the interdisciplinary trade in ideas as much as I did from preparing and chairing this ninth symposium of the Egon-Sohmen-Foundation.

I am happy to express my thanks to all participants, foremost the authors but also those who sent their comments to the authors. I would also like to express my thanks to Uwe Siegmund for intensive discussions before and after the meeting and for his organizational skill, and to him and Regine Sohmen for their editorial assistance.

Herbert Giersch   February 1998

Contents

Part I
Individualism in a Social Context

Self-Interest, Communalism, Welfarism

Gary B. Madison

Et il est heureux pour les hommes d'être dans une situation où, pendant que leurs passions leur inspirent la pensée d'être méchants, ils ont pourtant intérêt de ne pas l'être.

—Montesquieu, *De l'esprit des lois*

I   The New Challenge Confronting Liberalism

Only a few years ago, consequent upon the collapse of that form of communalism known as Communism, the definitive triumph of liberal democracy was being widely heralded.[1] Today, people are not nearly so confident that liberal values are destined to win out on the world scene. Talk abounds of impending "culture wars" and "intercivilizational conflict" (see Huntington, 1996). The traditional liberal values of freedom and individuality, it is said, are not truly universal values, as liberals have always proclaimed; not only are they strictly Western in origin ("culturally relative"), they are also, or so it is claimed, irrelevant to, and perhaps even incompatible with, the traditional values of non-Western cultures (see Madison, 1995a). This new attack on liberalism is as widespread in the West as it is in other parts of the world,

---

[1] The classic of the genre is, of course, Fukuyama's *The End of History and the Last Man* (1992), based on his earlier article, "The End of History" (1989). As I use it, "communalism" is a generic term; various species of it are: communism, socialism, communitarianism (left- and right-wing), fascism, and ethnonationalism (tribalism).

most notably East Asia. In the West the attack on liberal values is associated with what has come to be known as "communitarianism," while in the East it is advanced under the banner of "Asian values." Let us focus on the latter for a moment.

"[T]he most potent challenge today to the prevailing conception of democracy and human rights comes from Asia," write the editors of the *Journal of Democracy* (Plattner and Diamond, 1997, p. 9). The "culture argument" advanced by those in Singapore, the People's Republic of China, Burma, and other Asian countries asserts, as Zbigniew Brzezinski puts it, that "It is only the West ... that has cooked up these ideas [of human rights, human freedom, and the primacy of the individual], institutionalized them, formalized them, and proclaimed them" (Brzezinski, 1997, p. 4). Places like Singapore and China, it is further insisted, are imbued with their own "Asian values," ones which are not only distinctively "Eastern" but which are in fact incompatible with the Western emphasis on the rights of the individual. In contrast to the socially corrosive "individualism" said to be rampant in the West, "Asian values," their defenders allege, accord priority to the collectivity over the individual—for the sake of promoting peace and stability, social harmony, and the general welfare. In announcing the need to curb civil and political liberties in the former British colony of Hong Kong, Tung Chee-hwa, the Beijing-appointed chief executive of this new Special Administration Region of China, states: "We need to renew our commitment to the traditional Chinese values," ones which, as he says, include "an emphasis on obligations rather than individual rights, and the willingness to sacrifice one's interest for the common good" (see Gargan, 1997).

How does it stand with this line of reasoning? It is of course patently obvious that appeals to nonliberal "Asian values" and a concomitant downplaying of civil and political liberties and individual rights serves all too well the authoritarian, antidemocratic propensities of certain regimes. Nonetheless, how does it stand with the argument itself? Is it indeed the case that, as Tung suggests, the pursuit of their own self-interest on the part of individuals is inimical to the common good? Is it necessary to choose between the individual and the collectivity? Must individual liberties be sacrificed or greatly restricted if "community spirit" is to prevail? Is a civil market economy based on the rights of the individual incompatible with social obligations and community spirit and hostile to the promotion of (to use a Chinese expression) "social ethics"?[2] I have no doubt that many of our Western communitarians would side with Mr. Tung and answer in the affirmative. I do not believe that any such incompatibility exists, however. Indeed, as I wish to argue in this paper, the pursuit of individual self-interest within the context of a civil market economy is in fact the surest means for promoting the general welfare or what the Chinese call *gongtong fuyu*, "common prosperity."

II Self-Interest Rightly Understood

The notion of self-interest is by no means unambiguous, nor is there any general agreement in our culture as to whether or not, on the whole, it is a good or bad thing (see Hirschman, 1989). In the popular mind, self-interest (and the pursuit thereof) is often equated, without further ado, with selfishness and is deemed to be morally reprehensible. Decent people, it is held, should be concerned with the good of their neighbors and the good of society, and not merely with their own private well-being. Among the tribe of professional economists, a quite different view tends to prevail. Like their fellow laypersons, many neoclassical economists equate self-interest with selfishness, but they differ from ordinary people with less theoretical sophistication by arguing that selfishness is what makes the world go round and is what, as a matter of fact, confers untold benefits on society, in a way that naïve altruism never could. This stance flows from the proclivity mainstream welfare economists have for constructing idealized abstractions which—their mathematical attractiveness notwithstanding—have precious little to do with the real world. *Homo economicus*—an entity with "given" preferences which seeks merely to "maximize" its "utilities"—is as much a theoretical construct as is the notion of "general equilibrium" itself, the most sacrosanct of neoclassical constructs, and, like the

---

[2] I prefer the term *civil market economy* to that of *free market economy*, since the former is more specific than the latter. A civil market economy is a free market economy operating within the context of a legal system spelling out property rights and with laws of contract, tort, bankruptcy, etc. A market economy could be free (in the sense of not being centrally planned) and yet be of a sort to discourage legitimate business and honest enterprise, a situation that tended to prevail in some Eastern countries after the collapse of communism.

latter, it is equally remote from the real world of economic dealings inhabited by flesh and blood, acting human beings.[3]

As ordinary people well know, however, people do sometimes act out of "selfless" motives, and altruism is not always a smoke screen for the pursuit of selfish interests. That, however, is not the crucial issue. What both the common person—who extols the virtues of altruism over selfishness—and the neoclassical economist—who defends self-ishness by pointing to its "altruistic" by-products—share in common is a tendency to equate *self-interest* with *selfishness*, and that is what is unfortunate. Despite their differences, both the ordinary person and the neoclassical economist ignore a crucial distinction effected by early modern, Enlightenment thinkers.

In contrast to earlier political theorists and to the older tradition of civic humanism (much appealed to by present-day communitarians), Enlightenment thinkers such as Kant, James Madison, and Adam Smith did not believe that citizens had to act out of "benevolence" (the self-sacrificing "civic virtue" of Renaissance civic republicanism) in order to be good citizens. What in their various ways each of these theorists was attempting to argue was that a decent regard for one's own interests (the "bettering of one's condition," as Smith would say) need not be hostile to or incompatible with the good of society as a whole. Indeed, what they were actually saying is that when people are allowed to operate within a system which respects their individual rights and which allows them to pursue the "good life" in their own individual ways (a "system of natural liberty," as Smith called it), they can, out of self-interest, pure and simple, be expected to respect and help maintain the political-economic order that guarantees them these rights and liberties, and in so doing they are helping to promote the rights and liberties of all others to achieve a good life for themselves. The net result is one of mutual benefit and social harmony. As we would say nowadays, a free or civil market economy is one which simultaneously promotes both individual rights and social justice. It is a "system" which, by reason of the way in which it naturally operates,

---

[3] For a critique of the notion of "equilibrium" and other theoretical constructs central to mainstream neoclassical economics from an Austrian School perspective, see Madison (1998, ch. 5). For a history of the notion of "equilibrium," a concept imported into economics from physics, see Mirowski (1989).

encourages not only personal initiative and creativity but also public-mindedness and civility ("social ethics").

Crucial to this argument is the distinction all of these thinkers drew between *self-interest* (self-love or self-esteem) and *selfishness* (self-centeredness or egoism). Adam Smith, for instance, insisted that the pursuit of self-interest, while certainly not a virtue in the old, moral-istic sense of the term (i.e., self-sacrifice or self-denial), is certainly no vice either (i.e., selfishness or avariciousness). What Smith and other Enlightenment thinkers were arguing is that the public good is actually best served, not when people act out of "benevolism" (as the Earl of Shaftesbury referred to it), but when the interactions between indi-viduals are regulated by enlightened self-interest or what Alexis de Tocqueville was later to call "self-interest rightly understood." What the famous metaphor of the invisible hand (Hegel referred to this as the "cunning of reason," and it is a notion equally central to Madison's and Kant's thinking) was meant to express is the idea that improve-ments to the public good and an increase in the "wealth of nations" is actually the "unintended consequence" of the free pursuit of individual self-interest.

In arguing in this way, Enlightenment thinkers furnished the first theoretical justification for free markets and the enterprise economy ("capitalism"). When present-day mainstream economists ignore the crucial distinction between self-interest and selfishness and when, by means of their theoretical constructs, they reduce human beings to egoistic calculating machines and market catallactics to impersonal "equilibrating" forces, they are—by undermining the earlier rational for it—doing a great disservice to the cause they claim to be defending ("free enterprise"). As economist Israel Kirzner remarks: "There are grounds for believing that the character of much contemporary [eco-nomic] theory, especially in its emphasis on equilibrium conditions, is not well-suited for the explication of the social function of the market" (Kirzner, 1993, p. 106). These economists are playing directly into the hands of their communalistic critics who are ever ready to pounce on any apparent moral shortcomings in their adversaries so as to appro-priate the moral high ground for themselves and who have no great difficulty convincing the general public that "capitalism," whatever its utilitarian merits (which they may well grant), is nevertheless and most unfortunately a rather grubby and immoral sort of thing; that it is a system based on greed and selfishness ("possessive individualism")—

and that it needs, accordingly, to be carefully hemmed in and rigorously controlled by an all-powerful and beneficent state, so as to insure
that the common good is adequately served.

To be sure, human beings being what they are, the pursuit of
individual self-interest *can* have some very pernicious effects. In the
absence of *enlightened* self-interest, the passions of greed, avarice, and
domination can readily take over, and, when they do, the pursuit of
self-interest easily tends towards the subversion of the common good.
Human nature cannot easily be changed (this is perhaps the most salient
lesson to be learned from the grandiose failure of the Soviet experiment in creating the new "socialist man"), but, as Madison argued, its
defects can be compensated for. If the pursuit of self-interest is to contribute to the general welfare—if it is to result in a situation of "mutual
gain"—it is necessary that the right to the pursuit of one's own self-
interest be *reciprocally* recognized by all the members of a civil society.
This is why Enlightenment thinkers laid immense stress on the need for
institutional arrangements designed (*"par la distribution des choses,"*
in Montesquieu's words) to channel the expression of self-interest in
socially beneficial directions. For markets to demonstrate their merits,
what is required is (in the words of the contemporary French political
thinker, Claude Lefort) "a mutual recognition of liberties, a mutual
protection of the ability to exercise them" (Lefort, 1986, p. 366). In
short, what is required are *constitutional arrangements* of a political
and economic sort—without which people will be constrained to
make shortsighted, socially harmful choices dictated by the Prisoner's
Dilemma (see Buchanan, 1989). A "wise social system," as constitutional economist Wilhelm Röpke said, is one designed to release
human creativity ("the full activity of man"), while simultaneously
curbing those "tigerish tendencies" that are equally part of human
nature (Röpke, [1951/1957] 1987, p. 15). Liberalism, both political and
economic, is synonymous with constitutionalism.

III   The Individual and the Community

If liberalism—the political philosophy committed to liberal democracy
and market economics—is successfully to meet the challenges posed by
the new wave of communitarianism, in both its Eastern and Western
variants, it must divest itself of the scientistic or physicalistic view of

the human being dominant in much of present-day neoclassical economics. Not only are individuals not computer-like, utility-maximizing calculating machines driven by selfishness, they are also not isolated monads with their own self-defined "preference schedules"; nor is society the mere aggregation of these supposedly self-propelled, atomistic individuals. Marx was altogether right when he stigmatized this "Robinson Crusoe" view of society, and present-day communitarianism is in a position to score not a few points when it ridicules the atomistic individualism so prevalent in much of the libertarian defense of the market. Liberals would do well in this regard to follow the lead of Frank H. Knight when several decades ago he mounted an attack on the atomistic individualism of traditional laissez-faireism and sought to emphasize the "institutional character" of the individual (see Knight, [1947] 1982, pp. 242–243). Calling into question "our individualistic ethics," this leading liberal economist insisted that "[h]uman nature is a cultural phenomenon, and the individual exists as the bearer of a culture."

If, as Aristotle said, the human being is a *zoon politikon*, a social-political animal, and if individuals exist as bearers of cultures, it follows that what we now call *human rights* are not "natural" rights, somehow inscribed in the biological makeup of human beings. Human rights (i.e., individual rights, *les droits de la personne*) are *social* or cultural through and through. They are, in fact, "social constructs." One can enjoy individual rights and be free to pursue one's own self-interest ("happiness," as Jefferson called it) only if one lives in a *particular kind of society*, viz., a society which accords special legal status to "the individual." "Individuality" is not a *fact of nature* (most "traditional" societies afford extremely limited scope to it); it is a *cultural value*, the hallmark of liberal societies (see Madison, 1995b).

By reason of its analytic or decompositive (*partes extra partes*) approach to social issues and its methodological commitment to atomistic individualism, neoclassical economics tends to ignore the issue of *social order* (what German constitutional economists refer to as *Ordnungspolitik*). The problem of social order was, however, a matter of prime concern to political economists when they first sought to work out the philosophical basis for what we now call "capitalism." The issue of social order is in fact the central concern of traditional political philosophy. The present Chinese government is altogether right to be concerned with the problems of order and stability in that country, given its historically demonstrated tendency to degenerate into anarchy in the absence of an imperial iron fist. In the pursuit of this thoroughly reasonable goal, the Beijing authorities are, however (as I shall indicate below), acting in an irresponsible and, in fact, counterproductive manner.

There are, basically, two ways, and two ways only, for attempting to resolve the problem of social order, i.e., for fending off anarchy and dealing with the problem of reconciling the interests of individuals with the interests of society as a whole. The first, and by far the most common throughout history, is that of repression of individual creativity and exuberance (a potential source of social disruption, as all governments, democratic and undemocratic alike, have always known and which, being governments, they have always feared and attempted to censor). Since, however, brute repression is generally not terribly effective for any great length of time (and is, in any event, fairly costly), the repression method generally calls to its aid the would-be persuasive powers of ideology (e.g., the divine right of kings, the dictatorship of the proletariat, or, at the minimum, a ritualistic system demanding nothing more than lip service on the part of the populace).

The second way of achieving social order and of reconciling the interests of the individual and those of society is of far more recent vintage and is still, in some sense, an experiment that has yet to demonstrate convincingly its worth (and which, in any event, probably goes against the grain of human nature). This is the way of *civil society* and the *civil market economy*. The distinctive feature of a civil society, in both its political and economic forms, is that order emerges from below, or *spontaneously*, and is sustained by means of free agreement ("consensus") among the members of the society in question (the reason being that it is in their own personal interests to do so).

Both civil society and the civil market economy are quintessential examples of what F.A. Hayek called "spontaneous orders," about which he wrote in great detail. As he described them, spontaneous orders are "self-organizing or self-generating systems" (Hayek, 1973, p. 37). The most noteworthy feature of spontaneous orders is that they are not, in the details of their arrangement, the result of conscious planning or design on the part of a select number of individuals but are, rather, the unintended outcome of actions on the part of a myriad of individuals (who, more often than not, are unknown to one another [see Ebeling, 1995]) pursuing their own self-interests within the context of a common set of abstract rules of an institutional sort. The purpose that the abstract rules (rules which may themselves have been deliberately designed) of a spontaneous order (such as a democratic polity or a market economy) is meant to serve is that of facilitating interactions between individuals and providing for their coordination or reconciliation, such that an *order* of a certain type (e.g., what, in the economic sphere, neoclassical economists refer to, misleadingly, as "equilibrium") is thereby generated. A spontaneous order, in whatever realm of society, is, as Hayek said, an "abstract order of the whole which does not aim at the achievement of known particular results but is preserved as a means for assisting in the pursuit of individual purposes," i.e., of individual self-interests (Hayek, 1976, pp. 5–6). Civil society, including within itself the civil market economy, is itself an all-inclusive, multidimensional spontaneous order.

What I wish to argue is that the spontaneous order that is civil society (actually, a kind of overarching order comprising many interrelated suborders) embodies within itself—by reason of its very makeup —a *social ethics*.

IV Private Interests and Social Ethics

One of the great lessons bequeathed to us by the liberal thinkers of the Enlightenment is that, when seeking to understand the relation between the individual and the collectivity, it is absolutely crucial to avoid the error committed by premodern political thinkers, viz., the error of thinking that in order to be a good citizen one must also be a good ("virtuous") person, in the moralistic sense of the term (see Madison, 1986, ch. 7). The domains of politics and morality are separate and distinct domains (as Machiavelli pointed out in his own rather provocative way, calculated, as it were, to *épater les moralistes*), and private morality is not a prerequisite for public morality, or social ethics. In any event, preaching morality to people has never been a very effective means of making them be good, law-abiding citizens. "This sort of discourse," as Montesquieu said, "convinces everybody, but changes nobody" (Montesquieu, [1734] 1949, p. 112). As eighteenth-century writers were wont to say, if you want to make people be good citizens, you should appeal to their interests, not their conscience. This bit of sound advice has always been ignored by socialists (communalists). Take, for instance, the case of China.

Under the instigation of President Jiang Zemin, the Beijing authorities are currently waging an all-out propagandistic battle against corruption and for moral rectitude, baptized "spiritual civilization." As
well they should, it might be thought, given the corruption that is
pandemic in China. In a document entitled "Resolutions of the CCP
Central Committee Regarding Important Questions on Promoting
Socialist Ethical and Cultural Progress" (CCP, 1996), the insider
group of the Chinese Communist Party (CCP) listed as follows some
of the social evils currently plaguing China:

The standard of moral conduct has been lowered in some spheres, and the practice
of worshipping money, seeking pleasure and individualism has grown, feudal
superstitions and such social vices as pornography, gambling and drug abuse have
resurfaced; production of shoddy and fake goods and fraud have become a social
scourge; the cultural cause has been seriously affected by negative factors; things
that damage the physical and mental health of youngsters and children have not
been eliminated despite repeated prohibitions; the phenomenon of corruption has
been spreading in some places, seriously damaging the work style of the Party and
the government; and a number of people have a weak concept of the state, and
waver and doubt the future of socialism. In assessing the situation confronting the
promotion of ethical and cultural progress, on no account should we neglect the
existence of these problems. (sec. I [2])

Accordingly, in an attempt to promote "socialist ethical and cultural
progress under the condition of expanding a socialist market economy
and opening up" and "with the ultimate goal of realizing communism," the Central Committee called for an all-out struggle against
"bourgeois liberalism" and "the worship of money, hedonism and
individualism" and for "spiritual civilization," i.e., "socialist ethics."
The means to be employed to this end were purely (and oppressively)
propagandistic and called for all "comrades working in ideological,
cultural and educational fields" to be "'soul engineers' [!] of humanity."

As the historical record of experiments in "socialist ethics" clearly
demonstrates, however, a moralizing, ideological, and propagandistic
approach to social ethics simply does not work. Exhorting people to be
"good" and to be self-sacrificing for the sake of the common interest
("the willingness to sacrifice one's interests for the common good," in
Tung Chee-hwa's words) may have some effect in the short run, but it
fails miserably over the longer term. People, being what they are, will
not indefinitely sacrifice their own interests for the sake of the "com-

munity" and to the never-ending task of "building socialism." The current campaign for "spiritual civilization" in China is an ideological throwback to the "emulate Lei Feng" campaign of the Maoist 1960s, and has just as much a chance of success as did that naïve and ineffective (but greatly disruptive) campaign. Propagandizing on the part of the CCP is as effective—or ineffective—a means of making people be "good" as is the moralizing of pulpit preachers in the West (who themselves tend eventually to be arrested for embezzlement or association with prostitutes).

The chief reason why the "spiritual civilization" campaign has, on its own, no chance of success is because the source of corruption in China is *systemic*, not personal—as if the Chinese people were intrinsically less prone to be "good" than morally upstanding Westerners. It is the social (economic-political) order (or "system") that currently prevails in China, i.e., "market-Leninism," that is the source of the much-lamented corruption—indeed, which is itself corrupt, and thus, not surprisingly, corruption-producing. The system is corrupt (in the technical sense of the term) in that it is an unstable mixture of two quite different, and altogether incompatible, "systems," viz., the market economy (based on individual interests) and the planned economy (based on bureaucratic "administration control"). A system that is corrupt, logically speaking, is bound to call forth behavior on the part of individuals which is morally corrupt.

You cannot, as Deng Xiaoping did with superlative results, give people the idea that "To get rich is glorious" and not expect the worst forms of corruption to result—if, that is, you do not at the same time create the institutional framework that will direct the pursuit of self-interest in socially beneficial directions. And this you do by providing constitutional guarantees of individual (human) rights and by instituting the rule of law, something which the Chinese government has yet failed to do. It is not moralizing or propagandizing of a communitarian nature that effectively discourages corruption and encourages civility; it is, rather, institutional arrangements of a civic, political, and economic sort. The only thing that will do the trick is, in short, the creation of civil society and the civil market economy. This is the only truly effective way of getting people to be "civil." In his prescription for the betterment of China—the unleashing of personal initiative—Deng was half right. But in failing to mount a thoroughgoing reform of the system itself (a failure due to Deng's not wishing to jeopardize the purely private interests of the party), Deng was also half wrong. And when one is dealing with structural or institutional arrangements, a 50/50 mixture of right and wrong is a surefire recipe for social chaos. In such a "mixed" situation, the wrong usually tends to prevail over the right. If, therefore, the battle against corruption in China is to be won, this can only be by resolutely following through with the logic of the Dengist reforms begun in 1978, in such a way as to bring into being what never before has existed in China, viz., a full-fledged civil society grounded in a recognition of individual rights and freedoms.[4]

The CCP Central Committee was altogether right in its assessment of the current situation in China. Corruption *is* rampant and a socially disruptive "individualism" reigns supreme. The Chinese ideologues were, however, wrong in their diagnosis of the situation and, accordingly, in their prescription for treating this social disease. The problem has to do not with personal morality *per se* but with the *logic of systems*. If the Chinese people are currently seeking to "maximize their "utilities" in a socially injurious fashion, it is because the current social order—a structurally unstable mixture of communalism and individualism—gives them strong incentives for doing so. State socialism has failed in China, but, as yet, it has not been systematically replaced with the only other system that is viable in a developed economy, that of the civil market economy. Although it goes without saying that democratization poses a serious threat to the current monopolization of power on the part of the CCP, it is clearly in the long-term interests of the CCP (i.e., its very survival as a party) that it carry through with the political reforms that are required by the logic of modernization. Failure to do so would more than likely entail its suffering the same fate as the Qing dynasty and its going the way of the now extinct race of Manchus.

The important thing to note in this regard is that, unlike a socialist economy, a market economy possesses, as it were, built-in mechanisms ("incentives") which call forth civility and socially ethical behavior on the part of individuals—and that in a thoroughly *spontaneous*, non-coercive (and nonideological) fashion. The civil market economy is not

---

[4] For an excellent historical survey of the economic reforms undertaken in China since 1978 and an analysis of how these liberalizing reforms have created tensions tending to erode the conceptual hegemony of the regime's official ideology, see Chen (1995).

just an immensely effective way of creating wealth; it is also, though this is often overlooked, the best means yet devised for generating socially ethical behavior—*les moeurs douces*, as Montesquieu would say. As that staunch defender of "capitalism," Benjamin A. Rogge, once remarked:

I attach relatively little importance to the demonstrated efficiency of the free-market system in promoting economic growth, in raising levels of living. In fact, my central thesis is that *the most important part of the case for economic freedom is not its vaunted efficiency as a system for organizing resources, not its dramatic success in promoting economic growth, but rather its consistency with certain fundamental moral principles of life itself*.... [T]he significance I attach to those moral principles would lead me to prefer the free enterprise system even if it were demonstrably less efficient than alternative systems, even if it were to produce a *slower* rate of economic growth than systems of central direction and control. (Rogge, 1979, pp. 40–41; emphasis in original)

Not least among the merits of the market is the morality of the market. The ethical benefits of "democratic capitalism" are one of the overriding themes in the well-known work of Michael Novak, a resident scholar at the American Enterprise Institute, and accordingly I will not pursue the issue at any great length here (see, in particular, Novak, 1982, 1993). One of the main points that Novak makes is that a business corporation operating within a market economy not only has moral responsibilities but that, more important still, these responsibilities are "*internal* to it, which must be met simply for it to be a success in doing what it was founded to do" (Novak, 1996, p. 138; emphasis mine). The market economy operating under the rule of law, it could truly be said, is itself a form of institutionalized ethics. Or as Novak succinctly puts it: "The business corporation is in its essence a moral institution. It imposes some moral obligations that are inherent in its own ends, structure, and modes of operation" (1996, p. 158).

By reason of the very way the "system" works, a civil market economy provides incentives (of a structural—not psychological—nature) for people to be "virtuous" in their economic dealings with one another— and, conversely, such an economy ruthlessly punishes those who violate the ethical imperatives of the system. In a civil market economy, it is in peoples' own self-interest to be "good." As Novak says, "Too many analysts neglect a basic point: simply to succeed in business imposes remarkable moral responsibilities" (1996, p. 135). The *ethos* or way of life of democratic capitalism is the diametrical opposite of the uncivil "culture of violence" that prevailed in Mao's communalist China (see Mirsky, 1994). It amounts in fact to a kind of public morality. This is a properly *social* (as opposed to a personal) morality, and it is located not in the "good intentions" of individuals but rather in the rule-governed, social, and institutionally structured *practices* of the market economy.

For civic virtue to prevail, it is not necessary, as Tocqueville said in his reflections on constitutional democracy in America, that people set their self-interest aside; all that is required is that they be free to act out of "calculated personal interest." As a general rule, one's interests are best served by cooperating with others, and the cooperation of others is most likely to be secured when one respects the right of these others to pursue their own interests. The chief characteristic of a civil market economy, i.e., an economic order based on "calculated personal interest," is that of *reciprocity* and mutual *respect*. As Knight said, "The market rests on the ethical principle of mutuality, with each party respecting the equal freedom and rights of others" (Knight, [1947] 1982, p. 449). A civil market economy is characterized less by *competition* (in the dog-eat-dog, cut-throat sense of the term) than it is by enlightened *cooperation*. In the words of H.B. Acton:

Under this arrangement [the market economy] each party, in order to help himself, has to help the other, or, to put it another way, in helping the other, helps himself as well. There is no call for devotion to the community as a whole, no self-sacrifice or self-immolation.... [I]n taking part in this activity an individual does not make himself a burden on others but pays for what he gets with the product of his own efforts. Self-help is not helping oneself to what others have but cooperating in a system of mutual aid. (Acton, [1970] 1993, p. 17)

It is enlightened self-interest, not socialist, communitarian "solidarity," that produces "the best of all possible worlds." "Interest rules the world," eighteenth-century writers were fond of saying. Unfortunately, this is not quite true, at least as far as *enlightened* self-interest is concerned. In the absence of constitutional guarantees of individual rights, the pursuit of self-interest is, as often as not, inimical to the general welfare. And this is a situation that now, when the triumph of liberalism is still in doubt, prevails throughout much of the world. Thus, if in the emerging global economy more and more people were to be made democratically free to pursue their own self-interests under the rule of law—which would ensure that they would do so in a spirit of respect for the rights of all others to do likewise, with mutually beneficial results—this world would surely be a much better and more humane place.

V   To Promote the General Welfare

Political-moral philosophers have traditionally focused their attention on two fundamental questions: "What is the good life?" and "What is the good society?" These two questions—the personal and the social— are intimately related if it is indeed the case that individuals are social beings through and through and cannot realize their full potentialities except to the degree that they live in a society which has as its *raison d'être* the promotion of the welfare of the individuals who comprise it. The fundamental premise of a liberal society is that the state or polity should be so ordered that individuals enjoy the maximum freedom— consistent with the equal freedom of all and the demands of social order—to pursue their own interests. What this means is that the over- riding function of the liberal state is not only to protect its citizens from harm (police protection, national defense); it means also, and equally well, that it is the function of the liberal state to provide the "infrastructure" that is required if individuals are indeed to be free to pursue their own interests. It is, as Lincoln said, a function of the state to do whatever people need to have done, but which they "can not do, *at all*, or can not, *so well do*, for themselves—in their separate, and individual capacities" (Lincoln, [1854] 1989). This is the reason why the Preamble to the Madisonian Constitution of 1787 lists as its pur- pose, along with providing for the "common defense," the promotion of "the general Welfare."

The "father" of modern "capitalism," Adam Smith, also stressed the need for the state to provide the "public goods" that are required by any decent civil society. Public goods are those things that are ben- eficial to the people and the nation as a whole (such as good roads and control of pollution) but which, it is supposed, would not be provided, or provided in sufficient quantity, if government did not intervene in one way or another to do so. The public goods that Smith alluded to are mainly of an infrastructural nature and "are chiefly those for facil- itating the commerce of the society, and those for promoting the instruction of the people" (Smith, [1776] 1979, vol. 2, p. 723). In the new, postmodern, global economy that is now emerging, a nation's well-being ("wealth") is a function of its ability to compete in the global economy, and this is a function above all of the "human capital" at that society's disposal (see Drucker, 1993). Education—the production of "knowledge workers"—is the supremely important public good in any society that would seek to maintain its economic "edge" in the global economy. The general well-being of all the members of society, in both educational and health-care terms, is, or should be, a matter of concern to each and every individual. One of the beneficial spin-offs of globalization is that the more global the world's economy becomes, the more the interests of the individual and those of society as a whole in any particular society are indissolubly linked. This is because the more the poorer members of society are able to become productive economic agents, the more that society as a whole benefits in terms of enhanced competitiveness. It is thus in the mutual interest of all citizens of a civil society that the state, various subsidiary levels of government, and private, volunteer organizations should strive to promote the well-being of all the members of society, the poorer ones in particular.

Herein lies the rationale for what has come to be called "safety net" welfare. Unlike welfarism of the communalist or redistributionist sort, which operates under the assumption that people have a "right" to live indefinitely at other people's expense, safety net welfare is fully consistent with the liberal principle that tax revenues (the confiscation of private property by the state) should not be used to promote the individual interests of some at the expense of the interests of others, but may nevertheless legitimately be used as a supplement to the workings of the market, with the aim of aiding those who, in the short run, are not in a position to benefit from or to participate in market-generated prosperity. Transforming the indigent into productive citizens is a public good which, being in the general interest, serves the interests of all. The goal of welfare of this sort is precisely that of minimizing the chronic dependence on the state that is the result (and, indeed, the bureaucratic goal) of redistributionist welfare.

VI The General Welfare versus the Welfare State

In all discussions of welfare, critical attention should be focused primarily not on the extent of welfare measures (i.e., the financial outlay involved in pursuing them) but on the *form* that welfare spending takes, as well as the *purpose* welfare is intended to serve. This is why the creators of the original German Social Market Economy insisted that government intervention should, wherever possible, be *marktkonform*, i.e., should not seek to displace market mechanisms but, on the contrary, should as much as possible operate in and through them (as when the state provides vouchers for certain public services, such as education). The purpose of welfare, properly conceived, is to enable people to no longer have any need for it. A good welfare system is one which cancels out the need for it (as much as this is possible).

I stated above that the free market economy and the planned economy are logically incompatible. The same is true of the liberal state and the welfare state. They are incompatible because they rest on two fundamentally different, mutually exclusive premises. The former is premised on the belief that individuals, being autonomous moral agents, are the best judges of their own interests—and should, accordingly, be allowed the maximum of freedom to pursue them as best they see fit (with, when necessary, enabling assistance from the state); the second, being a form of bureaucratic communalism, operates on the assumption that it is the function of the state to determine what people's real needs are and how best directly to satisfy these needs.

One of the features of state-welfarism most worthy of note is that it is fundamentally *disabling*, in a number of ways. It is politically disabling in that it transforms free citizens into dependent clients. This has the unfortunate effect that it creates a "constituency" which is sure to demand ever more benefits, and this in turn calls forth an ever more extensive and powerful bureaucratic government. The attempt to create a "just society" by means of coercive legislation serves to make the beneficiaries of government handouts increasingly dependent on the government for their continued well-being and contributes directly to the weakening of civic spirit and active citizenship so bemoaned by communitarians. State welfarism is morally disabling as well. The "moral hazards" endemic to welfarism have been amply documented in recent years (see, for instance, Murray, 1994). It suffices in this context to note that the greatest of these moral hazards is the hazard that welfarism poses to morality itself, i.e., to the very notion of individual *autonomy* and *responsibility*, the basis (as Kant well knew) of any genuine ethics.

Not only is state welfare disabling, it is also corrupting. The sad fact of the matter is that when people come to believe that it is the function of government to guarantee them a *right* to whatever they desire (e.g., a certain standard of living, the "good life"—the right not just to "the pursuit of happiness" but to the actual possession of "happiness"), it is inevitable that individuals organized into special interest groups (what Madison called "factions") should compete among themselves for these special, state-conferred favors. It is inevitable that, as John Adams, one of the American founding fathers, said, we should then witness "a scramble for the loaves and fishes," a reversion from civility to a kind of Hobbesian *bellum omnia contra omnes*. The fact of the matter is that welfarism does not produce that which alone might conceivably justify it, viz., social harmony. For the more "entitlements" the welfare state hands out, the more the demand for them increases (the so-called ratchet effect), and the more citizen is pitted against citizen in a relentless battle for larger pieces of what tends to become a shrinking pie.

These arguments against welfarism are of a moral nature, but even if one were to assess welfarism in purely utilitarian terms, it would have to be deemed a dismal failure. It has now been clearly demonstrated that while state-welfare spending has increased dramatically over the last few decades—to the point of producing a serious fiscal crisis —social conditions have been worsening. The story of bureaucratic welfarism has increasingly been one of rising inputs and falling outputs. It has become obvious that governments can no longer hope to micromanage the affairs of their citizens so as to insure a "good life" for everyone regardless of what they choose to do, or not to do, for themselves. The old bureaucratic ideal of the modern welfare state dating back to that great nation-state builder, Prussia's Otto von Bismarck, has now proven to be a bankrupt form of bureaucratic-technocratic governance ill-suited to the new technological realities of the global market—as outdated a notion as is, in a world of ever freer trade, the "sovereign" nation-state itself. What we currently stand in need of is a new social paradigm. What, in short, the new postmodern times call for is a replacement of the "dependency culture" by an "enterprise culture." The welfare state is as morally—and technologically—bankrupt as is, after over one hundred years of failed attempts at social engineering, socialism itself.

The social evils of the traditional welfare state have been compounded in recent years by the emergence of a group-based, "identity politics" form of welfarism. What this form of welfarism is superbly

designed to promote is not social cooperation ("cooperation in anonymity"—social solidarity) but social strife, a ruthless competition for
a limited supply of public goods on the part of an ever-increasing
number of officially sponsored "minority" groups. Dividing society up
into "designated minorities" (a form of social "balkanization") as a
means for assigning benefits serves above all the interests of the welfare
bureaucracy. The more the public welfare is supposedly served in this
way, the more the bureaucracy benefits, and the more a spiraling circle
of a truly vicious sort is solidly implanted in the public realm.

VII "Living in Interesting Times"

One of the maladies of Western societies that communitarians have
assigned themselves the mission of exposing and combating is the
reputed decline in civic spirit and an increase in "consumerism" and
rampant "individualism." There can be no doubt that the communitarians have their finger on a real problem, even though they are likely
exaggerating the magnitude of the problem. Actually, given what was
just said about how state welfarism induces corruption in the body
politic, the social situation in the West has some interesting affinities
with that in China. Corruption is a real problem in both instances.
And in both cases the corruption is due to similar causes, of a structural or institutional nature. The situations in East and West are
actually much the same, and the causes are much the same, although
they parallel one another in, as it were, a structurally obverse fashion.
Let me explain.

In a country such as China, the breakdown of social order and
social ethics is due to a (systemic) failure to move sufficiently fast from
a socialist-communalist regime to a liberal-democratic regime, i.e., to a
full-fledged recognition of individual rights and the construction of a
full-fledged civil society. In the West, the breakdown in civility is due
to a similar, if opposite, move, a move away from the liberal state
towards the welfare state (a move that has been underway for several
decades). Contrary to what the communitarians allege, the much-
commented-upon weakening of civic spirit in Western societies is not,
I submit, a result of the liberal emphasis on individual rights.[5] It is,

---

[5] In regard to the communitarian critique of "rights-based" liberalism, see, for
instance, Glendon (1991), Beiner (1992), and Etzioni (1993, 1995).

rather, a result of a serious (communalist) misinterpretation of the nature of these rights. This has had as its result a serious weakening of them. The purported rise in incivility is, in a word, a result of the transformation of the liberal notion of civil society into the communalist notion of the welfare state.

The hallmark of the welfare state is its tendency increasingly to substitute the notion of group rights ("entitlements") for the traditional liberal notion of individual rights ("immunities"). What this amounts to, in political economic terms, is a corruption of "systems." As such, it must inevitably, when the logic of things works itself out, result in social corruption. Civic spirit must inevitably atrophy when government (the welfare state) assumes the role of "over-parent" (in the words of L.T. Hobhouse) to its citizenry and conceives of its chief function being that of directly satisfying peoples' "needs." By making everyone's personal interest increasingly a matter of political allocation, welfarism results in the *politicization* of society, which in turn results in an increase in the authority of the state and a concomitant impoverishment of the body politic and a weakening of the autonomous formations of civil society—*les forces vives de la nation.* For the stronger and more encompassing the state becomes, the weaker civil society necessarily must become (the omnipotent communalist state in imperial China representing perhaps the greatest degree of imbalance in this regard). As the Marxists would say, welfarism bears within itself a "contradiction." Setting out to improve the lot of individuals, it leads, by way of one of those ironic twists of fortune so prevalent in human history, to the subversion of the very thing—the public good—it was supposedly designed to promote. The public is indeed ill-served when, as that outspoken nineteenth-century critic of communalism, Frédéric Bastiat, said, "everybody tries to live at the expense of everybody else." The welfarist pursuit of public morality results in a decidedly immoral state of affairs and is a fine example of what Marx called "false consciousness." Welfarism is the *reductio ad absurdum* of human rights and individual interests wrongly understood.[6]

---

[6] It is ironic that communitarians who criticize (individualist) rights-based liberalism and defend the welfare state should appeal to the supposed right of the *individual* to government support (viewing this as an intrinsic right, as it were, of individuals purely as such), whereas liberalism justifies welfare to the degree only that it contributes to the *common* good.

At the beginning of this paper I alluded to the threat posed by the advocates of "Asian values" to universalist claims with respect to the traditional liberal values of freedom and individuality. As if in reaction to this threat, there are those in the West who would have us believe that an increasingly prosperous China is bound to seriously endanger Western interests (see Bernstein and Munro, 1997). To be sure, there is much in present-day China that should rightly be a matter of serious concern. But if one looks to the structural dynamics of China's ongoing reforms, the situation need not appear quite so grim. Sinologist Lucien Pye writes:

It could be that no people have ever outdone the Chinese in ascribing moral virtues to the state or in deprecating the worth of the individual.... At the core of Chinese ethics and morality there has always been the ideal of depressing self-interest and glorifying self-sacrifice for the collectivity.... Yet what is significant today is that the decline in the legitimacy of the Beijing regime is being accompanied by ... a marked increase in people seeking individual freedom. (Pye, 1996, pp. 16–18)

In what is beginning to appear to be one of the supreme ironies of history, while China is discovering the merits of the market and the open society and is advancing in the direction of civil society (albeit in a hesitant and restrained manner), the West, under the spell of welfarism and "groupism" (as the Chinese call it), seems almost to be moving in the opposite direction. The corruption that now seriously threatens civil society in Western democracies is a direct result of the communalist elements that have been introduced into them by state welfarism; this is the very same corruption from which China is now struggling mightily to escape. A curious state of affairs, to say the least.

The Chinese have a saying: "May you live in interesting times." To say this to people is not particularly to wish them well, since in China what historians would call "interesting times" have traditionally been those interdynastic periods marked by Hobbesian strife and civil disorder. In both China and the Western world, we can surely look forward to some "interesting times." Nothing guarantees that the leaders in Beijing will perceive wherein their true self-interests lie and that, consequently, developments there will not, because of this shortsightedness, spin out of control. Similarly, nothing guarantees that in the West, a hundred years of failed socialism notwithstanding, there will not be a renewed upsurge in the destructionistic passions of the communalist utopianism that has produced so many disasters in the past.

Perhaps, though, liberalism will triumph after all. Perhaps, thanks to the new global economy, the hopes and expectations of Enlightenment thinkers like Montesquieu who placed their faith in "commercial" democracy and the merit of markets will be vindicated. "Commerce cures destructive prejudices," Montesquieu wrote, "and it is an almost general rule that everywhere there are gentle mores [*des moeurs douces,* i.e., what eighteenth-century thinkers called *civilisation*], there is commerce and that everywhere there is commerce, there are gentle mores" (Montesquieu, [1734] 1989, XX, 2). Not only is getting rich "glorious," as Deng said, the pursuit of self-interest, when channeled by the appropriate liberal institutions, serves to promote a social ethics of civility and peaceful coexistence.

VIII   Conclusion

If our Enlightenment thinkers were right, people will always pursue their own self-interest, however they perceive it. They will do so in an especially perverse way—in a way that is inimical to the common good—in a welfare state. In such a state, benefits ("entitlements") can be had without economically productive work on the part of enterprising individuals, all that is required being political agitation on the part of group-based interest groups (lobbying that, as in Canada, is often funded by the welfarist government itself), with the result that benefits are arbitrarily conferred on some individuals at the expense of others. Given the incentives ("moral hazards") peculiar to state-welfarism, this spontaneous behavior on peoples' part has its own "unintended consequences" and results in a "spontaneous order" which is, in fact, social disorder, the corruption of the republic or commonwealth itself (or, as Tocqueville would say, of the common weal). When all is said and done, an outcome such as this is in no one's real interest. Everyone has a personal stake in the commonwealth (as Hobbes vividly showed). It is therefore in the interest of everyone, if they also wish to avoid living under a Hobbesian, despotic sovereign, that everyone pursue their self-interests in a manner that redounds (in a spontaneous, noncoercive way) to the interests of everyone else.

The "good life" is never to be had in a state which does not subscribe to the old liberal principle of the "equal liberty of all" and
which does not do its best to protect the rights and freedoms of all
its citizens. One of the central tasks of sound political economy should
be that of educating people as to where their true self-interests lie. The
good of society—the general welfare—and the good of individuals—the
freedom to pursue one's own self-interest—are inseparable and are mutually reinforcing, contributing in a synergetic manner to the achievement of both the good state and the good life. Therein lies the true
meaning of that so often misused word: *solidarity*. Solidarity, rightly
understood, does not mean stepping in and relieving people of the
responsibility that, as autonomous moral agents, they have for their
own well-being. It refers, rather, to a situation of mutual respect and
mutual benefit wherein the exercise of one's own freedom serves to
promote the equal freedom of all—"a mutual recognition of liberties, a
mutual protection of the ability to exercise them," in Claude Lefort's
words (1986, p. 366). Or, as that eighteenth-century thinker, Le Mercier
de la Rivière, said, speaking of the market economy: "It is of the
essence of [this] order that the practical intent of each individual can
never be separated from the common interest of all" (cited in Acton,
[1970] 1993, p. 45). This is solidarity as, in its struggle for civil society
over communalism, *Solidarnosc* understood it.

Bibliography

Acton, H.B. [1970] 1993. *The Morals of Markets and Related Essays*. Indianapolis:
    Liberty Fund.
Beiner, R. 1992. *What's the Matter with Liberalism*. Berkeley: University of
    California Press.
Bernstein, R., and R.H. Munro. 1997. *The Coming Conflict with China*. New
    York: Knopf.
Brzezinski, Z. 1997. "The New Challenges to Human Rights." *Journal of Democ-
    racy* 8(2):3–7.
Buchanan, J. 1989. "Constitutional Economics." In: J. Eatwell et al. (eds.), *The
    Invisible Hand (The New Palgrave)*, pp. 79–87. New York: Norton.
Chen, F. 1995. *Economic Transition and Political Legitimacy in Post-Mao China*.
    Albany: State University of New York Press.
CCP (Chinese Communist Party). 1996. "Resolution of the CCP Central Com-
    mittee Regarding Important Questions on Promoting Socialist Ethical and

Cultural Progress." Adopted at the Sixth Plenum of the 14th CCP Central Committee on October 10. *Beijing Review* (on-line).

Drucker, P. 1993. *The Post-Capitalist Society*. New York: Harper Business.

Ebeling, R.M. 1995. "Cooperation in Anonymity." In: D.L. Prychitko (ed.), *Individuals, Institutions, Interpretations: Hermeneutics Applied to Economics*, pp. 81–92. Aldershot: Avery.

Etzioni, A. 1993. *The Spirit of Community: The Reinvention of American Society*. New York: Simon and Schuster.

Etzioni, A. 1995. *Rights and the Common Good: The Communitarian Perspective*. New York: St. Martin's.

Fukuyama, F. 1989. "The End of History?" *The National Interest* (Summer):3–18.

Fukuyama, F. 1992. *The End of History and the Last Man*. New York: Free Press.

Gargan, E.A. 1997. "If Opportunity Knocks, They'll Be Home." *New York Times*, April 27.

Glendon, M.A. 1991. *Rights Talk: The Impoverishment of Political Discourse*. New York: Free Press.

Hayek, F.A. 1973. *Law, Legislation and Liberty*. Vol. 1: *Rules and Order*. Chicago: University of Chicago Press.

Hayek, F.A. 1976. *Law, Legislation and Liberty*. Vol. 2: *The Political Order of a Free People*. Chicago: University of Chicago Press.

Hirschman, A.O. 1989. "Interests." In: J. Eatwell et al. (eds.), *The Invisible Hand (The New Palgrave)*, pp. 156–167. New York: Norton.

Huntington, S.P. 1996. *The Clash of Civilizations and the Remaking of World Order*. New York: Simon and Schuster.

Kirzner, I.M. 1992. "The Ugly Market." In: M.W. Hendrickson (ed.), *The Morality of Capitalism*. Hudson, N.Y.: Foundation for Economic Education.

Knight, F. [1947] 1982. *Freedom and Reform: Essays in Economics and Social Philosophy*. Indianapolis: Liberty Press.

Kristol, I. 1979. *Two Cheers for Capitalism*. New York: Mentor Books.

Lefort, C. 1986. *The Political Forms of Modern Society: Bureaucracy, Democracy, Totalitarianism*. Cambridge, Mass.: MIT Press.

Lincoln, A. [1854] 1989. "Fragments on Government." In: *Abraham Lincoln: Speeches and Writings*. Volume 1 and 2, pp. 301–303. New York: Library of America.

Madison, G.B. 1986. *The Logic of Liberty*. Westport, Conn.: Greenwood Press.

Madison, G.B. 1995a. "Hermeneutics, the Lifeworld, and the Universality of Reason." *Dialogue and Universalism* (Polish Academy of Sciences) 7:79–106.

Madison, G.B. 1995b. "How Individualistic Is Methodological Individualism?" In: D.L. Prychitko (ed.), *Individuals, Institutions, Interpretations: Hermeneutics Applied to Economics*, pp. 36–56. Aldershot: Avery.

Madison, G.B. 1998. *The Political Economy of Civil Society and Human Rights*. London: Routledge.

Mirowski, P. 1989. *More Heat than Light: Economics as Social Physics*. Cambridge: Cambridge University Press.

Mirsky, J. 1994. "Unmasking the Monster." *New York Review of Books*, November 17.

Montesquieu. [1734] 1949. *Oeuvres Complètes*. Paris: Editions de la Pléiade.

Montesquieu. [1734] 1989. *The Spirit of the Laws*. Cambridge: Cambridge University Press.

Murray, C. 1994. "What to Do About Welfare." *Commentary* (December).

Novak, M. 1982. *The Spirit of Democratic Capitalism*. New York: Simon and Schuster.

Novak, M. 1993. *The Catholic Ethic and the Spirit of Capitalism*. New York: Free Press.

Novak, M. 1996. *Business as a Calling: Work and the Examined Life*. New York: Free Press.

Plattner, M.F., and L. Diamond. 1997. "Hong Kong, Singapore, and 'Asian Values.'" *Journal of Democracy* 8(2):9.

Pye, L.W. 1996. "The State and the Individual: An Overview Interpretation." In: B. Hook (ed.), *The Individual and the State in China*, pp. 16–42. Oxford: Clarendon.

Röpke, W. [1951/1957] 1987. *Two Essays by Wilhelm Röpke: The Problem of Economic Order; Welfare, Freedom and Inflation*. Lanham, Va.: University Press of America.

Rogge, B.A. 1979. *Can Capitalism Survive?* Indianapolis: Liberty Press.

Smith, A. [1776] 1979. *An Inquiry into the Nature and the Causes of the Wealth of Nations*. 2 vols. Oxford: Oxford University Press

Communitarian Approaches to the Economy

David M. Anderson

Since the early 1980s a distinguished group of philosophers, political theorists, and sociologists has been working in a tradition of thought that has come to be called the communitarian tradition. Many of the thinkers regarded as communitarians do not call themselves communitarians. The thinkers who are most self-identified as communitarians are Etzioni (1993), Galston (1991), and Selznick (1992). Etzioni and Galston, as well as Glendon (1991) cofounded the Communitarian Network in 1991.

The thinkers who do not use the label are also the ones who are regarded as the founders of the tradition, namely Sandel (1982), MacIntyre (1981), Walzer (1983), Taylor (1990), and Bellah and associates (1985, 1992; also see Gutmann, 1985; Bell, 1993; Mulhall and Smith, 1996; Paul et al., 1996). While these thinkers were critical of the American welfare state in the 1980s, they were even more concerned to criticize the dominant forms of liberal political philosophy: utilitarian

The ideas in this article have developed over a period of years. I wish to express my thanks to the following people for their help. A. Etzioni, W. Galston, P. Churchill, H. Giersch, U. Siegmund, W. Griffith, R. Coughlin, R. Ashford, M. Feldman, M. Burk, P. Selznick, D. Bell, B. Friedan, J. Anderson, B. Anderson, F. Abrams, S. Lipset, I. King, R. Fullinwider, P. Caws, M. Nadel, D. Millon, D. Doherty, V. Hoffman, W. Corson, J. Drogin, C. Fleet, M. Starik, M. Edwards, R. Hollingsworth, J. Fralley, K. Kretman, E. Grefe, G. Barker, L. Mitchell, P. Glynn, M. Bocian, L. Johnson, M. Daigneault, G. Laden, D. DeGrazia, D. Kane, M. Cornfield, B. Bergmann, M. Pauly, A. Peacock, A. Hilger, B. Jones, M. Aranha, R. Eisen, W. Harris, S. Tolchin, G. Weiss, M. Gray, J. Slade, I. Creppell, A. Lowenstein, E. Berkowitz, B. Catron, R. Willis, E. Chubin, M. Oppenheimer, D. Chang, E. West, B. Benson, L. Moersen, O. Kittrie, R. Beiner, H. Joas, B. Lehman, E. Lehman, S. Fleishman, and A. Goldsmith. Special thanks to A. Oleck and A. Altman.

welfare state liberalism (Brandt, 1979), Nozick's Kantian version of libertarianism (1974), and Rawls's Kantian version of welfare state liberalism (1971, 1993).

Since America in the 1970s and 1980s was more in line with Rawls's view than any other, the communitarian critics tended to criticize Rawls's theoretical political conception more than the others. The debate between liberalism and communitarianism has now gone on for fifteen years, and at times it intersects with various disputes between feminism and liberalism (Okin, 1989).

Communitarians have been critical of Rawls's theory of justice which, though it calls for substantial redistribution of wealth and power, does so in the name of providing citizens with the means to plan and implement their own views of the good with little if any concern with communal values over and above their own desires and needs. Communitarians have also objected to the abstract quality of universal theories of justice which fail to take seriously the crucial particulars which make up our identities and our relationships with others. Sandel updated the old criticism that liberalism has an impoverished view of the self when he argued that Rawlsian liberalism cannot build the vision of the just society it envisions because it rests on an attenuated view of the self, namely an "unencumbered self," a self not defined in terms of its relationships to others (Sandel, 1982).

The new communitarians, Etzioni, Galston, Glendon, and Selznick, represent what Bell (1994) regards as the "second wave" of communitarian theory. These communitarians, Etzioni above all, have made communitarianism into a public philosophy. Etzioni and Galston have also been involved in numerous ways with the Clinton administration. At the recent White House–Congressional Character Building Conference hosted by the Communitarian Network, Vice President Gore said numerous times during a major address (June 12, 1997) to 260 leaders in American elementary and high school education that Etzioni's ideas were at the heart of the major programs of the Clinton–Gore administration. Etzioni's influence on Tony Blair, especially when Blair was in the process of transforming the British Labor Party from a socialist into a progressive centrist party, is also well known. One British commentator refers to Etzioni as the "Father of Tony Blair's Big Idea" (Phillips, 1994).

Over the fifteen years of communitarian writing most of the discussion has centered around issues of political and moral philosophy but not economic philosophy. Communitarians are champions of the concept of virtue, even though most of them are either neoprogressives or social democrats rather than the traditional conservative proponents of an ethics of virtue.

Part of the explanation why there has not been a lot of attention to a communitarian economics is that one of the leading communitarian themes is that problems confronting Americans (and most citizens in the Western democracies) today are often best approached by families, schools, and businesses independent of government intervention. Another reason, though, is that much of the discussion in the early 1980s was conducted by philosophers who were engaged in major metaethical disputes over such topics as the role the concept of a person plays in a conception of political philosophy, the objective status of moral principles, and the best methodology for arriving at principles of right and justice.

In recent years, however, there has been more attention given to economic issues. This essay surveys some of the most prominent examples. In Section I, I focus on central themes from Amitai Etzioni's writings. In Section II, I discuss some central themes from the writings of Michael Sandel. Section III treats some of the central themes of William A. Galston's work. And Section IV contains some concluding remarks. At various points I also introduce some of my own ideas, which center around efforts to synthesize many core themes of feminism and environmentalism with communitarianism. I should emphasize at the outset that I write as a philosopher and social critic, not an economist. Nevertheless, I hope that this discussion will be useful for economists.

I   Amitai Etzioni: Communitarianism and Socioeconomics

Etzioni is the founding president of both the Communitarian Network and the Society for the Advancement of Socio-Economics. He has published numerous books to launch these projects (Etzioni, 1988, 1993, 1996; Etzioni and Lawrence, 1991; also see Sciulli, 1996). He is also Director of the Institute for Communitarian Policy Studies at The George Washington University. Etzioni has generated a social movement based on the concept of restoring social order in a way that promotes autonomy, and he has organized an academic movement based on the concept of the role society plays in shaping our economic behavior. Etzioni's work, academic and activist, has the mark of the sociologist.

Communitarianism, as Etzioni conceives of it, aims to strengthen the moral foundations of American society (and other societies as well) by calling on people to meet their responsibilities to others in the same way that they want others to respect their rights. We are a society out of balance. It is not his view, however, that we should give up the great gains in rights won by women and minorities in recent years. The problem is to find the right balance between rights and responsibilities, or as he now says, between moral order and autonomy (1996, pp. 34–57). "The communitarian paradigm," Etzioni (1997, p. 20) explains, "does not call for closing down the welfare state and replacing it with armies of volunteers. It envisages a triumvirate, in which the State, the private sector and various institutions of the community cooperate to shoulder social burdens." There is, as we will see below, a crucial place for the law in expressing the moral voice, but much of the responsibility that is needed is not directly about law (1996, pp. 119–159).

The concept of socioeconomics, which Etzioni introduced before he launched the Communitarian Movement, concerns the old question of whether human behavior, and here especially economic behavior, is based on rational self-interested motives. Classical economic theorists like Adam Smith and David Ricardo and neoclassical economists like Richard Posner, George Stigler, and Gary S. Becker think that it is. Amartya Sen, Albert O. Hirschman, Herbert Simon, Amos Tversky, Daniel Kahneman, David O. Sears, and Etzioni himself think that it is not.

Etzioni (1988) brought together a massive amount of evidence (the book has a 40 page bibliography) from across the social sciences to support the critics. He introduced a paradigm to house the existing criticism. His aim was to seek a new synthesis with the neoclassical paradigm and not to try to replace it, which he realized would be very unlikely. He called that alternative paradigm the "socioeconomic" paradigm, primarily because the evidence that is used to challenge the neoclassical theories comes from empirical studies of social institutions and social forces that shape personal preferences.

Some examples of socioeconomic views are as follows:

Socio-economic studies show: tax compliance is encouraged by social sanctions and moral commitments (disapproval of friends, value of honesty) as well as sanctions; energy use is affected by attitudes toward conservation as well as price incentives (Stern, 1984); job turnover is explained as much by social commitment as by economic factors such as pay opportunities (Price and Mueller, 1981); both deterrence and moral commitments significantly affect people's predispositions to commit crime (Grasmick and Green, 1981); voting behavior is more strongly determined by a sense of civic duty than by self-interest (Sears et al., 1980); and so on. (Etzioni and Laurence, 1991, p. 349)

Neoclassical theory, in short, is guilty of treating human behavior in isolation from crucial factors which influence it. It treats consumers in isolation because it regards them as rational maximizers of their own preferences (or utility). Because consumers know what they want, indeed because we should take their preferences as given, the path is short to laissez-faire policies which would protect consumers from state interference. Laissez-faire policies will foster the kind of efficiency in bringing about human welfare that individuals actually want.

Central to the critique is an attack on the very idea of rationality. Following Simon (1957), Kahneman and Tversky (1973), and others, Etzioni argues that much of human behavior is based on such non-rational factors (even irrational factors if taken from the neoclassical point of view) as commitments to values and the emotions. Rather than try to explain this irrationality away, we should recognize it, even celebrate it. In fact, it is helpful to separate the critique of the idea of self-interested motivation from the critique of the idea of motivation based on rationality.

Etzioni introduces a "normative-affective" approach to counter the dominant "logical-empirical" approach, namely the dominant rationality approach that is based on logical reasoning and empirical facts. Though Etzioni thinks we use both approaches, he clearly thinks that we use the "normative-affective" approach more of the time; and, indeed, he thinks that we should use both but continue to use the "normative-affective" approach more (Etzioni, 1988, p. 254). Etzioni also regards the socioeconomic paradigm as providing a "deonto-logical" corrective to the dominant "utilitarian" paradigm. The socio-economic paradigm also gives more emphasis to inductive, as opposed to deductive, reasoning (Etzioni, 1988, pp. 253–254).

We must also appreciate that a crucial feature of the socioeconomic paradigm is that values and the emotions play the dominant role in our evaluation of *means as well as ends*. Moreover, a crucial place is given to a theory of power to show citizens how they can control the free market rather than have it control them.

Etzioni and some of his sympathetic commentators have often spoken as though communitarianism and socioeconomics should develop independently (see Coughlin, 1996); I believe that they should develop in mutually supportive ways.[1] I regard them as a pair of ice dancers. In a slogan: *socioeconomics shows us how humans can act and communitarianism shows us how we should.* Communitarianism needs socioeconomics to explain how humans are capable of creating humane societies. If we are capable of acting for reasons other than rational self-interest, an argument is needed to undergird this point of view. The academic empirical research thus helps provide a basis for the moral structure of the activist movement. Moreover, communitarianism is clearly partly about economic issues. Therefore, it needs a systematic approach to explaining and predicting economic phenomena.

Etzioni's views on economic policy illustrate the complexity of his viewpoint overall. It seems best to say the following: As a communitarian, Etzioni thinks that we will solve our problems in America today by relying more on nongovernmental solutions than governmental ones. Although creating new government initiatives is not the animating theme of Etzioni's viewpoint, creating new governmental programs, especially those that are coordinated with new kinds of efforts in the private sector, is still crucial to the approach. His most recent book (1996) is packed with new policy proposals. In short, Etzioni thinks everyone must be more responsible, and that includes the federal government. It is probably best to regard communitarianism as an effort to find the "third way" in between the social welfare states of Europe and the individualistic welfare state of the United States (Baldwin, 1997).

Of the governmental changes that are needed, some will concern the economy quite directly while others will be more concerned with political and civil matters. Changes in economic policy will cover dis-

---

[1] Etzioni organized the first International Conference on Socio-Economics in 1989 at the Havard Business School. Today the organization has 1,100 members worldwide, about half of whom are from the United States. Its annual conferences have met in such places as Stockholm, Paris, Geneva, Montreal, and Washington, D.C. Coughlin served as executive director of the Society for the Advancement of Socio-Economics from 1993 to 1996.

tributive and regulative matters (more on this below) as well as the economics of politics, most notably campaign finance reform (Etzioni, 1993, pp. 210–246; also see 1984), a topic receiving more attention in Washington today than any time since the major reforms instituted after Watergate. Etzioni supports a seven part program that would transform the corrupt, unfair special interest system. His program calls for such things as publicly financing congressional elections, banning political action committees, and limiting individual contributions to candidates to $100.

In his most recent book, Etzioni (1996, pp. 85–257) unites his views on campaign finance reform with a sustained argument for major societal dialogues (megalogues) on critical value disputes. One condition of having megalogues in which average citizens have a genuine voice is to transform the special interest system with major campaign finance reform. In order to demand that individuals be more responsible citizens, obstacles that stand in the way of meaningful participation must be removed. Creating a society with healthy political and social debates is at the heart of Etzioni's attempt to create a responsive, open community rather than an authoritarian, closed community (1996, p. 130).

To be avoided at all costs is the view that Etzioni's "third way" is driven by the attempt to find innovative ways to motivate consumers and corporate leaders to do the right thing even as they maximize their own well-being. While he does support certain kinds of policies that would provide economic incentives, he is much more interested in finding innovative ways to motivate people to help others from a standpoint of moral responsibility. His views on both economic and noneconomic behavior are clearly driven by his concerns for the moral voice.

A   Two Common Objections and Etzioni's Responses

I want to mention two common objections to Etzioni's line of reasoning, even though I cannot address these objections or Etzioni's responses in any detail. One kind of objection neoclassical economists make is that the additional "factors" Etzioni brings into the explanations of economic behavior are often identified as "constraints" on the process of preference-formation. Therefore, preferences are still taken as given, but now some additional constraints have to be factored into the equation. Etzioni denies that this is an effective response because the factors in question are, he says, internalized in the motivational systems of economic actors and not external constraints (Etzioni 1988, p. 100; 1991a, pp. 68–69).

A second line of objection made by neoclassical economists (many of whom embrace some version of welfare economics) is that over the years economists have found ways to include various kinds of other-regarding (and/or moral) interests into utility functions themselves (creating so-called interdependent utility functions). Etzioni is well aware of these efforts and launches a penetrating critique of the various attempts (see especially 1988, pp. 21–87). He joins such eminent economists as Sen and Hirschman, who maintain that these attempts "trivialize" the very idea of "maximizing self-interest." Etzioni writes: "From a methodological viewpoint, the all-inclusive expansion of the concept of utility violates the rules of sound conceptualization. Once a concept is defined so that it encompasses all the incidents that are members of a given category (in the case at hand, the motives for all human activities), it ceases to enhance one's ability to explain" (1988, p. 27).

B   The Weberian Turn in American Economic Thought

Swedberg (1991) explains in an illuminating essay that Etzioni has essentially updated Max Weber's concept of "*Sozialökonomik*," which is translated as "socioeconomics." Weber sought to resolve the *Methodenstreit* that dominated European economics between 1880 and 1910. He sought to unite central components of the views of the main protagonists in the dispute: the Berlin economist Schmoller who defended the historical approach and the Viennese economist Menger who defended the mathematical approach. "Weber's thoughtful comments," Swedberg explains, "on the destructive potential of the *Methodenstreit* and the need for a new synthesis of neoclassical economics and the other social sciences, are part of the tradition of modern social science and should therefore be taken into account today when we are on the verge of a new *Methodenstreit*" (p. 15).

Yet Swedberg emphasizes that the distinctive feature of Etzioni's view is not that it is interdisciplinary but that it employs different factors in explaining economic behavior. The neoclassical camp, which employs a one factor model of explanation, took an interdisciplinary turn (away from the very compartmentalized period of mathematical economics that dominated the field from the 1920s to 1960s) with the work of Chicago school economists like Becker. Becker, a Nobel Prize laureate, used the one-factor model to explain behavior outside of the typical economist's domain, ranging from family to school and criminal behavior (Becker, 1957, 1976, 1981). The Becker approach has been regarded as a version of "economic imperialism" because it attempts to cover all areas of human behavior with one economic methodology.

Etzioni contrasts his approach with the neoclassical one:

Policy makers must deal with all of the major relevant factors; socio-economics, by incorporating economic, social, psychic, and political factors, obviously is more encompassing than mono-disciplinary approaches. (Etzioni, 1988, p. 238)

Policy analysis based on neoclassical economic theory tends to draw on pecuniary incentives such as tax incentives, raises, and bonuses, and to disregard or downplay the role of moral education and leadership (for example, from the White House "pulpit"). (Etzioni, 1988, p. 238)

Swedberg supports Etzioni's neo-Weberian turn:

Today there is a clear chance to steer things in a positive direction. Economic imperialism, however, does not represent a good minded vision on economics and its scientific neighbors, whereby it threatens to close the door to the new and promising developments of a multidisciplinary economics. Socio-economics, on the other hand, offers a possibility to keep the door open. (Swedberg, 1991, p. 29)

We can go a step further. We can say that in the same way that Weber explained the role played by nonmaterialist factors in the rise of modern industrial capitalism, Etzioni wants to explain the role nonmaterialist factors do play, and can further play, in the rise of a more communitarian version of capitalism.

Weber's classic argument ([1904–05] 1958) is that the "spirit" of the Protestant Reformation and its work ethic—its emphasis on a worldly calling, asceticism, hard work, individual conscience, the virtues of self-restraint and moderation, and the need to prove oneself through worldly success to be worthy of God's grace (a Calvinist rather than Lutherian thesis)—was needed to complete the Marxian materialistic explanation which was based solely on issues of the production system and economic class conflict. (Weber was responding to Marx as well as to Schmoller and Menger.) Thus Weber added the mental aspect of motivation to the material.

Compare the concluding sentences of each book.

For Etzioni:

At the same time, one should not deny that pleasure and self-interest constitute a major motivating force, and in their place—a legitimate one. Socio-economics is hence to view pleasure and self-interest within the broader context of human nature, society, and ultimate values, rather than either ignore the self-oriented force, or build a paradigm, theory, and morality focused entirely on self. (Etzioni, 1988, p. 251)

For Weber:

Here we have only attempted to trace the fact and the direction of its influence to their motives in one, though a very important, point.... But it is, of course, not my aim to substitute for a one-sided materialistic an equally one-sided spiritualistic causal interpretation of culture and history. Each is equally possible, but each, if it does not serve as the preparation, but as the conclusion of an investigation, accomplishes equally little in the interest of historical truth (Weber, 1958, p. 183).

The moral dimension to economic behavior that Etzioni uncovers (1988) is one of the central underlying premises of the argument for the spirit that should animate the responsive community (1993, 1996). And although he is very much dealing with the Durkheimian theme of uniting a concept of moral order with a concept of autonomy, Etzioni is also working in the Weberian tradition of finding core beliefs and spirit that could move us to action, recognizing that these motives will probably be intertwined with motives of self-interest.

C   Some Economic Policy Implications

One topic Etzioni discusses in various places is management theory. It took booms in Japanese and (former West) German industry to motivate American executives in the early 1980s to finally drop their top-down, authoritarian (Frederick) Tayloresque management style and turn to a decentralized, participative approach. But for years social scientists had been arguing that employees were motivated by "moral factors" (e.g., corporate culture, social acceptance, self-esteem, participation) as well as economic (Etzioni, 1988, p. 239). Social scientific evidence showed that decentralized firms are more cooperative and ultimately more efficient (Etzioni, 1988, pp. 196–198). American industry learned its lesson the hard way. We are, still, the most individualistic democracy in the world (Lipset, 1996).

The topic of centralized versus decentralized companies, and indeed governments, has emerged as one of the great themes for social theorists trying to develop a viable theory of the welfare state. The economic booms in post–World War II Japan and West Germany were based to a significant extent on the decentralized approaches to management (e.g., Total Quality Management, which they learned from Americans like W. Edwards Deming). Ironically, socioeconomic arguments provided a basis to create a more economically efficient workplace, even though socioeconomic arguments as a rule move us away from the concept of economic efficiency toward a view of equity.

The discussion about decentralization in recent years is informed by globalization and the negative as well as the positive effects of flattening corporate hierarchies. In the 1950s and 1960s Japan and West Germany used decentralized management (as well as the financial benefits of not having to build up defense) to create essentially full-employment societies. In the 1980s and 1990s, many major American companies decentralized, but they had to downsize the workforce in order to achieve the kind of efficiency the Japanese and the West Germans achieved without downsizing.

Globalized production, consumption, and financial markets, free trade, and especially the proliferation of developing democracies in the post–Cold War environment have meant that decentralization is no longer in the interest of all workers. The United States, which prides itself on being less in trouble than European social welfare states, has a growing contingent workforce which typically falls through the cracks of the social welfare system (e.g., contingent workers often lack health insurance).

Etzioni, drawing on the work of Dahrendorf (1995), briefly discusses the general problem of downsizing in an age of globalized markets and free trade. He writes: "Hence, the crowning contextual question for regeneration for the foreseeable future is *how far can a society tolerate public and corporate policies that give free rein to economic interests* and that seek to enhance global competitiveness, *without undermining the moral legitimacy of the social order?*" (Etzioni, 1996, p. 81).

Etzioni identifies a number of things (pp. 82–84) that a strong communitarian society can do to counteract the harshness of the globalized system, which I can only briefly mention here. Some of the things depend on new laws (providing community jobs using public funding and adopting a stronger safety net), some depend on corporations taking on moral responsibilities that are not legislated (work sharing and job security strategies), and some depend on moral responsibilities consumers take on themselves (e.g., adopting less materialistic lifestyles).

Thus, though communitarians oppose building walls around the United States (if not all countries), they also recognize that opening trade relations with other countries requires adjustments in other aspects of our social system, only some of which can be handled with legislation. The key to discovering the solution to trade dilemmas— including the question about incorporating labor, safety and health, and environmental standards in trade agreements—is to develop a collective responsibility solution. Communitarians reject top-down federal government solutions even though a vital role is given to the federal government.

A major task for those working in the socioeconomic tradition is to update the research on decentralized management. This new research would consider the relationship between efficiency and humane management styles in corporations and in government. It would also consider the relationship between various approaches to decentralization and the problems of leadership, corporate responsibility, and different ways that law can be used to motivate corporate executives and workers.

This research needs to be integrated with the developing literature in corporate law where a communitarian approach to corporate responsibility has emerged (e.g., Mitchell, 1992; Millon, 1993; Johnson, 1992) and the "stakeholder-stockholder" dispute in "business ethics" (e.g., Goodpaster, 1991; Freeman, 1984). Selznick's (1992, 1996) call for communitarians to focus more on institutional, especially corporate, responsibility, is crucial (see also Derber, 1994).

D   An Example of Communitarian Economic Thinking:
    Government, Business, and the Schools Working Together

In a very instructive article, Garfinkle (1997) outlines a communitarian approach to economics. He sees "communitarian economics" as representing a synthesis of "liberal" and "conservative" approaches to the economy (pp. 3–4). Communitarians should follow this rule of fiscal responsibility:

> Communitarians believe that government has an important role to play in regulating economic activities and improving social welfare. But the economic cost of the sum total of all regulatory and nonregulatory programs should be restained to avoid substantial negative effects on the growth of the economy. In order to avoid such negative effects, the total economic impact of the government's direct expenditures and regulatory programs should not grow more than the growth of GDP. (Garfinkle, 1997, p. 16)

Thus Communitarians should try to unite fiscal responsibility with progressive politics. Part of the new approach to fiscal discipline would involve embracing an "informed investment approach" along the lines presented by Shapiro (1995), of the Progressive Policy Institute, and Thurow (1996), the well-known MIT economist. The budget would be divided into an "Investment Account and a Consumption Account." "This approach," Garfinkle explains, "would limit the growth of government consumption spending plus depreciation of government investments to the growth of average per capita income" (1997, p. 12).

Consider the topic of government regulations. Garfinkle contrasts traditional "command and control" regulations that lead to "maximum costs both in expenses for government enforcement and the required industry investment for compliance" with a communitarian approach that is based more on "indirect or self-regulating methods" (p. 10).

Now consider the example of environmental regulations. Garfinkle says that a communitarian approach to environmental regulations would include "antipollution tax credits," and "publicizing pollution records of chemical manufacturers" (p. 10). The antipollution tax credits speak to an innovative way to motivate firms to be morally responsible and to maximize profits, and the publication of pollution records speaks to an innovative way to use public shaming to motivate corporate leaders to act responsibly. Neither approach, as I see it, is inconsistent with forming new international treaties or developing innovative ways of enforcing existing ones. But the public shaming approach does give special emphasis to community-based efforts (also see Estes, 1996).

An effort should also be made, I believe, to integrate a communitarian approach to environmental policy with communitarian approaches to environmental education, both scientific and moral. Consider the topic of moral education. Communitarians, among the leaders in character education in the United States (Etzioni, 1993, pp. 89–115), should treat the topic of environmental responsibility in the context of character education in the schools. In addition to learning about responsibility, discipline, caring, and moderation in connection with personal and family relationships, students should learn about these virtues in connection with the environment as well. Issues would range from recyling to voting for candidates who take a serious approach to environmental issues.

A place to start is Maryland, where Lieutenant Governor Kathleen Kennedy Townsend, Robert Kennedy's oldest child, is leading the way with a moral character program for Maryland's schools (*New York Times*, 1997). This program is currently funded by both the state of Maryland and the U.S. Department of Education. Townsend, who speaks with great respect for Etzioni, could probably integrate the topic of environmental responsibility in her existing program.

Maryland, which also has the only public service requirement for high school graduation, could thus also act as the laboratory for a communitarian approach to environmental education. In the communitarian school a new spirit of community would exist, one which would connect children to their teachers and their parents and their parents' employers. Issues of legal and moral responsibility are connected, and a basis is also provided for people with power (in this case, principals and teachers) to teach and to inspire others (in this case, students) to develop character traits that environmentally responsible citizens need.

II   The Keynesian Paradigm Is Missing a Moral Dimension: Michael Sandel's Efforts to Recover the Classical Republican Aspect of American History

In *Democracy's Discontent: America in Search of a Public Philosophy*, Sandel (1996), the distinguished Harvard political theorist, argues that the two dominant paradigms of the American welfare state—Keynesian economic theory and Rawlsian political theory—are seriously flawed because they fail to promote a notion of citizenship and especially an account of moral character which are needed to sustain a humane society. Like Etzioni, he draws on a wealth of scholarship to create the basis for an alternative paradigm, yet he draws more on philosophy and economic, political, and constitutional history than the social sciences.

The alternative paradigm that Sandel recommends, which he regards as a new public philosophy, is one that would unite the two grand traditions of American political history, the classical liberal and classical republican traditions, each of which represents an aspect of freedom. The liberal side concerns volunteerism and choice unimpeded by the constraints of others; while the republican side concerns self-government and developing moral character through political participation.

Sandel's narrative, which is quite extensive. shows how the two traditions have existed since our founding, but how in the years following World War II American leaders and thinkers essentially ignored the republican aspect of our heritage. He shows how the progressive administrations of Woodrow Wilson and both Theodore and Franklin Roosevelt centered around a "political economy of citizenship." While a dispute persisted from the early years of the Progressive Era through the end of the New Deal between "decentralizers" (like the early Wilson) and "planners" (like Herbert Croly and Franklin Roosevelt at certain stages), each side shared the historic commitment to use the national government to cultivate citizens with good moral character.

The massive spending needed to support our efforts in World War II and lift us out of the remains of the serious recession of 1937 (and the depression overall) served to transform our economic philosophy from one focused on the "political economy of citizenship" to one focused on "a political economy of growth and distributive justice" (Sandel, 1996, p. 262). We shifted from a series of federal efforts to engage in structural reform of the productive aspects of the capitalist system to an economic philosophy focused on accepting the basic structure of the productive system but stimulating it with a government spending fiscal policy that would increase growth overall, create full employment, and solve some of the grosser inequities in wealth and power. As Sandel explains: "Where earlier reformers had sought economic arrangements that would cultivate citizens of a certain kind, Keynesians undertook no formative mission; they proposed simply to accept existing consumer preferences and to regulate the economy by manipulating aggregate demand" (Sandel, 1996, p. 252).

This new approach to government spending, moreover, differed sharply from the early years of the New Deal and especially the great relief programs like the National Industrial Act, the Civil Conservation Corps, and the National Recovery Act. In the postwar period "[t]he economists urged that government spending no longer be viewed as a temporary emergency device but as permanent policy to compensate as necessary for slack in the private economy" (p. 261). Keynesians also increased "the purchasing power of lower-income families" by supporting social insurance and transfer programs for the aged, the ill, and the unemployed (p. 261).

Sandel offers a careful account of how the Keynesian paradigm linked up with the Rawlsian. For our purposes we can note the following crucial point. The fiscal policy of Keynesian economic theory was *neutral* about consumer preferences in the same way that the principles of justice of Rawlsian political theory (especially the equal opportunity and difference principles, namely the second principle of justice) were *neutral* about conceptions of the good life. While it is the job of government to correct for inequities in wealth and power, it is not the job of government to evaluate consumer preferences, so long as those preferences are not inconsistent with one's legal obligations.

Thus an economic and political philosophy of growth, distributive justice, and consumer preference satisfaction contrasts sharply with a dominant end of the republican tradition. Historically, the republicans "worried more about conditions of production than about conditions of consumption, because they viewed the world of work as the area in which, for better or worse, the character of citizens was formed. The activity of consumption was not decisive for self-government in the same way" (p. 268).

Sandel's solution to the moral and economic problems in America today is, roughly, to downplay though not discard the liberal-consumer ethic even as we recover the republican ethic. This process of recovery would include efforts on the part of our national leaders to "inspire" citizens to develop the kinds of character traits that make them better citizens in their private lives and more active citizens in the democratic state. Much of the work must be done, however, at the local level, since globalization is decreasing the influence of nation states.

The crucial connection with Etzioni's critique of the neoclassical tradition concerns the concept of taking ends as given. The welfare state theorists regard the agent as a consumer who should use the redistributed goods to advance his unreflective ends. It is this view of the self that Etzioni and Sandel oppose. What is striking is that Etzioni focuses his critique on neoclassical positions on rationality and motivation, while Sandel focuses his critique on the development of Keynesian economic theory and the consumer ethic of the post–World War II welfare state. In truth, Keynesians employ neoclassical assumptions about agency even though they depart from laissez-faire theorists who deduce free market conclusions from their neoclassical premises. If Sandel and Etzioni are both right, then Keynesianism is best regarded as a Band-Aid on the basic neoclassical paradigm.

Sandel and Etzioni are not critics of the welfare state so much as critics of a particular way of thinking about the welfare state. They each plainly agree that too much of the effort in constructing the American welfare state since the 1930s has focused on the role to be played by the federal government in developing and implementing economic policies. Indeed, their complaint about citizen-consumers who take ends as given (a complaint that applies more to Keynesians and American citizens themselves than Rawlsians) is as much about the fact that a theory of moral virtue is not built into the theory of the self as it is about the fact that the ends are not subject to criticism. Sandel and Etzioni both believe that virtue should be constitutive of the good life and the just community. Keynesians, American citizens, and even Rawlsians regard virtue, at best, as instrumental toward these ends.

III The Missing Republican Dimension Needs to Be United with the Realities of the Information Age: The Work of William Galston

Galston has argued for years (e.g., 1991) that Rawlsian political philosophy, like the American welfare state, is flawed because it fails to take seriously the concepts of virtue and moral character. In this regard, Galston and Sandel share the same target in American political philosophy. But Galston, a cofounder of the Communitarian Network and a leading voice at the Progressive Policy Institute—the think tank of the centrist Democratic Leadership Council, which President Clinton chaired during its early years in 1990—is currently working out an economic and political philosophy for America that would unite our forgotten republican ideals with the realities of globalization and the information age, all without violating our most cherished rights which animate the Lockean side of our American heritage. Unlike Sandel, he sees a greater role for the new political economy, yet one that differs in crucial ways from the Keynesian-driven vision of Johnson's Great Society.

Galston's ideas, like Etzioni's, are evident in central themes of the Clinton administration. Galston and his colleagues at the Progressive Policy Institute have issued a new book (Marshall, 1997)—which has a foreword by Vice President Gore and an afterword by Democratic Leadership Council Chairman Senator Joseph Lieberman—that they hope will inspire President Clinton and Vice President Gore to expand on their current vision. The lead essay, which Galston coauthored (Galston et al., 1997) outlines the new vision. The platform is meant to suit the Information Age in the same way progressive platforms at the turn of the century were meant to suit the Industrial Age, which was replacing the Agricultural Age.

A word about the Clinton administration is appropriate here, especially since Galston is a former domestic policy advisor and now a major voice in Democratic Party politics. While it is true that the president saved himself with quintessential political sagacity (especially with the help of political consultant Dick Morris) following the Republican takeover of the House in 1994, there is no denying that he helped formulate the centrist agenda for the Democrats in the mid-1980s. Galston was important in this restructuring process (Galston and Kamark, 1988; Shuman, 1994, p. 3). The liberal health care program of the early period of the first administration was not part of the original vision. Clinton embraced this theme after Senator Robert Kerry made it a national issue in the primaries. Admittedly there were other factors.

Galston's commitment to strengthening the American family (e.g., 1990/91), especially intact two-parent families—a commitment he shares with Etzioni and the whole communitarian movement and which is linked in many ways to school reform and civic education—animates his vision of a humane society.

In his article on family policy in the volume mentioned above, Galston states the "goals" of this policy quite explicitly:

First, strengthening intact, two-parent families to maximize the number of children who have the opportunity to grow up in such families; second, providing new supports for the millions of children in single-parent families, to create the closest possible functional equivalent of intact families, and third, radically changing our policies for children who lack even one caring, competent adult in light of what we know about the minimum conditions for normal child development. (1996, p. 150)

Among the measures that must be taken to implement these goals (pp. 155–161) are stronger divorce laws (at the state level) to encourage parents to consider working out their difficulties rather than breaking up their families, a family-friendly tax code that would "reduce the tax disadvantages of marriage," a mentor system for vulnerable children, "second-chance" homes for single mothers, and radical reform of foster care.

The new progressive platform places this family policy within the context of an economic vision that centers around concepts of decentralization, empowerment, and the progressive market. Yet the New Democrats differ sharply from the Republicans, Old and New:

The answer is not, as many conservatives assert, to simply disable government or abandon key public responsibilities. Rather it is to refocus government on enforcing fair rules of competition, cultivating an educated, public-spirited citizenry, and enabling individuals to succeed by dint of their own efforts.... The promise of America is the promise of equal opportunity, not equal results. (Galston et al. 1997, p. 22)

The policies and programs outlined in this platform and throughout the book include entitlement reform (e.g., of Medicare, Medicaid, and Social Security), school, crime, and environmental reform, and a new vision of America's role in the world. Etzioni would no doubt be sympathetic to many of these ideas, but he gives more emphasis to the moral voice than to the new market.

IV Concluding Remarks

I wish to conclude this article with some remarks about the direction of my own work, which aims to synthesize much that is of value in the communitarian/socioeconomic and feminist traditions, especially work in the ethics and politics of care tradition that grew out of the work of

Chodorow (1978) and Gilligan (1982). Etzioni himself says that some feminist values are clearly communitarian (1996, p. 252). Communitarianism needs both more compassion and more passion. Feminism can help. Etzioni makes a similar point about environmental values. He also calls for a "broad coalition" (p. 255).

The synthesis centers around a national family policy which would require that corporations and the federal government provide paid leave for parents with newborns and most of the cost of day care for most families (Anderson, 1994, 1996, forthcoming). This policy—"The Family Unity Act"—which is built on the arguments of numerous communitarians (including Etzioni's ideas on parental leave, 1993, pp. 54–88), feminists and progressives, aims to be the unifying theme for a theory of progressive politics.

One argument I am developing draws on the work of feminist social thinkers and management theorists (e.g., Kanter, 1993; Eisler, 1993) to show that The Family Unity Act blends nicely with a feminist view of decentralized management. The family policy would help decrease absenteeism, tardiness, and turnover at the same time that it engendered a new spirit of teamwork amongst men and women alike. This new spirit of cooperation would also lead to reductions in sexual harassment and other forms of workplace discrimination. Family life would also improve as a result of the improved relationships between managers and employees.

Moreover, The Family Unity Act (which would cost approximately 75 billion dollars a year) is not only compatible with Galston's family policies, but supportive of them. There are clearly numerous efforts needed to help the diversity of family types in the United States today.

Such a vision of a new spirit of community in the workplace and in society overall would succeed only if the family policy were combined with other communitarian-oriented policies and with the right kind of leadership in our corporations, in our government, and in our civil society. Leadership is a core communitarian notion (Etzioni, 1996, e.g., pp. 13, 27, 103) that is not quantifiable but among the most needed qualities in our society. A viable political philosophy for our time needs a theory of leadership. Communitarianism is the inspiration for developing such an account (also see Garfinkle, 1997, p. 23). The task is to unite the feminist focus on the special responsibilities men and corporate leaders must accept with the communitarian commitment to building a more responsible, more responsive community.

Finally, let us briefly consider whether it is fruitful to compare our age to the Progressive Era. While I think the comparison has much to teach us, I think that it is a serious error to think solely in these terms. The main problem with thinking in this way is that it is too narrow. Thinking about our society (and our world) largely in economic terms simply obscures crucial issues that, though they are intertwined with economic issues, are not reducible to economic issues. Our current "moral crisis" is not based solely on a response to the economic transformation underway.

Above all, critical issues about gender and race must not be subsumed under the economic category. Orthodox capitalists and orthodox Marxists have always made this error, and we owe thanks to various feminists and communitarians for opening our eyes to aspects of human experience that cannot be explained in terms of production, consumption, and employment. Many of the central problems facing Americans today concern our ambivalence about issues of gender and race. And that ambivalence stems from the 1960s, a period of great moral growth in our nation's history. Moreover, these struggles preceded the rise of the new global economy. Furthermore, the sense of moral decay many Americans feel is not a response to the changing economic situation. It is much more complicated. In truth, we live in an age beyond analogy.

Still, an era which may be even more instructive to think about is the Civil War Era. While we are not in the midst of a war we do live during a time of great moral strife. It is also a very violent time. In many ways we are as torn today as we were then. Only now it is not just race, and class, that divides us; it is also gender, sexuality, and ethnicity. A communitarian public philosophy, one animated by a new approach to strengthening our families, is perhaps the best hope we have for confronting the plurality of problems we face in this new age.

Bibliography

Anderson, D. 1994. "False Stability and Defensive Justification in Rawlsian Liberalism: A Feminist Critique." In: R.P. Churchill (ed.), *The Ethics of Liberal Democracy: Morality and Democracy in Theory and Practice*, pp. 47–70. Oxford: Berg.

Anderson, D. 1996. "The Family Unity Act." 8th International Conference on Socio-Economics, University of Geneva, Switzerland.

Anderson, D. In: J.M. Abbarno (ed.), *Inherent and Instrumental Value*, "Part of the Project of Building a Progressive Coalition: Uniting Working Mothers and Welfare Mothers Behind a National Family Policy." Bethesda, Maryland: Intentional Scholars Publications (forthcoming).

Baldwin, P. 1997. "The Past Rise of Social Security: Historical Trends and Patterns." In: H. Giersch (ed.), *Reforming the Welfare State*, pp. 3–24. Berlin: Springer.

Becker, G.S. 1957. *The Economics of Discrimination*. Chicago: University of Chicago Press.

Becker, G.S. 1976. *The Economic Approach to Human Behavior*. Chicago: University of Chicago Press.

Becker, G.S. 1981. *A Treatise on the Family*. Cambridge: Harvard University Press.

Bell, D.A. 1993. *Communitarianism and its Critics*. Oxford: Clarendon Press.

Bell, D.A. 1994. "Together Again?" (Review of *The Spirit of Community*.) *Times Literary Supplement*, November 25.

Bellah, R.N. et al. 1985. *Habits of the Heart*. Berkeley: University of California Press.

Bellah, R.N. et al. 1992. *The Good Society*. New York: Vintage Books.

Brandt, R.B. 1979. *A Theory of the Good and the Right*. Oxford: Clarendon Press.

Chodorow, N. 1978. *The Reproduction of Mothering: Psychoanalysis and the Sociology of Gender*. Berkeley: University of California Press.

Coughlin, R.M. 1996. "Whose Morality? Which Community? What Interests?: Socio-Economics and Communitarian Perspectives." *Journal of Socio-Economics* 25(3):135–155.

Dahrendorf, R. 1995. "Can We Combine Economic Opportunity with Civil Society and Political Liberty." *The Responsive Community* 5(3):13–39.

Derber, C. 1994. "Communitarian Economics: Criticisms and Suggestions from the Left." *The Responsive Community* 4(4):29–42.

Eisler, R. 1993. "Women, Men, and Management: Redesigning Our Future." In: P. Barrentine (ed.), *When the Canary Stops Singing: Women's Perspectives on Transforming Business*, pp. 27–42. San Francisco: Berrett-Koehler.

Estes, R. 1996. *Tyranny of the Bottom Line*. San Francisco: Berrett-Koehler.

Etzioni, A. 1984. *Capitol Corruption*. San Diego: Harcourt Brace Jovanovich.

Etzioni, A. 1988. *The Moral Dimension: Toward a New Economics*. New York: Free Press.

Etzioni, A. 1991a. "Contemporary Liberals, Communitarians, and Individual Choices." In: A. Etzioni and P. Laurence (eds.), *Socio-Economics: Toward a New Synthesis*, pp. 59–73. Armonk: Sharpe.

Etzioni, A. 1991b. "The Next Steps." In: A. Etzioni and P. Laurence, *Socio-Economics: Toward a New Synthesis*, pp. 347–352. Armonk: Sharpe.

Etzioni, A. 1993. *The Spirit of Community*. New York: Simon and Schuster.

Etzioni, A. 1996. *The New Golden Rule: Community and Morality in a Democratic Society*. New York: Basic Books.

Etzioni, A. 1997. "Tony Blair: A Communitarian in the Making?" *Sunday Times,* June 21, p. 20.

Etzioni, A., and P.R. Lawrence (eds.). 1991. *Socio-Economics: Toward a New Synthesis.* Armonk: Sharpe.

Freeman, R.E. 1994. *Strategic Management: A Stakeholder Approach.* Boston: Pitman.

Galston. W.A. 1990/91. "A Liberal-Democratic Case for the Two-Parent Family." *The Responsive Community* 1(1):14–26.

Galston, W.A. 1991. *Liberal Purposes: Goods, Virtues, and Diversity in the Liberal State.* Cambridge: Cambridge University Press.

Galston, W.A. 1997. "A Progressive Family Policy for the Twenty-First Century." In: W. Marshall (ed.), *Building the Bridge*, pp. 149–162. Lantham: Rowman & Littlefield.

Galston, W.A., and E. Kamark. 1988. "The Politics of Evasion." Washington, D.C.: Progressive Policy Institute.

Galston, W.A., W. Marshall, A. From, and D. Ross. 1997. "The New Progressive Declaration: A Political Philosophy for the Information Age." In: W. Marshall (ed.), *Building the Bridge*, pp. 17–38. Lantham: Rowman & Littlefield.

Garfinkle, N. 1997. "Communitarian Economics." *Journal of Socio-Economics* 26:1–24.

Gilligan, C. 1982. *In a Different Voice: Psychological Development and Women's Development.* Cambridge: Harvard University Press.

Glendon, M.A. 1991. *Rights Talk: The Impoverishment of Political Discourse.* New York: Free Press.

Goodpaster, K.E. 1991. "Business Ethics and Stakeholder Analysis." *Business Ethics Quarterly* 1(1):53–73.

Grasmick, H.G., and D.E. Green. 1981. "Deterrence and the Morally Comitted." *Sociological Quarterly* 22(1):1–14.

Gutmann, A. 1985. "Communitarian Critics of Liberalism." *Philosophy and Public Affairs* 14:308–322.

Johnson, L. 1992. "Individual and Collective Sovereignty in Corporate Enterprise." *Columbia Law Review* 92:2215–2249.

Kahneman, D., and A. Tversky. 1973. "On the Psychology of Prediction." *Psychological Review* 49(4):237–251.

Kanter, R.M. 1993. *Men and Women of the Corporation.* Second Edition. New York: Basic Books.

Lipset, S.M. 1996. *American Exceptionalism: A Double-Edged Sword.* New York: Norton.

MacIntyre, A. 1981. *After Virtue.* Notre Dame: Notre Dame Press.

Marshall, W. (ed.). 1997. *Building the Bridge: 10 Big Ideas to Transform America.* Lantham: Rowman & Littlefield.

Millon, D. 1993. "Introduction: Communitarians, Contractarians, and the Crisis in Corporate Law." *Washington and Lee Law Review* 50:373–1393.

Mitchell, L.E. 1992. "A Theoretical and Practical Framework for Enforcing Corporate Constituency Statutes." *Texas Law Review* 70:579–643.

Mulhall, S., and A. Smith. 1992. *Liberals and Communitarians*. Second Edition. Oxford: Blackwell.

New York Times. 1997. June 15. "Robert Kennedy's Children."

Nozick, R. 1974. *Anarchy, State, and Utopia*. New York: Basic Books.

Okin, S.M. 1989. *Justice, Gender, and the Family*. New York: Basic Books.

Paul, E.F., F.D. Miller, and J. Paul (eds.). 1996. *The Communitarian Challenge to Liberalism*. Cambridge: Cambridge University Press.

Phillips, M. 1994. "Father of Tony Blair's Big Idea." *Observer*, June 24.

Price, J.L., and C.W. Mueller. 1981. "A Causal Model of Turnover for Nurses." *Academy of Management Journal* 24(3):543–546.

Rawls, J. 1971. *A Theory of Justice*. Cambridge: Harvard University Press.

Rawls, J. 1993. *Political Liberalism*. New York: Columbia University Press.

Sandel, M.J. 1982. *Liberalism and the Limits of Justice*. Cambridge: Cambridge University Press.

Sandel, M.J. 1996. *Democracy's Discontent: America in Search of a Public Philosophy*. Cambridge: Harvard University Press.

Sciulli, D. (ed.). 1996. *Macro Socio-Economics: From Theory to Activism*. Armonk: Sharpe.

Sears, D.O. et al. 1980. "Self-Interest vs. Symbolic Politics in Policy Attitudes and Presidential Voting." *American Political Science Review* 74:670–684.

Selznick, P. 1992. *The Moral Commonwealth: Social Theory and the Promise of Community*. Berkeley: University of California Press.

Selznick, P. 1996. "Social Justice: A Communitarian Perspective." *The Responsive Community* 6(4):13–25.

Shapiro, R. 1995. "Cut and Invest: A Budget Strategy for the New Economy." Policy Report No. 2. Washington, D.C.: Progressive Policy Institute.

Shuman, M.H. 1994. "Introduction." In: R. Caplan and J. Feffer (eds.), *State of the Union 1994: The Clinton Administration and the Nation in Profile*, pp. 1–11. Boulder: Westview Press.

Simon, H. 1957. *Models of Man*. New York: Wiley.

Stern, P.C. 1984. *Improving Energy Demand Analysis*. Washington, D.C.: National Academy Press.

Swedberg, R.M. 1991. "The Battle of Methods: Toward a Paradigm Shift?" In: A. Etzioni and P. Lawrence (eds.), *Socio-Economics: Toward a New Synthesis*, pp. 13–33. Armonk: Sharpe.

Taylor, C. 1990. *Sources of the Self*. Cambridge: Cambridge University Press.

Thurow, L. 1996. *The Future of Capitalism*. New York: Penguin.

Walzer, M. 1983. *Spheres of Justice*. New York: Basic Books.

Weber, M. [1904–05] 1958. *The Protestant Ethic and the Spirit of Capitalism*. Translated by Talcott Parsons. New York: Charles Scribner's Sons.

Rational Choice and Human Agency in Economics and Sociology: Exploring the Weber–Austrian Connection

Peter J. Boettke

There has been a growing interest in the past decade or so in the intersection between economics and sociology. Much of the literature on this derives from a perceived disappointment by either economists or sociologists of the methods and approach to social questions of the other. Roughly, economic sociology is motivated mainly by the economist's perception of the lack of rigor in sociology. Social questions, it is argued, are too important to be left to poor methodological treatment. Thus, economic imperialism and rational choice sociology result.

On the other hand, sociologists criticize economists for ignoring the social dimension within economics. Economic science is sterile and, as such, cannot address the real issues it purports to examine. The treatment of individual actors as disembodied from institutional and historical context fails to account for how the social environment shapes individual desires and perceptions. Socioeconomics is proposed as a paradigm to replace neoclassical economics.

Both of these trends ignore an important historical school of social thought which sought neither to colonize sociology with economics

The ideas in this paper were originally stimulated by my participation in the 1992 summer faculty seminar on Economy, Culture and Values at the Institute for the Study of Economic Culture at Boston University, and by my graduate seminar on Economic Sociology at New York University in the fall of 1996. I would like to thank Peter Berger and Robert Hefner for providing me with the opportunity at ISEC, and to the students at NYU for interest in a broader conception of economics and political economy than is currently practiced within the mainstream of academic economics. In addition, I would like to thank Jeffrey Friedman, Israel Kirzner, Alan Peacock, Mario Rizzo, Uwe Siegmund, and the participants at the Egon-Sohmen-Foundation symposium for their comments and suggestions for revision. I gratefully acknowledge the financial assistance of the J.M. Kaplan Fund and the Egon-Sohmen-Foundation. The usual caveat applies.

nor eliminate universalistic economics with sociological analysis. Instead, economics and sociology were seen as existing within a symbiotic relationship. The approach of Max Weber and the Austrian School of Economics as represented by Carl Menger, Ludwig von Mises, and F. A. Hayek is seen as the foundation on which the proper relationship between economics and sociology should be grounded.

This paper highlights the Weberian roots of Austrian economics, *and* the Austrian roots of Weberian sociology. Menger ([[1871] 1981, [1883] 1985) influenced Weber (especially [1922] 1978) on two counts. First, the important distinction between levels of analysis (e.g., pure theory, applied theory, economic history) can be seen in both Menger and Weber. Second, the approach used in the social sciences, namely examining the origin and evolution of institutions, characterizes both the Austrian and Weberian research approaches. Weber's approach in constructing a unified interpretive social science was picked up by Ludwig von Mises and his development of praxeology. Mises's *Human Action* ([1949] 1966) was his most advancement statement, but this Weber–Mises connection has not been fully explored in the contemporary literature, despite Ludwig Lachmann's excellent treatment of the subject in *The Legacy of Max Weber* (1971).

Lachmann sought to articulate in that slim volume how the troublesome aspects of Weber's *Idealtypus* could be set aside by substituting the notion of *the plan*. Human action, according to Lachmann, exists in the form of plans—schemes designed to achieve imagined futures. The social scientist is able to provide an "intelligible account" of human society because of the centrality of the plan to human action, and it is precisely the notion of the plan which lies beyond the grasp of the natural sciences and vindicates the plea for the methodological autonomy of the social sciences. Lachmann continues his argument by linking the foundational concept of the plan to the praxeological approach, and by further arguing for the central role of "orientation" of human action by aid of institutions—as opposed to determinateness —for any causal-genetic theory of social processes, especially as they relate to the theory of economic growth and development. "A praxeological theory of society constructed on the firm basis of purpose and plan, such as emerges from Weber's work," Lachmann states earlier on in his essay, "is evidently not compatible with a functionalist view of life in society" (1971, p. 7). Unfortunately, the further development of this praxeological research approach, as traced by Lachmann, did not emerge—even with the crisis of positivism in the philosophy of science, and the resurgence of the Austrian School of Economics in the economics profession that has occurred over the past few decades.

I conjecture that the reason for the failure in the modern literature on economics and sociology to deal with the Weber and Austrian connection is threefold. First, Weber's approach was misunderstood in the Anglo-Saxon context because of the "translation" of his approach by Talcott Parsons. The Alfred Schütz–Talcott Parsons debate concerning this issue will be briefly discussed to tease out this point. Schütz, in fact, is the key component in this alternative account of the relationship between economics and sociology. He recast both Weber and Mises phenomenologically, offering an alternative path for sociological inquiry as a humanistic discipline concerned with meaning. In so doing, he was able to demonstrate that only by protecting the individualist-subjectivist point of reference would the social analyst be able to offer meaningful explanations for social phenomena.

Second, the basic anticlassical liberal (anti-individualist) strand of much of 20th-century sociological thought prevented scholars from overlooking Mises's classical liberal polemics and examining the substance of his thought. This development is due to Emile Durkheim, and, once again, Talcott Parsons's restatement of the Durkheimian approach which juxtaposed nonindividualist sociology against individualist economics. Here, as Viktor Vanberg has pointed out, there was a confusion of substantive and methodological criterion in social thought (1994, pp. 1–8). There is no reason whatsoever to believe that methodological individualism cannot account for the presence and importance of social institutions. In fact, as will be argued it is precisely here where the Weber–Austrian connection reveals its greatest potential for contributing to the contemporary discussion by avoiding both atomism and functionalism. There has also been an unfortunate tendency to conflate methodology and ideology. Methodological individualism is not the same as political individualism, and the failure to distinguish between these two different approaches is a major shortcoming of much of 20th-century sociological thought. This problem persists today in the modern communitarian and liberal dialogue.

Third, subsequent developments within the Misesian tradition did not explore the sociological heritage to which Mises's system belongs. Praxeology was treated exclusively as a methodological approach, rather than the substantive and comprehensive approach which it represented in Mises's mind. Praxeology is a term which simply means "the study of human action." Mises made certain justificationist methodological arguments in an attempt to ground this approach (apriorism and deductive reasoning) and other pragmatic arguments about the appropriate methods for praxeology (the method of imaginary constructions and the compositive approach).[1] But the overarching scientific vision which Mises had was not limited to methodology and the analytical methods. Rather, Mises's vision was the completion of Weber's approach in interpretative sociology. Mises sought to demonstrate that the human sciences were at once distinct from the natural sciences, yet were also distinct from history. Praxeology promised a unified social science that could strive for conceptual universalism for the purpose of improving particularistic historical understanding. The modern Austrian school has been myopic on two fronts—a reading of praxeology as exclusively a methodological position, and a narrow fixation on praxeology as catallaxy (or economics). This paper will try to redress this state of affairs by way of attempting to place the praxeological approach within the modern discourse on economics and sociology.

I   The Modern Discourse

The social sciences have been in a state of turmoil for over 30 years. An uneasy tension between the various heterodox schools of thought and the mainstream of social science is evident. Sociology, for example, has split between classic sociology and modern quantitative and formal sociology (see Wolfe, 1992). Economics, which may appear less vulnerable, has nevertheless suffered a crisis of thought (see, e.g., McCloskey, 1985, 1994; Heilbroner and Milberg, 1995). The real reason for this state of affairs is the crisis in the philosophical status of the social sciences and modernity in general. Postmodern developments in thought challenge the hegemony of mainstream formalist and positivist thought across the disciplines. The inertia of institutional forms is all that has prevented the complete fracturing of academic disciplines conceived along positivistic grounds.

The interpretative turn in social thought demands a fundamental rethinking of the basic questions that are to be asked and what are to be judged as acceptable answers. But, the modern discourse concerning

---

[1] On Mises's methodological approach, see Boettke (1998).

economics and sociology seems stalled at this point—concentrating on the merits or demerits of the rational choice framework for social analysis (see Swedberg, 1990).

Modern sociology came late to the academic table. It was left only the scraps of the social world. History claimed the past, and anthropology claimed the exotic. Psychology dealt with the mind, economics with the market, and political science with the state. The family, crime, race, gender, and other social problems were left for sociology. This division of labor was an arbitrary and unstable equilibrium. Trespassing was inevitable.

The founders of modern sociology, for example, differentiated themselves from the other social sciences by claiming that the "social" was in everything. Social forces, stratification, systems effects, class analysis, etc., became the hallmark of sociological analysis. Emile Durkheim, for example, insisted that social study required an examination of the social (as opposed to individual or psychological or material) causes of all phenomena. His famous studies of the division of labor, and suicide, as well as his interest in religion and morality all reflect this *imperialistic* approach of Durkheim ([1893] 1884, [1897] 1963). The general overriding principle of his approach was that religious, juridical, moral, and economic phenomena must be explained in reference to the particular social milieu within which they are found.

Max Weber, on the other hand, represented a different approach to sociology. But, modern sociology did not develop along the Weberian lines that I will highlight. Weber's approach was a causal-genetic approach which employed ideal-type methodology to aid the task of interpretive sociology. But Durkheim's influence dominated sociological thought. Even with the developments pioneered by Talcott Parsons, social systems explanations dominated sociology, i.e., functionalism. Functionalism seeks to examine the consequences of social patterns and practices without really addressing their underlying cause. In examining family relations and monogamous marriage in Western society, for example, a functionalist approach would contrast this form of family system with alternative forms and investigate the consequences with regard to the wider social milieu of Western civilization.

Functional analysis is not necessarily in conflict with causal-genetic analysis, but the way it was practiced by modern sociology forced a split between these two traditions of social analysis. Economic theory, which at heart is a causal theory, was forced into conflict with sociology.

When Gary Becker (1957) first decided to use economic tools to examine subjects that were the domain of sociologists, such as discrimination, his work was met with great skepticism. Becker provided something which traditional sociology did not—a theory grounded in the rational behavior of individuals. Discrimination was a nonpecuniary "taste" which within market interaction generated pecuniary costs. Discrimination in the market place by any group reduces its own real incomes as well as the real incomes of those that it discriminates against. Becker's study was not only theoretically coherent, it appeared to be consistent with the data.

Rational choice studies of investment in human capital (education, skills, etc.) followed with the same kind of results. Crime, politics, family relations, and social interaction in general all came to be examined using the tools of economics. The economic approach became synonymous with the study of human behavior in all walks of life and realms of society.[2] Becker defines the economic approach as the relentless and unflinching use of the combined assumptions of maximizing behavior, market equilibrium, and stable preferences (1976, p. 5).

Becker's economic imperialism has been criticized for having an "undersocialized" view of the individual. Classic Durkheimian and (Karl) Polanyian themes of social systems of rules and values, the embeddedness of culture, etc., have been resurrected in a modern sociological critique of the neoclassical view of the individual. Non-rational processes, it is argued, form the basis of our choices. The influence of our parents, our situation within the community, and the religious morals of that community form the basis of human behavior, not rational choice (see, for example, Etzioni, 1988). With this shift away from utilitarian rational choice, comes an entire package of reassessment of the social sciences, from methodology to discourse within the polity to public policy.

Mark Granovetter's alternative approach, for example, focuses attention on the social structures, organizations and groups within which economic activity is embedded, including the state in its capacity of shaping ownership, authority, and financial relationships between business groups. Granovetter's intent is to overcome both

---

[2] Perhaps one of the most ambitious studies influenced by Becker in this regard was Richard Posner's examination of the history of sexual practices. See Posner (1992). For my own assessment of this work, see Boettke (1995).

the problems of the *under-* and *oversocialized* view of the individual that is evident in standard economics and standard sociology. "Actors do not behave or decide as atoms outside a social context, nor do they adhere slavishly to a script written for them by the particular intersection of social categories that they happen to occupy" (Granovetter, 1985, p. 487). But this does not necessarily imply a rejection of rational choice theorizing. "Insofar as rational choice arguments are narrowly construed as referring to atomized individuals and economic goals," Granovetter states, "they are inconsistent with the embeddedness position presented here. In a broader formulation of rational choice, however, the two views have much in common" (1985, p. 505). In this statement Granovetter's approach is quite consistent with the one I associate with the Weber–Mises formulation of methodological individualism, but Granovetter's actual argument proceeds as if the arrow of influence runs in only one direction—from the social context to the individual. That individuals are the source of institutions is not an avenue that is pursued, and, thus, the meaning of these structures remain incomplete. A sophisticated version of methodological individualism would see institutions as both the product and shaper of individual choice. In this perspective, the problem with the modern discourse is that while sociology asks the interesting questions, it remains hobbled by a lack of analytical structure. On the other hand, while economics possesses an analytical structure, it remains hobbled by an undue restriction of the questions it can ask and answer. Praxeological reasoning requires a more flexible form of thought, which does not mechanically "close" the system as in equilibrium styles of reasoning, but nevertheless enables us to establish the boundaries of action. The task before us is one of simultaneously broadening the questions and yet retaining structure. Granovetter's concern with embedding individual action within a social context is an important first step, but it is neither enough in itself nor is it unique to him.

At its best, economics is caught between being "dismal science" and "worldly philosophy" without becoming exclusively either. The aproach here is one which recognizes that the best contributions in political economy combine the analytical rigor of economic theory with methodological and philosophical sophistication, and political theory. In the intersection between politics, philosophy, and economics —whatever ideological perspective—the truly interesting work in the social sciences takes place. By myopically pursuing only the formal aspects of the discipline, economics has been reduced to its present state, in which we continually know more and more about less and less. The narrowness of modern economics, combined with the imperialistic tendencies of its formalist and positivist research, has led many to not only resist "economism" but to launch organized intellectual and political efforts to overturn individualist and market-oriented economics (see, e.g., Coughlin, 1996). It will be useful for our purposes to invoke this socioeconomic and communitarian approach as a foil, with which to contrast the alternative Weber–Mises approach for social inquiry that is being advocated.

Perhaps the most ambitious attempt to coordinate the efforts of those who find rational choice social science particularly lacking can be found in the activities of Amitai Etzioni. The Etzioni approach to socioeconomics, however, possesses some serious intellectual problems. First, several social theories are conflated where they should be differentiated. An appreciation of the dynamic adjustment qualities of markets does not automatically translate into a spirited defense of rugged individualism and radical libertarianism. It may, but it also may not. Second, this conflation is based on questionable readings of the various scholars in question. Not all understandings (or defenses) of the market order are based on an isolated view of the individual. Moreover, classical liberalism should not be contrasted with a concern with civil society. Instead, classical liberalism is a political theory grounded in the voluntarism that is reflected in a vibrant civil society. The rather simplistic categories which scholars are placed in within this literature does not aid serious social inquiry into, and engagement in, important issues. Third, the stated choice between economic imperialism or sociological imperialism is a false choice. Fourth, the communitarian ethos needs to be debated critically, not simply asserted. It is not at all clear whether Etzioni's approach can successfully steer between moral authoritarianism and spirited individualism.

II An Alternative to the Modern Discourse

The great problem in social theory is to steer a course between either an undersocialized or oversocialized view of the individual. Whereas the undersocialized view eliminates the social context within which preferences are formed and choices are made, the oversocialized view eliminates the power of human agency to shape the social world. Neither approach is very fruitful.

The classic historicist/institutionalist critique of economics is that culture and history are core concepts that have been eliminated in the strive for universalistic explanation. What standard economists assume to be characteristics of human nature are instead behavioral regularities that are specific to time and place and persist because of enculturation. Choose a different time and place, with different history-specific enculturation processes, and the assumptions of economic theory (as standard theory understands them) do not hold. Beyond developed capitalism, economic theory—understood as modern price theory—does not hold. One cannot look to economic theory to solve the problems of poverty and deprivation in non-Western cultures (see, e.g., Heilbroner, 1996). Solutions there must be found in the historical and cultural practices of the time and place under consideration. Culture and historicity are the core concepts of social analysis, and work not based on these concepts will be faulty and misleading.

The major problem with relying on culture and historicity as the core concepts is that it slights the simple fact that in order to understand a people and their culture and history, we must presuppose the validity of some universal propositions about human behavior. Theory is logically prior to historical interpretation, and thus the question is never one of theory versus no theory, but articulated theory versus unarticulated theory. The gulf between historicism and economism simply reflects the classic social science dichotomy between "thick" and "thin" description. Economists possess a penchant for "thin" description (and the scientific value of parsimony), while area studies scholars and historians value "thick" description (and the scholarly value of thoroughness). The social scientific methodological question for over a century has been whether meaningful "thick" description is possible without the guidance of "thin" description. On the one hand, "thin" description unconcerned with the underlying reality conveyed in "thick" descriptions describes little of relevance to our daily lives.[3] On

---

[3] In his recent critique of modern economics and the political-cultural implications which mainstream economics has had for U.S. society, Robert Kuttner (1997, p. 34) makes the following telling observation about economists' penchant for "thin" description: "Apprentice economists, and fellow travelers in other disciplines, were spared the time-consuming process of reading history or

the other hand, "thick" description unaided by an articulated theory cannot help but bring on board theoretical baggage that defies critical scrutiny. The social world is far too complex to access directly; our understanding must of necessity be theory-impregnated.

We need, in other words, both "thin" and "thick" description for our social theory to possess both meaning and relevance—coherence and correspondence, so to speak. To put it bluntly, if there were nothing universal in the human experience (the basis for "thin" description), then even our "thick" description of different people would remain beyond our ability to understand. Alien cultural practices would for-ever remain *alien* and inaccessible to others. At the same time, if all there were to the human condition were the universal, then culture and history and area studies in general would disappear. We could learn as much about a people by sitting at our computer as we would by studying their history. Both extremes of exclusivity in social explana-tion are to be avoided. We need universal theory to understand, but we need uniqueness to whet our desire to understand *the other*. We are enough alike to learn from one another, but we are also different enough so as to have something to learn.

Thus, contrary to the traditional dichotomization, economic theory must not be contrasted with the diversity of humanity and the partic-ularities of time and place (see Rutherford, 1994). Instead, economic theory is a necessary (though not sufficient) component of a social analysis which hopes to make sense of that human diversity and those particularities. Institutions are constraints as well as shapers of human behavior, and social analysis must be prepared to deal with this com-plex interaction. All human behavior is mediated through specific institutional filters. The justification for the "thin description" of eco-nomic theory is that it affords us more compelling "thick descriptions" of the social experience of particular times and places.

---

studying the details of complex institutions. They had only to devise the models, collect the statistics and crunch the numbers. . . . You didn't really need to know anything, and you could know everything about everything. Some of the most prestigious economists today are astonishingly expert in everything from trade to labor markets to income distribution to financial markets to macroeconomic policy—and by the age of thirty-five. It suggests either remarkably protean intellects—or dubious shortcuts." In an otherwise quite confusing work, Kuttner touches the right cord with regard to the rather dubious shortcuts which "thin" description, taken alone, can lead.

It is precisely at this juncture—between "thick" and "thin"—that institutional individualism offers an alternative to either atomistic individualism or naïve holism (see Prychitko, 1995, pp. 9–56). "Rationality" in this formulation of individual action is nothing more than a basic notion of instrumental rationality and must be understood as being entirely individually subjective and forward-looking. Following Mises ([1933] 1981, pp. 68–129), an open-ended notion of human agency in economics and sociology can subsume the Weberian categories of action—valuational, emotional, and traditional—under the rubric of the purposive-rational, which in turn is simply "meaningful action." The essence of the sciences of human action lies in "grasping the meaning of action" (ibid., p. 132). The universalistic approach based on purpose-rational action is made possible by introducing degrees of typification, including the most abstract anonymous typification to the more concrete typification of historical agents. (This is a methodological modification of Mises's system that is attributable to Alfred Schütz; Mises himself actually relied on Kantian categories rather than on the degrees of typification.) Since the scientific goal in interpretative sociology (i.e., praxeology) is *Verstehen*, not prediction and falsifiability, broadening of the concept of rationality to near tautological status does not present the problem it would in alternative concepts of science. The point to emphasize for my purposes here is that it is the *institutional context of choice* that gives meaning to individual choices within a social system, and provides the basis for the scientific ability to grasp the meaning of human action both through discursive reasoning (conception) and through empathetic intuition (understanding).

Functionalist or social systems theories are not necessarily in conflict with rational choice theories. In fact, one of the most ambitious enterprises in contemporary sociology is that associated with James Coleman's attempt to bridge the gap between rational choice and functionalism (see Coleman, 1990). As in Gary Becker's approach, rational choice is synonymous with maximizing behavior, and a functionalist explanation is equivalent to an equilibrium one. Neither maximizing nor equilibrium are concepts intended to get at *meaning* in human affairs.[4] The goal of social science is not intelligibility, but pre-

---

[4] Kirzner (1976) provides a classic presentation of the Austrian argument for significance of purposeful action. Also see Berger's (1963, pp. 164–176) discus-

dictability—and parsimony and theoretical elegance are valued, not detailed and thorough historical understanding.

Like Etzioni, the Becker–Coleman approach suffers from serious problems. First, it does not eliminate the problem of under- and over-socialization, but rather constructs an oversocialized view of the social system from an undersocialized view of the individual. Second, as a result, the approach cannot adequately deal with either social embeddedness or human agency.[5] The buffoonery, as well as the wonder, of social life as individuals steer a course between alluring hopes and haunting fears is lost to the analyst, and with that his/her ability to understand the human condition. A precise set of propositions about maximizing entities and social forces not subject to human will is produced, but in a fundamental sense the analyst is blind to *humanity*.

The strict assumption that individuals maximize their behaviour eliminates the conscious component from the choice problem faced by individuals in a world of uncertainty. Choice is instead reduced to a simple exercise within a given ends-means framework. The individual's attempts to discover not only which ends to pursue but also the appropriate means to use in pursuing these ends is left out of the equation.

The maximizing assumption eliminates not only the social construction of individual preferences, but also the individual's own construction of preferences through time (see Buchanan, 1979).[6] The

---

sion of sociology as a humanistic discipline, and especially his comments on "humorless scientism" which produces a situation in which sociology "may find that it has acquired a foolproof methodology, only to lose the world of phenomena that it originally set out to explore—a fate as sad as that of the magician who has finally found the formula that will release the mighty *jinn* from the bottle, but cannot recollect what it was that he wanted to ask of the *jinn* in the first place" (p. 165). Modern economics has been in this sad state of affairs for most of the 20th century (see Boettke, 1997).

[5] Becker (1991), for example, has written a very interesting paper on the social influences on economic behavior. But, in Becker's analysis social and cultural influences constitute the constraints within which maximizing behavior takes place. This approach, while an improvement over the isolated view of individual utility maximization, nevertheless does not fully capture the meaning of embeddedness.

[6] Buchanan's paper was a critique of the Becker–Stigler formulation of the individual inspired by his reading of Shackle's *Epistemics and Economics* (1972). Buchanan has often taken a dual position with regard to the individual actor

rationality postulate can only generate formal proofs of equilibrium if the future (with its novelty, uncertainty, and ignorance) is excluded. A static conception of rationality is inconsistent with the passage of real time (see O'Driscoll and Rizzo, 1985, pp. 52–70). If an understanding of economic and social life requires the examination of both the passage of real time and rational behavior, then modeling human interaction in a fashion which excludes either drains the explanation of essential details, to the detriment of social scientific thought.

My contention is that certain traditions within classical political economy and the neoclassical revolution, and classical sociology do, in fact, attempt to explore human interaction in a manner which does not exclude the details of novelty, uncertainty, and ignorance. The conjectural history of the Scottish moral philosophers and the interpretative sociology of Max Weber should be, and was among some economists, the general theoretical framework for a social theory that attempts to steer between under- and oversocialized views of the individual (see Boettke, 1990). This framework promises a unified social science, within which economics represents a subset of the broader discipline of sociology. Sociology, as Weber put it, "is a science concerning itself with the interpretive understanding of social action and thereby with a causal explanation of its course and consequences" ([1922] 1978, p. 4).

Weber was deeply influenced in this regard by the Austrian school of economics. Weber had read and appreciated Carl Menger's and

---

in economics. On the one hand, Buchanan has been one of the foremost proponents of the subjectivist perspective in economics and embraced the open-endedness of human choice. On the other hand, Buchanan admits that within that open-ended quest we often act "as if" we were rats. In other words, maximizing is not an all-encompassing picture of man, but sometimes we are maximizing agents. To the extent we act as rats, then the standard model of man—as captured by Becker–Stigler—is an appropriate scientific tool. To the extent we act as humans, however, the neoclassical conception of the individual is not an appropriate tool. In addition, Buchanan has developed an argument for using the maximizing model in political economy that is not a descriptive/predictive argument, but rather a tool in theory construction. By modeling the polity as a revenue-maximizing Leviathan, Buchanan generates an argument for structural rules which prevent political opportunism even in the worst-case scenario. This last use of the maximizing model—as purely an analytical construct—cannot be objected to in the same manner that the predictive-descriptive use of maximizing can from a praxeological viewpoint.

Eugen Böhm-Bawerk's contributions to economic theory and methodology. He invited both Friedrich von Wieser and Joseph Schumpeter to contribute volumes to his encyclopedic project in social theory. And, in Weber's magnum opus, *Economy and Society*, he, at key junctures in the development of his own arguments concerning monetary circulation and economic calculation (Weber, [1922] 1978, pp. 78, 93, 107), favorably references Ludwig von Mises's *Theory of Money and Credit* ([1912] 1980) and Mises's 1920 essay on the problem of economic calculation under socialism. Mises, in turn, devoted considerable attention to the systemic, critical study of Weber, which is reflected in his *Epistemological Problems of Economics* ([1933] 1981) and *Human Action* ([1949] 1966). As Ludwig Lachmann stated in his review of Mises's *Human Action*, "In reading this book we must never forget that it is the work of Max Weber that is being carried on here" ([1951] 1977, p. 94).

Weber's connection to the Austrians was quite close, though this is not really appreciated by traditional sociologists.[7] This should be a natural starting point for a discussion of the interface between economics and sociology. Yet, it is an avenue not explored at all in contemporary scholarship. In Richard Swedberg's (1980) interviews with the leading scholars at the edge of both disciplines, Max Weber's name is referenced 34 times, but Hayek is referenced only once and Mises not at all. Schumpeter is referred to 16 times, but Menger is only referred to twice, neither reference being substantive, and Lachmann (who wrote a book on the Weberian legacy in economics) is not referenced at all. Etzioni's *The Moral Dimension* (1988) cites neither Mises nor Hayek, though Machlup is cited a few times with respect to methodological points. Hayek's *Law, Legislation and Liberty* (1973–1979), on the other hand, makes the bibliography and warrants a few references to the concept of spontaneous order in James Coleman's *Foundations of Social Theory* (1990). But, Hayek's work does not play a prominent role in Coleman's theory construction, nor does Coleman deal with the intellectual history issue of Weber's connection to the Austrians. In the index of *The Handbook of Economic Sociology* (Swelser and Swedborg, 1994), Hayek is referenced 6 times, and Mises 2 times, while there are 36 references to Weber and 17 to Schumpeter. Even George Stigler is referenced more often than Mises and Hayek

---

[7] Though see the discussion in Holton and Turner (1989, pp. 30–67).

combined, namely 11 times. Clearly, in the modern discourse, the Austrian economists are not considered important potential contributors.

The relationship between the Austrians and Weber, however, was a mutually beneficial one in which both learned from the other and influenced the development of their respective work. Weber's connection to the Austrians was obscured by Talcott Parsons. While Parsons is largely responsible for introducing Weber to the English-speaking community, his "prejudices" were imported along with his translation of Weber's ideas.[8] Alfred Schütz (the Austrian economist and Weberian sociologist), for example, charged Parsons with only nodding to the theory of subjectivism.[9] Parsons did not, according to Schütz, "safeguard the subjectivist point of view" from the unwarranted intrusion of objectivism ([1940] 1978, p. 50). But, Schütz added that it was only by safeguarding the subjectivist point of view that we will have a guarantee "that the social sciences do in fact deal with the real social world, the one and unitary life-world of us all, and not with a strange world of fancy that is independent of and has no connection with our world of everyday life" ([1940] 1978, p. 60).

The postulate of subjective interpretation demands that the social theorist include "first-level" reference to the meaning actions possess for actors, i.e., to their purpose, in his/her construct of the social world. *Verstehen* as a "second-level" reference, that is, from the point of view of the scientist, refers to his/her attempt to understand the implications of purposive behavior among individuals. In understanding human understanding, the task is first and foremost one of rendering intelligible the purposes and plans of the social actors involved, and second, to trace the unintended consequences of those actions. As Schütz argued in *The Phenomenology of the Social World* ([1932] 1967), we must first achieve a genuine understanding of the actions of the individual. Second, we must understand the "communicative intent" and significance of meaningful actions to others, and how the interpretation of these actions leads to the complex coordination of human activity.

---

[8] See Bernstein (1976, p. 252, fn. 26) for a discussion of Parsons's influence on the English language reading of Weber.

[9] See Grathoff (1978) for the correspondence between Alfred Schütz and Talcott Parsons with respect to the theory of social action. Also, see Fitzhenry (1986). In addition, see Prendergast (1986) for a discussion of Schütz's relationship with the Austrian School of Economics.

III   Theory and Application

The Austrian–Weberian theoretical approach entailed a commitment
to three principles: (1) methodological individualism, (2) methodological subjectivism, and (3) unintended consequences and spontaneous order. In this approach, the sociologist raises general questions
such as Georg Simmel (1908) raised concerning "How is Society Possible?" The economist, on the other hand, concentrates on the subset
question of how market coordination is possible without central
design. This approach does not commit the social theorist to either an
under- or oversocialized view of the individual. Instead, as Holton and
Turner have pointed out:

> Weber and the Austrian School are not obliged to deny the reality of institutions
> or the idea that actors may act under institutional constraints, or that this con-
> straint may be experienced as an external compulsive force or imperative. Nor
> need they hold to a social contract or design theory of institutions. Only two
> propositions are excluded. The first is that social life can be explained without ref-
> erence to the causal consequences of the meaning individuals give to their actions.
> The second is that institutions act as organic, causally effective entities through the
> structural imposition of rules or constraints on unwilling actors, and irrespective of
> the actions of such actors. (1989, pp. 42–43)

What emerges in the Weber–Austrian approach is what could be
termed an "action-systems theory" consisting of three components:
pure theory, institutional or applied theory, and history and policy.
Individuals are not assumed to maximize within an institutionless
vacuum, nor are they assumed to be merely puppets of structural
forces beyond their control. Reasonableness substitutes for hyper-
rationality, and spontaneous ordering processes substitute for equilibrium end-states.

Schütz's phenomenological sociology, for example, developed a
continuum of ideal-type constructions which made pure universal
theory as well as concrete historical case studies possible. Typification
of anonymous human action is employed to develop pure theory. Pure
theory enables theorists to reflect on universal characteristics of human
agency. Economic principles, such as marginal utility and opportunity
cost, are examples of such anonymous typification. Man's purposive
activity as evidenced in the forming of plans is the most general principle in Schütz's sociological approach. We are thus, in this respect,

teleological creatures. The fact that we have imagined ends and we seek to arrange means to satisfy those ends does not imply strict instrumental rationality in a close-ended sense. Maximizing behavior is only a subset of human goal-oriented behavior. Our understanding of human actions derives, Schütz argues, from our intuitive understanding of the actions of "others" within the life-world. Though anonymous, therefore, the individual, according to Schütz's approach, can only be understood as man acting as a result of his social embeddedness.[10]

Institutionally contingent theory construction is the second component mentioned above. Moving ideal typification of anonymous action to more concrete action within specific institutional constraints generates certain positive propositions concerning individual incentives and the social use of information. Individual goal-oriented behavior is not independent of the social context of action. Again, social embeddedness is at the forefront of theory construction, not an afterthought.

Human intercourse is also radically altered by the social and institutional context. Patterns of exchange and production that would emerge within one institutional setting may not be expected to emerge in another. Social patterns are not invariant to institutional contexts. Goal-oriented behavior in one setting (say one involving private property ownership) may lead to the rational allocation of scarce resources, whereas goal-oriented behavior in another setting (say one involving collective ownership) may produce "the tragedy of the commons." Not only is individual behavior dependent on the social context of decision, but so are the consequences of the interaction of participants on the social scene (both intended and unintended). The Weber–Austrian argument concerning socialist calculation, for example, was an institutional argument. The institutions of socialism radically changed the social context within which decisions concerning resource use were made.[11]

The purpose of the first two components of the actions-systems

---

[10] On this intersubjective "introspection" as the source of knowledge in the social sciences and its implication for social theory construction, see Hayek ([1943] 1980, [1952] 1979, pp. 41–92).

[11] One of the most serious weaknesses of Lange's model of market socialism was his explicit denial of the importance of the institutional context of decisions ([1936] 1964, p. 62).

theory is to develop an analytical and interpretive framework within which a qualitative and quantitative narrative of a concrete historical or contemporary episode can be constructed, this being the third component. The justification for the first two components is, in other words, to enable scholars to produce better historical accounts.

IV   Where Sociologists and the Austrian's Went Wrong

In 1922, when Mises published his *Socialism*, he chose as a subtitle, *An Economic and Sociological Analysis*. By the time Mises would write *Human Action*, he substituted the word praxeology for sociology. Sociology had been corrupted, according to Mises, by Durkheim's influence, and, thus, had become both methodologically and politically collectivistic. Praxeology, on the other hand, represented the general science of human action. The sciences of human action could be divided into praxeology and historical science. Historical sciences include the history of political and military action, of ideas and philosophy, of economic episodes, of technological developments, of literature, art, and science, of religion, morals, and customs. Ethnography and anthropology as well as psychology are historical sciences to the extent they are not part of biology or physiology.

In contrast, praxeology is a theoretical discipline which concerns itself with human action in the abstract as opposed to the concrete of historical conditions. It aims at deriving universally valid principles of human behavior. These theoretical concepts, Mises contended, were "a necessary requirement of any intellectual grasp of historical events. Without them we should not be able to see in the course of events anything else than kaleidoscopic change and chaotic muddle" ([1949] 1966, p. 32).

The general intellectual climate of the day was not receptive to Mises's epistemology or politics. Positivistic notions of science increasingly dominated the social scientific community. And, nonpositivistic social science tended to reject classical liberalism. Mises was caught between a rock and a hard place. Positivistic economics rejected Mises methodology, but sometimes generated similar conclusions concerning the importance of economic principles for public policy. Humanistic social science accepted aspects of Mises's methodology, but rejected the public policy conclusions he held dear. Mises's reconstruction of Weber simply had a very limited to nonexistent professional audience.

But, Mises's strong opposition to socialism was grounded in an economic and sociological understanding of the basic problem of production and exchange.[12] The exchange ratios established in the market represent the social mosaic upon which rational economic calculation is based. Individual action is embedded in a web of social meaning. Far from being a problem, the social nature of human action is the major source of our knowledge about one another. It is only within the specific context of market activity that individuals have access to the knowledge required to appraise alternative courses of productive activity. Outside of that social context, the requisite knowledge does not exist. Without these shared meanings, economic life would be forever chaotic.[13]

Mises's (and Weber's) argument against socialism was in this sense an embeddedness argument. The social context of choice under capitalism cannot be replicated by socialism. Liberalism was the only viable social and political theory that could be a progressive force. Intellectuals and academics thought, however, that liberalism lacked a critical edge. A stale conservativism permeated the liberalism of early 20th-century thought.

Mises had no natural alliance within the intellectual community. Economics had gone in a different philosophical direction; sociology had gone in a different political direction. Mises was not without fault. He could have put aside political polemics, focusing instead on building a purely academic bridge to phenomenological sociology. In spite of his natural affinity with Alfred Schütz, many sociologists simply could not get past Mises's classical liberal polemics. On the other hand, Mises did not try to tone down his polemics. Political polemics were tied up with his science—and in a very important respect it was legitimate, for his argument against socialism was a scientific argument grounded in socioeconomics, and the consequences for humanity were huge.

In addition, Schütz unfortunately died at an early age. Machlup con-

---

[12] For a discussion of Mises and Hayek's contributions to the socialist calculation debate which emphasizes both the intellectual context of their respective contributions and the role of the institutional context of choice and the contextual nature of knowledge in general, see Boettke (1996a).

[13] See Horwitz (1992) for a discussion of the social nature and significance of money.

cerned himself with influencing mainstream economics and appeared to have developed ideal-type methodological arguments to defend neoclassical assumptions of maximizing behavior and profit.[14] Hayek increasingly turned his attention to political and legal theory, rather than economic and sociological theory. Mises's American students Israel Kirzner and Murray Rothbard each pursued scholarly careers which did not emphasize the sociological heritage of Austrian economics. The Austrian economists simply did not attempt to maintain their close contact with sociology during the post–World War II period.

As the Austrian economists and sociologists turned their backs on one another, other trends developed with regard to the interface between sociology and economics. Both Weberian sociology and Austrian economics moved to the far reaches of their respective disciplines. However, modern economic sociology can be reconstructed along precisely these lines.

This reconstruction is important because it is generally recognized that modern neoclassical economics suffers an institutional deficiency. Economics without institutions is reduced to a sterile set of propositions and irrelevant mental gymnastics. The rise of new institutionalism within economics, including such intellectual movements as public choice theory, law and economics, new economic history, and the new economics of organization, all derive from this perceived shortcoming in the formal body of neoclassical theory as it developed in the post–World War II era. The question is whether the institutional deficiency in economics can be remedied without first repairing the behavioral model.[15] If this is indeed the case, then the current efforts to incorpo-

---

[14] Though it should be pointed out that Machlup always added the caveat that what differentiated him from Friedman's position were the criteria of understandability and intelligibility. Machlup, in invoking the criteria of understandability and intelligibility, as opposed to either verification or falsifiability, was alluding to the phenomenological roots of his thought in Schütz and his approach to understanding *meaning*. An explanation which offers nothing beyond the successful prediction of observable events does not satisfy the intellectual curiosity of those who hope to understand a phenomenon. This aspect of Machlup's thought was simply lost on his American academic audience.

[15] To the best of my knowledge, this challenge to neoinstitutionalism owes its origin to Hans Albert. It is common in the literature to distinguish between neo- and new-institutionalism. Neoinstitutionalism retains the behavioral model used by neoclassical economics, namely a model based on complete ratio-

rate institutions fully into economic analysis will be doomed unless the basic conception of the individual is modified. The Becker–Coleman approach is a prime example of neoinstitutionalism, in which the basic neoclassical conception of man is retained and institutions are introduced as another set of constraints against which to maximize, and in which functionalist equilibrium outcomes result. But there is an alternative formulation, which retains the methodological individualist (rational choice) structure of argument, but complexifies the social environment within which human actors must develop mechanisms for coping with uncertainty and imperfections in their judgment and knowledge, and yet find meaning in goals they pursue and the lives they lead (see Boettke, 1996c). The Weber–Austrian approach to political economy offers a wider set of behavioral postulates for economic theory, and has already suggested a way to incorporate institutions into economic analysis.

Schluchter (1996), for example, attempts to deal with problems of how modernity emerged and the issue of meaning within modernity in relation to Weberian theory. Weber's theory was a comparative and developmental one which dealt not only with economics, but also with ethics, values, religion, etc. Modern market process theory also attempts to integrate similar concepts, such incentives, information, institutions, and ideology, into a coherent account of the social developmental process (see, e.g., Boettke, 1996b). Development issues can be divided usefully into two types of issues. First, there are issues of a technical nature which concern how inputs are channeled into output and how individuals within the system discover better ways of mixing inputs to expand output. These issues have to be addressed independent of whatever given set of institutions individuals find themselves operating within, and are addressed by the theory of entrepreneurship and technological innovation. Second, there are issues concerning how alternative political and social environments affect entrepreneurial decision-making. Different institutions produce different results in terms of how entrepreneurial behavior is exhibited. Which enviromments are most conducive to entrepreneurship and which ones are not? In the Weber–Austrian connection, the Austrians have significantly addressed

---

nality, while new-institutionalism substitutes a model of bounded rationality. The model of bounded rationality does not suffice in my mind to adequately address the type of criticisms which Albert raises.

the first set of issues, while Weberian analysis (combined with recent work on social capital) can be said to have addressed the second set of issues. A comparative theory of social development must address both sets of questions, and it is precisely at this juncture that the Weber–Austrian connection has the most to offer in the contemporary dialogue concerning economics and sociology.

V   Sociology and Liberalism

There can be little dispute over the fact that Mises was overly polemical. But so was Marx. And like Marx, Mises thought that his argument concerning the limits of socialism was not just an academic argument, it was one that concerned the life and death of civilization. Passion should not disqualify a scholar from being seriously examined. Mises was a passionate *and* a sophisticated scholar.

The arguments that Mises put forward concerning the negative aspects of socialism and the positive aspects of liberalism were, as he termed them, the product of an economic and sociological analysis. His methodological individualism did not rely on an undersocialized view of the individual, as does neoclassical theory, for which it is often criticized. Liberalism in the hands of Mises (and Hayek) was a complex social theory that highlighted not only rational action and incentives, but also cultural traditions and institutional infrastructure, and how alternative institutional arrangements influence the use and transmission of knowledge in society.

Some of today's issues demonstrate the socioeconomic component of liberalism. Issues concerning economic development, for example, occupy a priority in the intellectual community. The Third World is seeking ways of getting on the road to economic prosperity. The second world is trying to find their way in the transition from authoritarian political economies to market economies with political democracy. Even the first world is attempting to address issues ranging from technological innovation to sustainable development to environmental tradeoffs.

Historical economic sociology has given rise to a metadiscourse concerning the preconditions for economic development in Western civilizations. Historical success has not emerged from the brow of any genius, but rather as the result of the accidental process of trial and error. Civilization is not the product of man's intelligence. In fact, precisely the opposite is true—man's intelligence grew because of his existence within civilization, as Hayek emphasized.

This does not mean that we must acquiesce to the accidental forces of history. Rather, by examining historical discussions over the emergence of capitalism, we can glean a certain social wisdom about economic "takeoff" and the emergence of political freedom. We do possess some metahistorical hypotheses concerning the emergence of capitalism. Max Weber ([1904–1905] 1979) conjectured that certain cultural and religious values were necessary components in economic development. This thesis has recently been reasserted by Gianfranco Poggi (1983) and Peter Berger (1986). Harold Berman (1983) has argued that Western civilization developed out of legal and political polycentricism, and this has also been stressed by Jean Baechler (1975), Nathan Rosenberg, and L.E. Birdzell (1985). And, Fernand Braudel (1982) has emphasized the peculiar conflation of religious, political, and economic practices that laid the ground for the development of capitalism and Western civilization.

Capitalism developed in some regions and not in others precisely because certain institutionalized practices which were conducive to economic experimentation were adopted and reinforced. Market activities, for example, existed throughout the world. Monetary circulation and even certain elementary banking operations had existed for centuries. But, the development of capitalism went beyond the mere existence of these market activities.

What we find in common with all historical examples of "takeoff" is the adoption of practices and rules which protect from predation, namely the establishment, clarification, and enforcement of property rights. It seems sensible to put forward the hypothesis that economic takeoff is associated with the extension of property ownership to capital goods. As property ownership is respected in goods further remote from consumption, then practices emerge which lead to capitalistic development. The banking system, for example, is transformed so as to provide it with an additional role as a financial intermediary— private savings are channeled into investment funds. The transformed banking system facilitates the growth of the capital market. Longer-term investments in productive activity (which promise greater returns in the form of consumer goods) are undertaken and prove to be the vehicle by which sustainable growth is achieved.

The extension of property ownership to capital goods has proven fundamental for several reasons. First, recognized property ownership establishes the legal certainty necessary for individuals to commit resources.[16] The threat of confiscation, by either other market participants or political actors, undermines confidence in market activity and limits investment opportunities (see Olson, 1996). Individuals tend to get around the lack of *de jure* property rights through (1) the tacit acceptance of *de facto* rights which is self-enforced because of the discipline engendered by repeated dealings, (2) the use of extensive family networks, or (3) the employment of extralegal contract enforcement. These allow "markets" to develop without clear property ownership, and these markets may even provide the basis for the emergence of a new order. Nevertheless, markets without clearly defined rules tend to be limited and constrained as vehicles for economic development.

Second, recognized property rights generate incentives for the use of scarce resources, whereas markets without recognized property rights do not. Absent property rights, for example, the time discount on resource use will tend to be higher, and resource conservation will be discouraged. With clear property ownership, however, economic actors have an incentive to pay close attention to resource use and the discounted value of the future employment of scarce resources.

Third, recognized property rights is a precondition for the emergence of stable capital markets. The market for capital goods establishes the exchange ratios for scarce resources (reflected in the relative money price of capital goods) which guide investment activity. In other words, recognized property rights in the means of production, combined with a sound monetary system, allow the process of economic calculation to work. Economic calculation provides economic actors with vital knowledge which enables the social system of production to separate endeavors

---

[16] North and Weingast (1989) argue that the emergence of new institutions in the wake of the "Glorious Revolution" of 1688 enabled the government to credibly commit to upholding property rights. This ability by the government to successfully commit to not confiscate wealth led to a tremendous growth in investment activity. A subsidiary component of the North and Weingast argument which is particularly relevant to the post-Soviet era is the tortuous path that history takes as it stumbles toward constitution building. Seventeenth-century England, for example, experienced a crisis of the monarchy, a civil war, a Parliamentary crisis, a restoration of the monarchy, and a Glorious Revolution, all before institutions developed which restricted the state's ability to manipulate the economic rules for its, and its constituents, personal gain.

which are economically feasible from those which are technologically feasible. Without economic calculation, as Mises often stated, industrial production would be reduced to so many steps in the dark.

Liberalism is a political philosophy based on a sociological understanding of human agency, an appreciation of economic forces, and a close reading of social, political, and economic history. It is far from the atomistic and armchair doctrine of which it is often accused of being.

Liberalism is also fundamental to the debates over communitarianism. In fact, the contrast between liberalism and communitarianism is a false one. Communitarianism presupposes certain liberal values which govern the discourse over values. Not only does communitarian discourse rely on liberal values to govern the discourse over values, communitarianism does not preclude liberal experimentation. Neither Charles Taylor nor Etzioni have effectively demonstrated that communitarianism necessarily conflicts with liberalism. They are correct that liberalism does undermine some traditional values, but the framework for permissive social and individual experimentation is grounded (just like the value discourse over experimentation) in respect for personhood. If communitarianism is possible, then so is liberalism, for both presuppose the sustainability of the same basic values—respect for personhood and the community of discourse.

Neither does liberalism conflict with communitarianism. Within a liberal society, communitarian values of family, virtue, duty, social consciousness, etc., can be adopted by various communities. The key point is that civil society requires a value infrastructure consistent with liberalism within which the virtuous and unvirtuous can nevertheless live together in peace. This is, of course, the great irony that the Soviet experience taught us. Without securing and protecting the private domain, a meaningful public domain canot be obtained. Instead, by making public what had previously been private, the communist experiment led to a truncated public life and a retreat into an isolated private life (see Gellner, 1994, pp. 30–43, 87–96).

In both cases, economic development and the communitarian-liberal debate, a liberal argument can be formulated which is steeped in a historical and theoretical sociology based on the rational activity of individuals. Liberal theory in the Weber–Austrian rendition is not based on a faulty conception of human nature (Benthamite utilitarianism), but rather emerges from an understanding of human intercourse in its rich complexity.

VI Conclusion

The cross-fertilization of Weberian sociology and Austrian economics promises a way back from scientistic models of irrelevance in the social sciences, and a return to the "life-world" of human existence. Methodological individualism in this tradition does not postulate man as being disembodied from his social environment. Atomism is not an appropriate criticism of liberalism, and thus the critical stance that socioeconomists take against the contributions of Mises and Hayek to liberalism have to be reexamined. Using criticisms of neoclassical conceptions of man to dismiss Mises and Hayek's understanding of the progressive influence of markets in social development simply does not engage the issue. Similarly, criticizing liberalism for failing to deal with the community also fails to engage the issue. Communitarians have yet to show how they can avoid moral authoritarianism unless they constrain their approach by referring to the autonomy of the individual—in which case the communitarian position is nothing more than the advocacy of a particular way of life within a framework of liberal pluralism.

The obstacles that prevent engaging the issues in the current dialogue over the economics and the sociology of the Weber–Austrian approach have to be overcome. The interaction between Weberian sociology and Austrian economics has been quite fruitful in the past, and the gains from this interaction have not been exhausted—especially in developing a comparative political economy of developmental processes. The resulting hybrid approach may represent what has appeared so elusive in the 20th century: a social theory which is at the same time logically coherent, empirically useful, humanistic in its method, and humanitarian in its concerns. If so, then the Weber–Austrian connection would provide exactly what we need as we head toward the 21st century.

Bibliography

Baechler, J. 1975. *The Origins of Capitalism*. Oxford: Blackwell.
Becker, G. 1957. *The Economics of Discrimination*. Chicago: University of Chicago Press.
Becker, G. 1976. *The Economic Approach to Human Behavior*. Chicago: University of Chicago Press.

Becker, G. 1991. "A Note on Restaurant Pricing and Other Examples of Social Influences on Price." *Journal of Political Economy* 99(5):1109–1116.

Berger, P. 1963. *Invitation to Sociology*. New York: Double Day.

Berger, P. 1986. *The Capitalist Revolution*. New York: Basic Books.

Berman, H. 1983. *Law and Revolution*. Cambridge: Harvard University Press.

Bernstein, R. 1976. *Restructuring Political and Social Theory*. Philadelphia: University of Pennsylvania Press.

Boettke, P.J. 1990. "Interpretive Reasoning and the Study of Social Life." *Methodus* 2(Dec.):35–45.

Boettke, P.J. 1995. "Good Economics, Bad Sex (And Even Worse Philosophy): A Review Essay of Richard Posner *Sex and Reason*." *Review of Political Economy* 7(3):360–373.

Boettke, P.J. 1996a. "Economic Calculation: *The* Austrian Contribution to Political Economy." (mimeo).

Boettke, P.J. 1996b. "L'economia, la politica e il segno della storia." *Nuova Economia E Storia* 3:189–214. Translated from "Why Culture Matters: Economics, Politics and the Imprint of History." (mimeo).

Boettke, P.J. 1996c. "What is Wrong with Neoclassical Economics (And What is Still Wrong with Austrian Economics)." In: F. Foldvary (ed.), *Beyond Neoclassical Economics*, pp. 22–40. Aldershot: Elgar.

Boettke, P.J. 1997. "Where Did Economics Go Wrong? Modern Economics as a Flight from Reality." *Critical Review* 11(1):11–64.

Boettke, P.J. 1998. "Ludwig von Mises." In: J. Davis, W. Hands and U. Makii (eds.), *The Handbook of Economic Methodology*. Aldershot: Elgar (forthcoming).

Braudel, F. 1982. *Civilization and Capitalism*. New York: Harper and Row.

Buchanan, J. 1979. "Natural and Artifactual Man." In: *What Should Economists Do?*, pp. 93–112. Indianapolis: Liberty Press.

Coleman, J. 1990. *Foundations of Social Theory*. Cambridge: Harvard University Press.

Coughlin, R. 1996. "Whose Morality? Which Community? What Interests? Socio-Economics and Communitarian Perspectives." *Journal of Socio-Economics* 25(2):135–155.

Durkheim, E. [1893] 1984. *The Division of Labor*. New York: Free Press.

Durkheim, E. [1897] 1963. *Suicide: A Sociological Study*. New York: Free Press.

Etzioni, A. 1988. *The Moral Dimension*. New York: Free Press.

Fitzhenry, R. 1986. "Parsons, Schütz and the Problem of *Verstehen*." In: R. Holton and B. Turner (eds.), *Talcott Parsons on Economy and Society*. London: Routledge.

Gellner, E. 1994. *Conditions of Liberty: Civil Society and Its Rivals*. New York: Penguin.

Granovetter, M. 1985. "Economic Action and Social Structure: The Problem of Embeddedness." *American Journal of Sociology* 91(3):481–510.

Grathoff, R. (ed.). 1978. *The Theory of Social Action: The Correspondence of Alfred Schütz and Talcott Parsons*. Bloomington: Indiana University Press.

Hayek, F.A. [1943] 1980. "The Facts of the Social Sciences." In: *Individualism and Economic Order*, pp. 57–76. Chicago: University of Chicago Press.

Hayek, F.A. [1952] 1979. *The Counter-Revolution of Science*. Indianapolis: Liberty Press.

Hayek, F.A. 1973–79. *Law, Legislation and Liberty*. Volumes 1–3. Chicago: University of Chicago Press.

Heilbroner, R. 1996. "The Embarrassment of Economics." *Challenge* (Nov./Dec.): 46–49.

Heilbroner, R., and W. Milberg. 1995. *The Crisis of Vision in Modern Economic Thought*. New York: Cambridge University Press.

Holton, R., and B. Turner. 1989. *Max Weber on Economy and Society*. New York: Routledge.

Horwitz, S. 1992. *Monetary Evolution, Free Banking and Economic Order*. Boulder: Westview Press.

Kirzner, I. 1976. "On the Method of Austrian Economics." In: E. Dolan (ed.), *The Foundations of Modern Austrian Economics*, pp. 40–51. Kansas City: Sheed & Ward.

Kuttner, R. 1997. *Everything for Sale: The Virtues and Limits of Markets*. New York: Knopf.

Lachmann, L. [1951] 1977. "The Science of Human Action." In: *Capital, Expectations and the Market Process*, pp. 94–111. Kansas City: Sheed Andrews and McMeel.

Lachmann, L. 1971. *The Legacy of Max Weber*. Berkeley: University of California Press.

Lange, O. [1936] 1964. "On the Economic Theory of Socialism." In: B. Lippincott (ed.), *On the Economic Theory of Socialism*, pp. 57–142. New York: McGraw-Hill.

McCloskey, D. 1985. *The Rhetoric of Economics*. Madison: University of Wisconsin Press.

McCloskey, D. 1994. *Knowledge and Persuasion in Economics*. New York: Cambridge University Press.

Menger, C. [1871] 1981. *Principles of Economics*. New York: New York University Press.

Menger, C. [1883] 1985. *Investigations into the Methods of the Social Sciences with Special Reference to Economics*. New York: New York University Press.

Mises, L. [1912] 1980. *The Theory of Money and Credit*. Indianapolis: Liberty Press.

Mises, L. [1922] 1981. *Socialism: An Economic and Sociological Investigation*. Indianapolis: Liberty Press.

Mises, L. [1933] 1981. *Epistemological Problems of Economics*. New York: New York University Press.

Mises, L. [1949] 1966. *Human Action: A Treatise on Economics*. Chicago: Regnery.

North, G., and B. Weingast. 1989. "Constitutions and Commitment: The Evolution of Institutions of Governing Public Choice in Seventeenth-Century England." *Journal of Economic History* 59(Dec.):803–832.

O'Driscoll, G., and M. Rizzo. 1985. *The Economics of Time and Ignorance*. New York: Blackwell.

Olson, M. 1996. "Big Bills Left on the Sidewalk: Why Some Nations Are Rich, and Others Poor." *Journal of Economic Perspectives* 10(2):3–24

Poggi, G. 1983. *Capitalism and the Calvinist Spirit*. Amherst: University of Massachusetts Press.

Posner, R. 1992. *Sex and Reason*. Cambridge: Harvard University Press.

Prendergast, C. 1986. "Alfred Schütz and the Austrian School of Economics." *American Journal of Sociology* 92(July):1–26.

Prychitko, D. (ed.). 1995. *Individuals, Institutions, Interpretations: Hermeneutics Applied to Economics*. Aldershot: Avebury.

Rosenberg, N., and L.E. Birdzell. 1985. *How the West Grew Rich*. New York: Basic Books.

Rutherford, M. 1994. *Institutions in Economics*. New York: Cambridge University Press.

Schluchter, W. 1996. *Paradoxes of Modernity: Culture and Conduct in the Theory of Max Weber*. Stanford: Stanford University Press.

Schütz, A. [1932] 1967. *The Phenomenology of the Social World*. Evanston: Northwestern University Press.

Schütz, A. [1940] 1978. "Parsons' *Theory of Social Action*: A Critical Review." In: R. Grathoff (ed.), *The Theory of Social Action: The Correspondence of Alfred Schütz and Talcott Parsons*, pp. 8–60. Bloomington: Indiana University Press.

Shackle, G.L.S. 1972. *Epistemics and Economics*. Cambridge, Mass.: Cambridge University Press.

Smelser, N., and R. Swedberg (eds.). 1994. *The Handbook of Economic Sociology*. Princeton: Princeton University Press.

Swedberg, R. 1990. *Economics and Sociology: Redefining Their Boundaries. Conversations with Economists and Sociologists*. Princeton: Princeton University Press.

Vanberg, V. 1994. *Rules and Choice in Economics*. New York: Routledge.

Weber, M. [1904–05] 1979. *The Protestant Ethic and the Spirit of Capitalism*. London: Allen and Unwin.

Weber, M. [1922] 1978. *Economy and Society*. Berkeley: University of California Press.

Wolfe, A. 1992. "Weak Sociology/Strong Sociologists: Consequences and Contradictions of a Field in Turmoil." *Social Research* 59(Winter).

The Role and Evolution of Beliefs, Habits, Moral Norms, and Institutions

Stefan Voigt and Daniel Kiwit

It is impossible to conceive of a prosperous economic order in the absence of any institutions. Indeed, in the absence of institutions, it is impossible to conceive of any kind of order in the sense of "a state of affairs in which a multiplicity of elements of various kinds are so related to each other that we may learn from our acquaintance with some spatial or temporal part of the whole to form correct expectations concerning the rest, or at least expectations which have a good chance of proving correct" (Hayek, 1973, p. 36).

It is thus the role of institutions to bring about order. In this paper, we will argue that not only those institutions which can be set up by design but also those institutions which emerge and develop, i.e., evolve, as the spontaneous result of individual action are relevant for the economic development of a society.

Methodological individualism will be the basis of our analysis of the evolution of institutions. Collectively beneficial results will still have to be explained by drawing on expected individual advantage. Everything else would be equivalent to committing the functionalist fallacy. We will, however, not draw on the notion of atomistic, rational individuals trying to maximize narrowly defined self-interest, a notion which has already been critized by Hume ([1777] 1985), who therefore wrote about the useless fiction of the original contract. Instead, we will focus on individuals already connected to one another via several social relationships such as kinship, friendship, etc.

Three areas of inquiry will be distinguished:

(1) The relevance of institutions in influencing individual behavior and thus social outcomes. Institutions are considered as exogenous variables. In this area of inquiry, we will search for hypotheses that link institutions with social outcomes that are of interest to the

economist, such as per capita income or economic growth. This area corresponds with the "Role" in the title of our paper.

(2) The explanation of the emergence and development of institutions. Institutions are considered as endogenous variables. In this area of inquiry we will search for possible inputs that lead to their emergence. This is in accord with the modern conception of economics, which is defined not by its subject matter but by its method of analysis. This area corresponds with the "Evolution" in the title of our paper.

(3) The analysis of possibilities to steer societies by deliberately changing or setting up institutions as possible constraints for economic policy. In this area, we will try to explore the possibilities to influence the evolution of institutions via public policy.

We will proceed as follows: in the next section, we will propose a taxonomy of institutions and define key concepts. In Section II, we will deal with the role of institutions in economic development. Section III is devoted to approaches that try to explain the emergence and development of institutions and Section IV deals with possible implications for economic policy. The title of the paper is very ambitious but space is severely limited. The paper is therefore more a *tour d'horizon* that presents some possible avenues for future research rather than presenting such research itself.

I   A Taxonomy of Institutions, Norms, Beliefs, and Habits

In this section, we will not only define the four central terms that appear in the title of our paper but also try to establish some links between them. As has already become apparent in the introduction, most of the emphasis will be put on institutions because it is the most encompassing of the four terms, because it is the term that has received most attention by economists, and because it is directly relevant for the emergence and development of order. Institutions are rules or norms that are subject to an enforcement mechanism.

To illustrate the function of institutions in bringing about order, imagine an anarchic society. As soon as two individuals begin to interact, strategic uncertainty is present. If the respective individuals had a set of rules at their disposal, strategic uncertainty could be reduced by excluding theoretically possible actions from the range of actions to be expected from other actors. Following Ostrom (1986, p. 5), rules

refer to prescriptions commonly known and used by a set of participants to order repetitive, interdependent relationships. Prescriptions refer to which actions (or states of the world) are *required, prohibited,* or *permitted.* Rules are the result of implicit or explicit efforts by a set of individuals to achieve order and predictability within defined situations.

To be effective, rules have to be supported by an enforcement mechanism. As already stated, rules that are supported by an enforcement mechanism are called institutions here. We also classify institutions with regard to the kind of enforcement mechanism used. A general dichotomy could differentiate between external institutions which are backed by the coercive monopoly of the state and internal institutions which rely on private enforcement, or enforcement internal to society, thus their name.[1] Among the five types of institutions, four types of internal institutions can be distinguished according to the enforcement mechanism used (see Table 1).

Let us start with conventions. In pure coordination games, all participants are better off if they coordinate their behavior. There is no conflictual element, so no participant has a preference for any particular Nash equilibrium in case there is more than one.[2] Once a particular equilibrium, a convention, has emerged, nobody is able to make him- or herself better off by deviating from it unilaterally. It is thus self-enforcing. Some authors (e.g., Sugden, 1986) have extended the con-

---

[1] Our overall approach towards institutions is similar to that chosen by North (1990), yet markedly different in important details. North distinguishes between informal constraints and formal rules with an enforcement mechanism. It seems that his distinction focuses on the process of how constraints come into being. The criteria for evaluating a constraint as formal or informal are, however, unclear as North (1990, p. 46) admits. According to North (1990, p. 47), "(f)ormal rules include political (and judicial) rules, economic rules, and contracts." According to our definition, rules need to be commonly known. In the majority of cases, the contents of contracts are, however, not commonly known. It is therefore more appropriate to qualify contract law as a set of institutions, rather than to qualify contracts themselves as institutions.

[2] A Nash equilibrium is a payoff-combination from which no player can make himself better off given that the other player chooses to repeat his move.

Table 1. Types of Institutions

Kind of Rule/Norm	Kind of Enforcement	Type of Institution
1. Convention	Self-enforcing	Type 1 internal
2. Ethical rule	Self-commitment of the actor; possibly amplified by religious convictions	Type 2 internal
3. Custom	Via non-organized societal control	Type 3 internal
4. Private rules	Organized private enforcement	Type 4 internal
5. State law	Organized state enforcement	External

vention concept to games that do involve a certain amount of conflict and are thus mixed-motive games. Since unilateral defection still does not make any player better off, conventions remain self-enforcing, and are called type 1 institutions here.

Ethical rules are a second kind of institution to be discussed now. Prisoners' dilemma (PD) games only have one Nash equilibrium. In one-shot games, it is always instrumentally rational to defect. If participants in games that seem to be of the PD type are observed to be reaching the cooperative solution, they must have been able to transform the PD into a different game. Individuals might have internalized the strategy to cooperate as "the right thing to do." In other words: as a result of internalization, the payoff for defecting has been substantially decreased or the payoff for cooperating substantially increased. Participants thus internalize specific institutions in such a way as to comply with them intrinsically even if they conflict with narrowly defined self-interest. Internally enforced institutions are called type 2 institutions here.

We now turn to customs. Whereas the first two ways of enforcement are rooted within the structure of the game or the actor himself, there are other ways of enforcement which rely on other actors. Enforcement via societal control is one of them. An unspecified variety of persons surveys compliance by way of spontaneous control. This is the third type of enforcement, one possible example being to punish non-compliance by informing others about this behavior in order to diminish the reputation of the person who did not comply. Customs that are enforced via nonorganized societal control are called type 3 institutions here.

We call the fourth type of internal institutions private rules. Enforcement that makes use of other actors, i.e., third-party enforcement, can also be based on some kind of organization. Organized private enforcement may, for example, rely on private courts of arbitration that monitor compliance with private rules. The enforcement of rules by private organizations is called type 4 institutions here.

Rules whose noncompliance is punished by the state, i.e., a very specific organization, are called external institutions because the act of punishing is external to society. Laws and decrees are examples of external institutions.

Having introduced a definition of institutions and a typology of different types of them, we now turn to our understanding of values. They are sometimes differentiated from norms or rules. *The International Encyclopedia of the Social Sciences* defines values as

conceptions of the desirable, influencing selective behavior.... Values are not the same as norms for conduct. .. Values are standards of desirability that are more nearly independent of specific situations. The same value may be a point of reference for a great many specific norms; a particular norm may represent the simultaneous application of several separable values. ("Values," 1968, p. 248)

We now turn to discuss another concept named in the title of our paper, namely beliefs. Shared values and norms imply shared conceptions of the desirable. In order to coordinate one's behavior using shared conceptions of the desirable, i.e., of the "ought," the group that is sharing those conceptions must have achieved some shared perception of the "is" as well. In different interaction situations, different norms may apply. Interaction situations do not classify themselves but have to be classified by the participants. Norms will only stabilize expectations if the people sharing them have a similar way of classifying the interaction situations they are confronted with. If two people believe to be confronted with different interaction situations, their expectations might be disappointed although both faithfully try to stick to the norms applicable to the respective situation they believe to be confronted with. We will therefore assume that shared norms imply not only shared normative conceptions but also shared cognitive perceptions. Conjectures, or ideosyncratic hypotheses, about how the world is and how it functions can also be called beliefs.

Habits are factual regularities in behavior. As emanations of individual rules of thumb, they reduce information or decision costs.

Simon (1955) introduced the notion of bounded rationality into economics, which simply recognizes the fact that obtaining and processing information is costly. It can therefore be rational to use rules of
thumb (Heiner, 1983). These are, however, individual rules that are not
socially enforced. They do not, as such, entail any normative expectation that somebody *should* act in a specific way in a given situation.
They can, however, contain the seeds of socially relevant institutions.
This will be discussed below.

II   The Role of Institutions in Economic Development

Throughout this section, we will assume that there is uncertainty in
human actions and that transaction costs are thus positive. Coase
(1937) introduced the concept of transaction costs to draw attention to
the fact that market exchange is costly. But he also drew attention to
the fact that organizations do not function costlessly either. We will
use the term "coordination costs" to include the costs of using markets
as well as the costs of using organizations (see also Streit and Wegner,
1992). The coordination costs members of a society face in their interactions determine, inter alia, the amount of interactions that will take
place. If they are too high, exchange that could make all participants
better off, will not take place. If the institutions prevalent in a society
have a substantial influence on the amount of coordination costs, their
potential relevance to the allocation and distribution and thus to economic development becomes apparent. It is conceivable that institutions lead to lower as well as to higher coordination costs. To evaluate
the relevance of institutions for the economic development of a society,
one thus needs to specify the material content of the institutions shared
by most members of the society in question.

Three classes of interactions in which coordination costs can be influenced by institutions will be distinguished: (1) horizontal exchange, or
interactions on markets; (2) voluntarily entered into vertical exchange,
or interactions within firms; and (3) vertical exchange backed by force,
or interactions between citizens and state.

(1) Markets are based on the "exchange paradigm." If two persons
voluntarily agree to exchange goods, both expect to be better off as a

result. Otherwise, they would not enter into an exchange in the first place. Norms that prevent the *emergence of a market* altogether by substantially increasing coordination costs lead to a division of labor that is lower than it could be if a market could emerge. It can therefore be expected to reduce the potential for material welfare. This is the case when some goods are exempt from the range of tradable goods altogether, as, for instance, drugs, pork, parts of the human body, etc.

But suppose a market can emerge. Institutions might then constrain the *extent of the market:* They might reduce the number of potential trading partners (by forbidding trade with anyone of a different race, religion, nationality, etc.) or alter the terms of trade (when credit financing or bargaining is socially not acceptable). Some terms of trade might be perceived as unfair and might therefore not be accepted. Scholars of descriptive decision theory have presented vast evidence that economic actors are ready to incur some costs if they feel that others are offending their concept of fairness (for empirical evidence, see, e.g., Kahnemann, Knetsch, and Thaler [1986]). An example can frequently be observed at gas stations when the major brands are trying to increase the price of fuel: long queues will build up quickly at unaffiliated stations, with consumers waiting a long time just to save a couple of cents. This description of the possible relevance of institutions might mediate the impression that by their constraining either the existence of a market altogether or by constraining at least its extent, they would generally be a hindrance to economic development. This conclusion is, however, obviously wrong. Institutions can also substantially lower coordination costs in markets, e.g., if they promote honesty or punctuality.

Widely shared cooperation norms will lead to mutual trust among members of a society even if the interacting persons do not know each other. If, a priori, potential trading partners are expected to cooperate rather than to behave opportunistically given the smallest chance, this will increase the amount of potentially welfare-increasing transactions. The importance of trust in facilitating exchange relationships has been described with regard to Italy. This is especially interesting because its external institutions are identical all over the country, whereas people in the south often share different norms than people in the north, i.e., its internal institutions vary in different regions. Banfield (1958) describes the dominant norm prevalent in the village of Montegrano in southern Italy as: "Maximize the material, short-run advantage of the nuclear family; assume that all others will do likewise" (p. 85).[3] The differences in economic development between northern and southern Italy are, inter alia, due to these differences in internal institutions.

(2) In interaction situations within firms, institutions can also influence coordination costs. An often quoted institution is the solidarity among employees who refuse to train junior colleagues who do the same work but receive lower wages (Akerlof, 1980). The resulting wage rigidity not only influences the wage structure within firms but also the unemployment rate. Another example of the relevance of institutions within firms is the informal control among employees who monitor their own work effort, which can have various effects: if institutions exist that punish overachievers, the productivity of a company will remain below its potential. On the other hand, institutions that promote teamwork can lead to substantial savings in formal monitoring costs as one kind of coordination costs.

(3) In interactions between citizens and the state, the relationship between internal and external institutions becomes relevant. Recall that internal institutions are enforced within society, whereas external ones are enforced by the state. Drawing on simple logic, four possible relationships between internal and external institutions can be conceived of:

(1) A *neutral* relationship, i.e., the institutions regulate different areas of human interaction.
(2) A *complementary* relationship, i.e., the institutions constrain human behavior in an identical or similar fashion and rule-breaking behavior is punished by private individuals as well as representatives of the state.
(3) A *substitutive* relationship, i.e., the institutions constrain human behavior in a similar fashion but rule-breaking behavior is punished *either* by private individuals *or* by representatives of the state.
(4) A *conflicting* relationship, i.e., the institutions constrain human

---

[3] See also Putnam (1993); Voigt (1993) attempts to compare the value systems of the Central and Eastern European societies and draw conclusions concerning their potential for economic growth.

behavior in different ways. Abiding by an internal institution would then be equivalent to breaking an external one and vice versa.

If the relationship between internal and external institutions is a conflicting one, this will increase coordination costs. If it is complementary, it will decrease them because the state has to provide fewer resources for the enforcement of its institutions. Trust may also play an important role in the relationship between citizens and their state. In modern social philosophy, the state is often conceptualized as being created by the citizens by way of a contract. This would mean that the citizens are the principal, and the state is their agent. In many real world situations one has, however, exactly the opposite impression: the state tells the citizens to pay taxes, and the citizens often appear to be agents of the state. Now, if the state "trusts" its citizens to pay their taxes and does not control their taxpaying behavior closely, this might have two effects: (1) the citizens might be more willing to pay their taxes because they feel they are being treated as responsible citizens (Frey, 1997; see Deci and Ryan [1985] for a more general treatment of intrinsic motivation) and (2) the state budget for tax administration can be smaller, which can lead to lower tax rates.

To sum up: Institutions can indeed be relevant to economic development. Whether they enhance or reduce a society's prospects for economic development depends on their material content and on the degree of their enforcement.

As a next step, we will therefore present a list of rules that are supposedly favorable to economic development if they are enforced to a considerable extent. The list names some of the rules that seem to be either necessary for, or favorable to, growth in an economic system based on individual liberty. The fundamental hypothesis underlying our "list of rules conducive to economic development" is that economic systems that are based on individual liberty have proven to provide individuals with the greatest opportunity to enhance their wealth (recent studies that find a positive correlation between economic freedom and growth rates are Bhalla [1994] and Gwartney, Lawson, and Block [1996]). Giersch (1995, p. 7f.) divides the morality that led to the rise of Western civilization into (1) a morality of property, (2) a morality of contract, (3) a morality of individualism, and (4) a republican morality.

(1) The morality of property can be translated into the rule "Respect the property of others." The significance of this rule for the economic development of a society is almost self-explanatory. As the property rights theory shows, we can only expect individuals to economize on resources if they can internalize the fruits of their efforts while also having to bear the possibly negative consequences of these efforts.

(2) The morality of contract can be translated into the rule *"Pacta sunt servanda."* The economic relevance of this rule is also obvious. If it is absent, the amount of profitable exchange and the productivity-enhancing division of labor will remain low.

(3) The morality of individualism can be translated into the rule "Become active in order to reach your own goals." It is the individual actor who is responsible for decision-making, for carrying out the decisions and for reaching—or not reaching—his or her goals. If success in life is, however, perceived of as being largely out of the individual's control and as being determined by God, destiny, or some organic entity, we would not expect a market economy that is based on private autonomy and that depends on entrepreneurial spirit to develop.

(4) The morality of republicanism is hard to translate into one specific rule. This morality requires that individuals be able to assume the standpoint of an impartial spectator (Smith [1759] 1984, p. 112) and to act accordingly. This means that they must have some propensity to contribute voluntarily to the production of collective goods, e.g., to vote. Voluntary contributions are especially relevant if individual behavior cannot be observed and therefore cannot be punished by others.

III   Explaining the Emergence of Norms

If moral rules are defined as rules which aim at structuring interaction situations involving some conflict, self-enforcing conventions, as results of pure coordination games, do not fall within the range of institutions whose emergence needs to be explained. We will therefore restrict ourselves to discussing some approaches that have been advanced to explain type 2 and type 3 institutions, i.e., institutions that are either enforced via internalization or via nonorganized social control.

A   Drawing on Other (Social) Sciences?

Ullmann-Margalit (1977, p. 8) has called attempts to explain the emergence of specific norms as futile as attempts to explain the origins of languages or of a joke. Rather than attempting to explain the emergence of specific norms, we are interested in general mechanisms that lead to their emergence, diffusion, and development. Above, we equated behavior in accordance with norms with behavior deviating from narrow instrumental rationality or *Homo economicus* as often modeled in economics. If, however, conformity with norms is observed daily on a large scale and is furthermore relevant to the economic development of entire societies, the question of whether the explanatory power of the economic approach can be enhanced by drawing on other disciplines almost suggests itself. Because of space restrictions here, our treatment of this question in the following might be somewhat distorted and thus might not do justice to these disciplines.

Traditional sociology, which is based on the model of *Homo sociologicus*, who is attributed various roles by society and is assumed to conform to the normative expectations that come with his or her various roles, is not a good starting point for our purposes because functional sociology takes norms as exogenously given and is thus of little help.

Over the last decades, a competing approach to sociology which is based on the rational choice paradigm has emerged. In his *Foundations of Social Theory*, James S. Coleman (1990) tries to show that the presence of externalities is a necessary condition for a demand for effective norms to arise. A second condition (see below) could secure that the demand will be satisfied. In an earlier paper, Coleman (1987, p. 140) had poignantly described his view: "The central premise ... is that norms arise when actions have external effects, including the extreme cases of public goods or public bads. Further, norms arise in those cases in which markets cannot easily be established, or transaction costs are high." In other words, norms structure social interaction. Externalities being absent, there is hardly any need for social norms.

On the other hand, externalities are either omnipresent or they can be created such that they are omnipresent. If they are omnipresent, norms can arise that regulate pretty much any interaction situation. This does not, however, mean that one could deduce a similarly omnipresent demand for social norms because externalities are not objectively given but subjectively created by the affected individuals. One therefore has to determine which externalities society has created as a consequence of a plurality of persons having perceived a particular phenomenon similarly. To give an example: A noisy motorcyclist riding the narrow streets of Naples, Italy, at ten o'clock at night will supposedly be evaluated as producing fewer negative externalities than the same motorcyclist at the same time in any German town. This means that explaining the emergence of norms by drawing on externalities is impossible without taking the perception of the underlying interactions by possibly affected parties, and thus their cognition, explicitly into account.[4]

The second condition Coleman mentions is that there must be an individual readiness to punish norm-deviating behavior. In order to structure social interactions, a norm needs to be accompanied by some means of punishing individuals when they deviate from the norm. Punishing norm-deviating behavior is, however, costly and any rational choice approach will have to explain why some people are willing to engage in this costly business. Coleman describes this as "the second-order public good problem" of norms. The second condition reads (Coleman 1990, p. 273):

Stated simply, this condition is that under which the second-order free-rider problem will be overcome by rational holders of a norm. To put it differently, the condition is that under which beneficiaries of a norm, acting rationally, either will be able to share appropriately the costs of sanctioning the target actors or will be able

---

[4] Littlechild and Wiseman (1986, p. 166) have a nice example of how diversely externalities can be perceived and constructed:

Consider some of the various ways in which smoking by one person A might be argued adversely to affect a nonsmoker B:

a) B's health may be adversely affected, in ways that can be verified by persuasive empirical evidence.
b) Even without such evidence, B may *believe* that his health is adversely affected.
c) B may be simply annoyed by tabacco smoke.
d) B may be concerned about the effect of smoking on A's health.
e) B may be concerned about the effect of A's smoking on the happiness of third party C, who is exposed to A's smoke, or on third party D, who is a concerned friend or relative of A.
f) B may be annoyed at what he believes is A's lack of awareness of the suffering he is causing.

to generate second order sanctions among the set of beneficiaries that are sufficient to induce effective sanctions of the target actors by one or more of the beneficiaries.

This, however, is not an explanation but a logically consistent reformulation of the problem.

Evolutionary approaches, just as traditional sociology, do away with explicit individual rational choice. They are not interested in the choices of individuals, but rather in the chances that competing behavioral strategies have of surviving in a competitive environment. Rationality is then defined as maximizing one's chances of surviving, and those who do survive must have acted *as if* they were rational (Alchian, 1950; Friedman, 1953). Arguments explicitly based on genetic evolution are relatively seldom because they only apply to the very long run. With regard to explaining the emergence of norms, they seem to be utterly misleading because they are incapable of explaining the vast differences in behavior of different individuals as well as the vast differences of norms between different societies (see also Kirchgässner [1996] who uses the argument against sociobiology).

Often, evolutionary approaches are not based on genes but on "memes" (Dawkins, 1989). These are cultural traits which are sustained and transmitted by memory and mimicry. Colman (1982, p. 267) describes the notion as follows: "A meme will spread through a population rapidly if there is something about it that makes it better able than the available alternatives to infect people's minds, just as germs spread when they are able to infect peoples bodies. This analogy draws attention to the fact that the fittest memes are not necessarily ones that are beneficial to society as a whole." In their anthropological view towards the evolution of norms, Boyd and Richerson (1994) use the concept of memes, whose diffusion they model analogously to the diffusion of innovations. Norms are defined as those memes which influence standards of behavior.

One merit of their approach is that it takes the approaches of anthropology and traditional sociology explicitly into account. It also stresses the importance of beliefs, rules, and values, i.e., the cognitive side, for explaining the emergence of norms, which is also an advantage. They try to manage the splits between anthropology and economics by drawing on three forces of cultural evolution, namely biased transmission, which is based on explicit choices by the actors, unbiased transmission, which takes place during a person's childhood, and nat-

ural selection, which functions just as genetic variation. Biased transmission is described in analogy to the diffusion of innovations. Just as
a person has the choice of adopting an innovation, a person also has
the choice of adopting those memes for which he/she has preferences.
Notice that this is not compatible with the diffusion mechanism of
memes described above. In our view, the assumption that norms are
subject to deliberate choice is mistaken. Norms structure our interactions even if we explicitly refuse to accept them individually or if we
do not perceive the necessity of choosing at all. The analogy is mistaken because the adoption of an innovation is subject to deliberate
choice, which norms are not. Because of the behavioral strategies perspective prevalent in evolutionary approaches, the social interactions
by which norms get diffused remain unspecified. These interactions,
however, should be the very essence of an explanation of the diffusion
of norms if norms are deemed to structure social interaction.

Furthermore, evolutionary approaches remain unsatisfactory because the existence of a set of memes out of which the participants
individually choose those that suit them best has to be assumed. The
emergence of memes is thus not dealt with within evolutionary
approaches.

Evolutionary game theory is the analytical tool used by many representatives of an evolutionary approach. Compared with standard
game theory, it has the advantage of not making such demanding
assumptions concerning the computational capacity of the players. A
bird or a rat that structures its behavior using trial and error will do
for the purposes of this approach. This, however, can also be seen as
a disadvantage: it remains unclear what role the human capacity to
reason, to conjecture, or to hypothesize plays in such models. Majeski
(1990, p. 277f.) notes that most empirical work on the evolution of
strategies rests on a biological birthdeath mechanism: "This is not surprising since it is the only approach that can be formalized and tested
without developing a model of individual cognition. It is, however, the
least persuasive approach for explaining the effects of norms on social
behavior.... A rejection of a biological perspective leaves only
approaches that have some form of human cognition."

Having perused some of the approaches that try to explain the
emergence of norms and having evaluated them as uniformly unsatisfactory, it might seem promising to turn back to a somehow modified
rational choice approach.

B Trying to Broaden the Traditional Notion of *Homo Economicus*

Instrumental rationality has traditionally been interpreted very narrowly. If the time horizons of the actors are assumed to comprise only one round, solutions to repeated games cannot be incorporated. As soon as the actors are able to structure interaction situations as repeated games, the range of possible solutions rises considerably. It may even rise when the actors that play two-person games repeatedly are not always the same actors, as long as they can communicate information cheaply and reliably on how a specific actor has behaved in previous rounds. It has been shown that conditional cooperation is one among many strategies that can be sustained in an indefinitely repeated PD (the so-called folk theorem, Fudenberg and Maskin [1986]). It might even be possible to sustain a cooperative solution in finite PDs for a number of rounds. If actors can transmit information among themselves cheaply and reliably, uncooperative behavior can destroy a participant's reputation and thus diminish the value of his or her future payoffs.

For this to be the case, however, three necessary conditions have to be fulfilled: (1) the uncooperative behavior must have a certain amount of publicness, i.e., it must be known by not directly involved third parties; (2) these parties must all be aware of the same facts concerning this behavior, i.e., they must all know about the same interaction situation; and (3) they must evaluate the relevant facts concerning this behavior in this situation similarly, i.e., they must share the norms underlying the evaluation of this behavior. This means that the cognitive side of behavior, i.e., the shared beliefs, comes into play again. It also means that reputation is based on something like proto-norms. Since the ability of reputation to induce people to cooperate depends on the existence of (proto-)norms, reputation itself cannot be used to explain the emergence of norms but only to explain norm-abiding behavior.

Pointing towards reputation and repeated games rationalizes apparently nonselfish behavior as more subtle selfish behavior. This still leaves cooperative behavior in nonrepeated games between anonymous participants who stand very low chances of ever meeting again unexplained. To explain such cooperative behavior, broadening the notion of *Homo economicus* would then not refer to the presumed time horizon of the actors but to their assumed rationality. The standard model for evaluating such behavior is based on instrumental rationality, on actors who are supposed to be able to compute very complex operations in an error-free manner. A broadened notion of *Homo economicus* could incorporate trial and error processes.

There have been numerous attempts to explain the emergence of norms without taking recourse to standard game theory. Axelrod (1986), e.g., explicitly departs from using this analytical tool: "empirical examples of changing norms suggest that real people are more likely to use trial and error behavior than detailed calculations based on accurate beliefs about the future" (p. 1097). In his *Evolutionary Approach to Norms*, Axelrod asks how one can explain the viability of norms given that punishing norm-deviating behavior is costly. He names eight mechanisms which can serve to support norms, among which metanorms, internalization, social proof, and reputation are named. His approach thus hinges on the people's readiness to punish norm-deviating behavior. How this readiness emerges must then be shown if one is interested in explaining the emergence of norms. Unfortunately, these meta-norms are introduced exogenously.

Sugden (1989, p. 89) also explicitly rejects standard game theory: "The ideally rational but completely inexperienced players of classical game theory would find that they had insufficient data to determine what they should do. In contrast, ordinary people with limited rationality but some degree of experience and imagination might have no difficulty in coordinating their behavior." It is thus experience and empathy that enable people to coordinate their behavior. Sugden continues by drawing on Schelling's (1960) concept of prominence or focal point solutions. Conventions and norms that are susceptible to analogy —i.e., that can be transferred from one known solution of a coordination situation to a similar, yet new coordination situation—could spread best. Here, the danger of getting caught up in "infinite regress" looms large: if one goes back to explaining a norm using an analogous norm, one will end up with one "last" norm which is not susceptible to analogy.

C   An Emerging Synthesis?

So far, we have tried to explain the emergence of norms by drawing on other concepts used in the social sciences and by trying to broaden the notion of *Homo economicus*. None of these attempts has been fully satisfactory. We think, however, that the broadened notion of *Homo economicus* is most promising. The main problem with that notion has to do with one of three necessary conditions of the reputation mechanism to work, namely the existence of shared (proto-)norms. A satisfactory approach should allow for an explanation of the emergence of such norms. In this section, we will try to give one possible explanation for the emergence of these norms. This will be done using the methodological tool of conjectural history.

Drawing on the notion of broadened *Homo economicus*, it can be shown that factual regularities in cooperative behavior can emerge. This holds for pure coordination games without any conflictual element as well as for mixed motive games involving a considerable amount of conflict. Factual regularities in cooperative behavior do not have to imply the existence of any normative claim that people should behave in the way they actually do. We argue that factual regularities in cooperative behavior can acquire normative status. Suppose that some person has demonstrated clear-cut regularities in his or her behavior towards others, who have as a consequence formed expectations concerning his or her behavior. If their expectations are frustrated, this will lead to resentment among them and anger towards the person who has frustrated them. Regularities in individual behavior can, then, lead to expectations of others that the individual will act in the same way in the future. Because individuals have to rely on regularities in the behavior of others in order to coordinate their actions successfully, the expectation that individuals will behave in the future as they did in the past can become a normative expectation in the course of time. If we assume that humans strive for the approval of others, this can constitute an additional incentive to conform with a rule that has acquired normative status. This story is, of course, not new. It was David Hume ([1740] 1990) who first used it. In his account of the emergence of norms, Sugden (1986; 1989) draws heavily on it: "Our desire to keep the good will of others . . . is more than a means to some other end. It seems to be a basic human desire. That we have such a desire is presumably the product of biological evolution" (1986, p. 152). This amounts to a reintroduction of biological evolution. Using conjectural history and some group selection mechanism, one can conjecture that biological evolution has negatively selected those persons who were not endowed with genes that caused them to strive for the approval of others.

Striving for the approval of others means that their approval enters as one argument into our utility functions and thus does away with the concept of atomized individuals. Ever since Hobbes, social scientists and philosophers alike have tried to solve the problem he first formulated, namely how to explain the emergence of order from an institution-free state of anarchy drawing solely on atomized individuals who—due to the absence of institutions—are incapable of credibly committing themselves to certain actions which would make the respective interaction partner worse off. Kliemt (1991, p. 194f.) argues that the Hobbesian problem has only apparently been solved because the capacity to commit oneself has often been smuggled in (Kliemt [1991, p. 194f.] names Schotter [1981] as an example in which this capacity is smuggled in; Gauthier [1986] would be another one). Frank's (1988) "commitment model" can be read as an approach to solve the commitment problem by taking recourse to emotions. He argues that emotions like anger or guilt can serve as signals as to what type of person one is. If they are costly to fake, they can become a valuable clue in predicting other people's behavior. The commitment problem would thus be mitigated by hard-wired commitment mechanisms. Frank reports that in 14 out of 16 studies, the reliability of predicting cooperation based on such clues was significantly better than chance. The benefit of being a cooperator would lie in being able to recognize other potential cooperators and to interact selectively with them.

Above, we showed that cooperation can emerge in repeated games even if they entail a relatively high amount of conflict. It can, however, be observed that some groups are more successful than others in bringing about regularities in cooperative behavior. We argue here that after having cooperated in a game with little or no inherent conflict, people will have learned, step by step, to cooperate in games involving ever more conflict. The rationale of this hypothesis is very simple: the greater the inherent conflict in a game, the greater the risk of being exploited by the opponent. But if the members of a society were able to successfully cooperate in a game involving a certain amount of conflict, x, the probability that they will try to cooperate in another game involving a greater amount of conflict, $x + \varepsilon$, should be higher than in the case in which the members of the society reached a low level of cooperation (for a measure of amount of conflict involved in games, see Axelrod [1970]).

This hypothesis suggests that the emergence of moral norms might very well be a path-dependent phenomenon in the sense that it is a self-reinforcing process. It can also remind us not to neglect the cognitive side of behavior, which can be crucial to solving interaction problems: an apparently identical interaction situation might be constructed by members of society A to contain a certain amount of conflict, x, whereas the members of a society B might reconstruct it as containing twice the amount of conflict, namely $2x$. Different societies can thus differ in their ability to successfully coordinate their behavior.

Ullman-Margalit's (1978, pp. 121–127) approach to the emergence of norms seems to be very similar to the one advanced here: she discusses the game of stag hunt as an intermediary case between a pure coordination game and the PD and argues that the PD can be turned into a game of stag hunt "given, first, a general belief that people's choices will display some habitual stability and, second, a favourable starting-point where cooperation has somehow been initially established" (p. 124).[5]

---

[5] The stag hunt game is described by the following payoff matrix:

	C1 (stag)	C2 (rabbit)
R1 (stag)	3 3	0 2
R2 (rabbit)	2 0	2 2

In order to catch a stag which promises higher utility than a rabbit to both players in this game, the row chooser and the column chooser have to coordinate their behavior. After having promised each other to cooperate and after having separated, it is not entirely clear whether they will stick to their promise as soon as they see a rabbit which each can catch on his own—and therefore with certainty. Both might end up catching rabbits and might therefore be worse off than they could be if they had been able to coordinate their actions.

Binmore (1994, pp. 120–125) contains a discussion of the stag hunt game. Our argument is that the probability that two opponents will cooperate in a prisoners' dilemma is substantially higher if they belong to a society in which the R1–C1 solution to the stag hunt game is a firmly established norm. We have thus left the firm grounds of game theory because our prediction of how two actors will behave depends on how they have behaved in other games and is thus not contained in the matrix of the current game played.

We think we might be dealing with an emerging synthesis because many authors have told similar stories concerning the emergence of norms largely independently of one another. Here is Majeski's (1990, p. 276) story:

Walliser (1989) ironically describes the game-theoretic state of the art as being capable of explaining the solution to minor coordination problems such as traffic lights but not being able to explain more complex ones. As we have seen, being able to explain how people solve minor coordination problems might provide a clue for the explanation of more complex ones. In a somehow related vein, Binmore (1994, p. 186) argues that normative (i.e., cooperative) behavior will not survive in situations "that are genuinely crucial to what holds societies together." Binmore seems to say that as the stakes are increased, people will eventually switch to uncooperative (nonmoral) behavior. This is, of course, one of the most basic assumptions of utility theory and we think it is a realistic description of most human behavior (not of all though, because we do not want to exclude the possibility of lexicographic preferences, i.e., preferences where no amount of good β can make up for a missing good α, by assumption). We think, however, that the consequences Binmore infers from this assumption do not necessarily follow: Society does not need heroes and saints with lexicographic preferences to cohere. Instead, if many people are willing to incur low costs in order to produce public goods voluntarily, society can cohere and prosper. An example is participation in elections (for a theory of low-cost decisions, see Kliemt [1986] and Kirchgässner [1992]).

Our story of how conventions and norms might evolve does not hinge upon the instrumental rationality often used in standard game theory. Indeed, people who possess that sort of instrumental rationality would supposedly be unable to bring about social norms. What consequences does this insight have for the way we try to model behavior? If our actors possess a capacity to learn, it makes sense to model

---

The first time a rule that eventually becomes a norm is invoked by an individual in the group it is *not* a norm. It is an individual contextually generated decision rule.... An individual rule becomes a norm when the application of the rule by other members of the social group is justified by appeal to the precedent application, or when the application is justified by the individual as the expected and/or appropriate behavior of a member of the group. Also, an individual rule becomes a norm when the rule is so established in the group that individuals perceive it to be the only plausible alternative.

Other authors from different fields and with different backgrounds include Max Weber ([1922] 1985, p. 191f.), Friedrich A. Hayek (1973, p. 96), William Graham Sumner ([1906] 1992, p. 358), and D. Lewis (1969, p. 99). This line of thought can be traced back to Aristotle and his *Nicomachaen Ethics*.

them not only as forward-looking but also as backward-looking. They take into account the experiences they have made in previous rounds. Mueller (1986, p. 9) writes: "More generally, an effort to model human behavior based on realistic assumptions about 'how men think'; as opposed to 'how they would think if they were rational' would place more emphasis on the experience of the individual in relationship to the context in which the decision is posed, and less on the consequences of the decision." Mueller thus pleads for a model of "adaptive egoism" (instead of rational egoism) which takes path-dependence explicitly into account.[6]

He proposes that economics be oriented towards behavioral psychology. He argues that actors who have been educated to cooperate in many situations, can be predicted to cooperate even if they do not get the immediate reward anymore that they got when they were children. If this is taken into account, it almost suggests itself to model human behavior using a two-step procedure: The first step consists of a decision rule that tells the actor how to classify a problem: if a cooperation norm is involved and the monetary stakes are rather low, the actor will supposedly stick to the behavior he or she has been taught, i.e., instrumental rationality in the economic sense of a cost-benefit calculus will not come into play. As the monetary stakes are gradually increased, more and more actors will at least begin to classify the problem in which costs and benefits have to be weighted in a rational, future-oriented manner. Supposedly, only a small number of decision problems are totally immune from ever becoming subject to an explicit cost-benefit calculus. As long as this switch in the treatment of a specific decision problem does not exhibit any regularities, this model is of little help to the scientist. The task of research would thus consist of developing hypotheses concerning the "switch" (see also Kliemt, 1991, p. 199).

---

[6] However, we are not prepared to follow him in his conclusion that over time those institutions will survive and prosper that "maximize group survival chances" (1986, p. 18f.). Precisely because path-dependence is potentially relevant, this cannot be assumed. Various authors (e.g., Ullmann-Margalit, 1977; Sugden, 1986) have observed that a norm—or more generally, an institution— need not be efficient simply because it has survived. The stability of norms can have the consequence that they are still abided by although they have long lost their functionality. Norms can thus prevent (welfare-increasing) change. Kiwit and Voigt (1995) and Kiwit (1996) discuss possible path-dependences in the development of institutions.

Lindenberg (1992) is a first step in that direction. He claims that three instrumental goals exist universally: gain, norm-conformity, and loss avoidance. Depending on the framing of a situation, one of them will be more important to the actor than the other two (which is not to say that the other two become completely unimportant). If one is able to influence the way people structure various interaction situations, one can influence the way they behave.

IV Policy Implications

Some time ago, one of us was discussing the relevance of values and norms to the development of Russia with a Russian advisor to a leading Russian politician. He stated that they had understood the relevance of values and norms and that they were about to introduce Weber's Protestant Ethics to Russia. He did not mean that Weber's book would be translated into Russian but that some central agency would tell the people to behave according to the ethics of Protestant sects. This story reminds us of the fact that values and norms usually emerge and develop over very long periods of time without anybody having preconceived them. They are thus the result of human action but not of human design (Ferguson, [1767] 1988). It can also remind us that no central agency will be able to control their development. The degree to which policies concerning values and norms can do any good might therefore be severely limited.

In modern societies with many members and a high degree in the division of labor, relying primarily on internal institutions is not only impossible but also undesirable because rights would be unsecure. External institutions are thus needed. We have seen above that coordination costs increase if internal and external institutions conflict with each other. Since internal institutions are not subject to deliberate change, whereas external institutions are, one policy implication is thus that the external institutions of a society should be shaped in such a way that they do not flatly contradict its internal institutions. If a large majority of a society strongly shares the value of (outcome) equality and its external institutions do not contain any (re-)distributive element, the external institutions will have a hard time gaining legitimacy among the population. Trying to establish external institutions compatible with the concept of a market economy but incompatible with the internal institutions of a society might then lead to outcomes worse than those that might result if the content of the internal institutions were explicitly taken into account when modifying the external institutions. This can be the case if the external institutions do not gain any legitimacy, the order appears unstable, investment is therefore low, etc.

The necessity to rely on external institutions is not questioned by Frey (1997). But he claims that external institutions which assume everybody is a "knave" and that aim at minimizing opportunistic behavior can lead to a crowding-out of civic virtue. A constitution that is built on citizens' trust in their politicians and politicians' trust in their citizens could, in turn, lead to a crowding-in of civic virtues. Republican rules could be maintained by allowing popular initiatives and referenda.

Values and norms have traditionally been thought to be an independent variable, whereas the potential for economic development has been thought to be the dependent variable. Up to a certain degree, it might also be possible to conceptualize values and norms as the dependent variable. One could, e.g., try to establish an education system in which rules favorable to economic growth are promoted. If a person's value system develops primarily during his or her childhood and remains rather stable for the rest of his or her life, this is only straightforward. But there are severe limits: a theoretical education alone will supposedly not suffice because people learn by imitation, i.e., the instructors would have to live the values and norms they teach in order for them to spread.

Bibliography

Akerlof, G. 1980. "A Theory of Social Custom, of Which Unemployment May Be One Consequence." *Quarterly Journal of Economics* 94:749–775.

Alchian, A. 1950. "Uncertainty, Evolution, and Economic Theory," *Journal of Political Economy* 58:211–221.

Axelrod, R. 1970. *Conflict of Interest*. Chicago: Markham.

Axelrod, R. 1986. "An Evolutionary Approach to Norms." *American Political Science Review* 80(4):1095–1111.

Banfield, E. 1958. *The Moral Basis of a Backward Society*. Chicago: The Free Press.

Binmore, K. 1994. *Game Theory and the Social Contract*. Volume 1: *Playing Fair*. Cambridge, Mass.: MIT Press.

Boyd, R, and P. Richerson. 1994. "The Evolution of Norms: An Anthropological View." *Journal of Institutional and Theoretical Economics* 150(1):72–87.

Coase, R. 1937. "The Nature of the Firm." *Economica* 4:386–405.

Coleman, J. 1987. "Norms as Social Capital." In: G. Radnitzky and P. Bernholz (eds.), *Economic Imperialism*, pp. 133–155. New York: Paragon House.

Coleman, J. 1990. *Foundations of Social Theory*. Cambridge: Belknap.

Colman, A. 1982. *Game Theory and Experimental Games: The Study of Strategic Interaction*. Oxford: Pergamon Press.

Dawkins, R. 1989. *The Selfish Gene*. New Edition. Oxford: Oxford University Press.

Deci, E., and R. Ryan. 1985. *Instrinsic Motivation and Self-Determination in Human Behavior*. New York: Plenum.

Ferguson, A. [1767] 1988. *Versuch über die Geschichte der bürgerlichen Gesellschaft*. Frankfurt: Suhrkamp.

Frank, R. 1988. *Passions Within Reason*. New York: Norton.

Frey, B.S. 1997. "A Constitution for Knaves Crowds Out Civic Virtues." *The Economic Journal* 107:1043–1053.

Friedman, M. 1953. "The Methodology of Positive Economics." In: *Essays in Positive Economics*, pp. 3–43. Chicago: University of Chicago Press.

Fudenberg, D., and E. Maskin. 1986. "The Folk Theorem in Repeated Games With Discounting or With Incomplete Information." *Econometrica* 54:533–545.

Gauthier, D. 1986. *Morals by Agreement*. Oxford: Oxford University Press.

Giersch, H. 1995. "Wirtschaftsmoral als Standortfaktor." Lectiones Jenenses. Jena: Max-Planck-Institute for Reserach Into Economic Systems.

Hayek, F. 1973. *Law, Legislation and Liberty*. Volume 1: *Rules and Order*. Chicago: University of Chicago Press.

Heiner, R. 1983. "The Origin of Predictable Behavior." *American Economic Review* 73:560–595.

Hume, D. [1740] 1990. *A Treatise of Human Nature*. Edited by L.A. Selby-Bigge. Second Edition. Oxford: Clarendon.

Hume, D. [1777] 1987. *Essays: Moral, Political, and Literary*. Edited and with a Foreword, Notes, and Glossary by E.F. Miller. Indianapolis: Liberty Classics.

Kahnemann, D., J. Knetsch, and R. Thaler. 1986. "Fairness as a Constraint on Profit Seeking: Entitlements in the Market." *American Economic Review* 76: 728–741.

Kirchgässner, G. 1992. "Towards a Theory of Low-Cost Decisions." *European Journal of Political Economy* 8:305–320.

Kirchgässner, G. 1996. "Bemerkungen zur Minimalmoral." *Zeitschrift für Wirtschafts- und Sozialwissenschaften* 116:223–251.

Kiwit, D. 1996. "Path-Dependence in Technological and Institutional Change: Some Criticisms and Suggestions." *Journal des Economistes et des Etudes Humaines* 7(1):69–93.

Kiwit, D., and S. Voigt. 1995. "Überlegungen zum institutionellen Wandel unter Berücksichtigung des Verhältnisses interner und externer Institutionen." *ORDO* 46:117–147.

Kliemt H. 1991. "Der Homo oeconomicus in der Klemme: Der Beitrag der Spieltheorie zur Erzeugung und Lösung des Hobbesschen Ordnungsproblems." In: H. Esser and K.G. Troitzsch (eds.), *Modellierung sozialer Prozesse*, pp. 179–204. Bonn: Informationszentrum Sozialwissenschaften.

Kliemt, H. 1986. "The Veil of Insignificance." *European Journal of Political Economy* 2:333–344.

Lewis, D. 1969. *Convention: A Philosophical Study.* Cambridge: Harvard University Press.

Lindenberg, S. 1992. "An Extended Theory of Institutions and Contractual Discipline." *Journal of Institutional and Theoretical Economics* 148:125–154.

Littlechild, S., and J. Wiseman. 1986. "The Political Economy of Restriction of Choice." *Public Choice* 51:161–172.

Majeski, S. 1990. "Comment: An Alternative Approach to the Generation and Maintenance of Norms." In: K. Coo and M. Levi (eds.), *The Limits of Rationality*, pp. 273–281. Chicago: Chicago University Press.

Mueller, D. 1986. "Rational Egoism versus Adaptive Egoism as Fundamental Postulate for a Descriptive Theory of Human Behavior." *Public Choice* 51:3–23.

North, D. 1990. *Institutions, Institutional Change and Economic Performance.* Cambridge: Cambridge University Press.

Ostrom, E. 1986. "An Agenda for the Study of Institutions." *Public Choice* 48:3–25.

Putnam, R. 1993. *Making Democracy Work: Civic Traditions in Modern Italy.* Princeton: Princeton University Press.

Schelling, T. 1960. *The Strategy of Conflict.* Cambridge, Mass.: Harvard University Press.

Schotter, A. 1981. *The Economic Theory of Institutions.* Cambridge: Cambridge University Press.

Simon, H. 1955. "A Behavioral Model of Rational Choice." *Quarterly Journal of Economics*, 69:99–118.

Smith, A. [1759] 1984. *The Theory of Moral Sentiments.* Indianapolis: Liberty Press.

Streit, M.E., and G. Wegner. 1992. "Information, Transactions, and Catallaxy: Reflections on Some Key Concepts of Evolutionary Market Theory." In: U. Witt (ed.), *Explaining Process and Change: Contributions to Evolutionary Economics*, pp. 125–149. Ann Arbor: Michigan University Press.

Sugden, R. 1986. *The Economics of Rights, Cooperation and Welfare.* New York: Blackwell.

Sugden, R. 1989. "Spontaneous Order." *Journal of Economic Perspectives* 3(4): 85–97.

Sumner, W.G. [1906] 1992. "Folkways." In: R.C. Bannister (ed.), *The Essential Essays of William Graham Sumner*, pp. 357–372. Indianapolis: Liberty Press.

Ullmann-Margalit, E. 1977. *The Emergence of Norms*. Oxford: Clarendon Press.
"*Values*". 1968. In: D.L. Sills (ed.), *The International Encyclopedia of the Social Sciences*. New York: Macmillan.
Voigt, S. 1993. "Values, Norms, Institutions, and the Prospects for Economic Growth in Central and Eastern Europe." *Journal des Economistes et des Etudes Humaines* 4(4):495–529.
Walliser, B. 1989. "Théorie des Jeux et Genèse des Institutions." *Recherches Economiques de Louvain* 55(4):339–64.
Weber, M. [1922] 1985. *Wirtschaft und Gesellschaft*. 5th Revised Edition by J. Winckelmann. Tübingen: Mohr.

Part II
The Frontiers of Markets

Privatization of Legal and Administrative Services

Bruce L. Benson

Law and order is frequently characterized as one of the "important examples of production of public goods," and it is further contended that "private provision of these public goods will not occur" (Samuelson and Nordhaus, 1985, pp. 48–49). For instance, the public good justification for tax-supported police is explained by Tullock (1970, pp. 83–84):

> Let us say that hiring a police force having a reasonable degree of efficiency would cost each individual ten dollars a year. If I refuse to contribute my yearly allotment, I will receive almost as much protection as if I did make the contribution ... and I would, on the whole, be wiser not to pay. On the other hand, if everybody made this calculation, we would have no police force and thus would all be worse off than if each paid the ten dollars. Therefore, we join together and form a police force that has as one of its duties coercing people into paying the ten dollars.

Similarly, Brunet (1987, pp. 19, 14–15) contends that "the output of conventional litigation should be viewed as a public good—society gains more from litigation than would be produced if litigation were left to the private market" because the results of private alternative dispute resolution (ADR) processes are "internal" to the parties involved, so they will either not produce or underproduce precedents.

In light of such views, relatively little has been written by economists regarding the potential for market provision of legal and administrative functions until recently, but questions are now being raised regarding the presumption that the state must be the source of these

Parts of this paper draw from my forthcoming book, *To Serve and Protect: Privatization and Community in Criminal Justice* (1998b), written with financial support from the Independent Institute, the Earhart Foundation, and the Carthage Foundation, and parts draw from two papers (Benson, 1997, 1998a).

functions. One reason for such questions is recognition of the growing private provision of policing and dispute resolution, as well as some of the other functions of a jurisdiction's legal system. Section I provides an overview of these activities. Public good and other market failure arguments applied to private policing are examined critically in Section II, and Section III considers similar arguments applied to dispute resolution. Section IV explains that some so-called market failure arguments may be quite valid when government units contract with private firms for various legal system functions, suggesting that "government failure" may actually be the source of significant limitations on market performance in the provision of these services. Brief conclusions appear in Section V.

I   Markets in Legal and Administrative Services

A   Policing and Security

Sherman (1983, pp. 145–149) observes that "[f]ew developments are more indicative of public concern about crime—and declining faith in the ability of public institutions to cope with it—than the burgeoning growth in private policing.... Rather than approving funds for more police, the voters have turned to volunteer and paid private watchers." Indeed, while a 1970 estimate put the number of privately employed security personnel in the United States at roughly equal to the number of public police, public police employment has not changed dramatically since then and by 1991 there were roughly 2.5 private security personnel (about 1.5 million in total) to every public police officer (Cunningham et al., 1991), and this ratio is rapidly approaching three to one (Reynolds, 1994).[1] Security personnel include minimum-wage night watchmen, of course, but they also include fully qualified police

---

[1] Even these estimates "greatly underestimate the extent of private policing. Surveillance of private places and transactions is being conducted by actors who traditionally have not been counted as among the rank and file of private police" (Reichman, 1987, p. 246), such as insurance adjusters, and corporate risk managers. Furthermore, voluntary watching and patrol organizations are increasingly widespread.

officers (many public police moonlight as private security, while many others have resigned to enter the private security market), and highly trained and skilled electronic-security experts. In fact, growing demand for detection and deterrent equipment and technological advances that are lowering the price of such equipment stimulate demand for more educated, skilled, and specialized labor. As a consequence, "there is emerging a new security person, highly trained, more highly educated and better able to satisfy the growing intricacies of the security profession" (Ricks et al., 1981, p. 13).

Crime prevention and protection are not the only "policing" products available through markets. Insurance companies' employees investigate many crimes (e.g., if their losses are large enough to warrant the cost of investigating), for instance, and private firms provide similar services to some of these companies. Many other organizations and businesses also employ private criminal investigators. The American Banking Association and the American Hotel-Motel Association both contract with the Wm. J. Burns International Detective Agency, for example, because they do not get satisfactory results from public police (Reynolds, 1994, p. 12). Similarly, a complete and autonomous private police force was established at the end of World War I to both prevent crimes against railroads in the United States and investigate those committed.

Numerous other examples of markets for policing and security services could be cited, but by now it should be clear that private markets in at least some of the services associated with policing do in fact occur, in contrast to the implications of public goods/free rider analysis (Samuelson and Nordhaus, 1985, pp. 48–49; Tullock, 1970, pp. 83–84). The same is true of dispute resolution.

B Alternative Dispute Resolution

The vast majority of all disputes are resolved through private means. These include direct negotiation backed by reciprocity incentives, informal procedures backed by reputation threats, and formal mediation and/or arbitration often backed by formal group boycott threats. The actual level of such private dispute resolution relative to publicly provided litigation is unmeasurable, although a few surveys have been conducted that provide some indications of the level of some formal arbitration. It has been estimated, for instance, that by the 1950s at least 75% of all disputes between businesses in the United States that could not be negotiated or mediated were settled through private arbitration rather than litigation (Auerbach, 1983, p. 113), and the use of arbitration has continued to expand at a rapid pace since then. Indeed, commercial arbitration has made "the courts secondary recourse in many areas and completely superfluous in others" (Wooldridge, 1970, p. 101). Arbitration is even more dominant for disputes between international traders. Almost all international trade contracts expressly exclude adjudication by the national courts of the trading parties and refer any dispute that cannot be resolved through negotiation (perhaps with the aid of a mediator) to arbitration. A large number of international trade associations have their own conflict resolution procedures, using arbitrators with special expertise in matters of concern to association members (Benson, 1992). Other traders rely on organizations like the International Chamber of Commerce arbitration institution.

Arbitration is also increasingly important for disputes between businessmen and employees, and between businessmen and customers in the United States (Benson, 1997), and ADR is moving into non-commercial areas as well. Mediation of environmental disputes is increasingly widespread, for instance, and since the 1960s, arbitration or mediation has been used in a large number of programs to resolve "conflicts that courts may find too trivial or too elusive: domestic quarrels, squabbles between neighbors and similar animosities among ethnic groups" (Denenberg and Denenberg, 1981, p. 15). Many are designed to seek compromise solutions to disputes by using neighborhood volunteers as mediators or arbitrators. Minor criminal cases are also moving into other neighborhood justice centers (Denenberg and Denenberg, 1981, p. 18). Many other examples of ADR could be cited, but the last two decades have seen an even more interesting market development.

In 1976, two California lawyers who wanted a complex case quickly settled discovered an 1872 statute recognizing that individuals in a dispute have the right to a full court hearing before any referee they choose (Pruitt, 1982, pp. 49–57). At that time, California had a 70,000 case public court backlog, with a median pretrial delay of 50 and one-half months (Poole, 1980, p. 2). The lawyers found a retired judge with expertise in the area of the dispute, paid him at attorney's fee rates, and saved their clients a tremendous amount of time and expense. The practice quickly caught on, and while there is no count of the number of so-called rent-a-judge cases tried since 1976, the civil court coordinator of the Los Angeles County Superior Court estimated that several hundred disputes had been so settled during the next five years. Most of the early cases involved complex business disputes that litigants "feel the public courts cannot quickly and adequately" try (Pruitt, 1982, p. 51), but entrepreneurs quickly recognized an opportunity and private for-profit firms actually began entering the judicial market in the late 1970s and early 1980s, offering to resolve a much wider variety of disputes, including personal injury disputes, divorces, construction warranty disputes, disputes over loan defaults, and so on. The industry has continued to grow and competition is increasing. More than fifty private-for-profit dispute resolution firms were operating in the United States in 1992. The two largest firms in this market, Judicial Arbitration and Mediation Services Company (JAMS) (started in 1979 by a California state trial judge who retired early to do so), and Endispute (formed in 1982), recently attracted large investments by venture capitalists, not as start-up money, but as "late-stage expansion investments that have enabled ... [the firms] to push their hearing rooms into big-city markets ... that should add significantly to revenues" (Phalon, 1992, p. 126). These two companies enjoyed gross revenue growth of 130% (Endispute) and 826% (JAMS) between 1988 and 1992 in reflection of the "demand for relief from the jammed dockets and killer jury awards of the courts" (Phalon, 1992, p. 126).

ADR is often characterized exclusively as a procedural option for resolution of disputes,[2] but it can also be an attractive jurisdictional option. Lew's (1978, pp. 582–583) detailed examination of international commercial arbitration records demonstrates this, as arbitrators intentionally "denationalize" disputes, looking instead to

---

[2] For instance, arbitration provides many benefits as a procedural alternative in contract disputes, including the facts that: (1) arbitrators can be selected for their expertise in matters pertinent to a dispute, thus reducing the potential for judicial error as well as the time costs of and expenditures on dispute resolution relative to litigation; (2) as a less adversarial procedure than litigation, arbitration is more likely to sustain repeated-dealing relationships; (3) if desired, privacy can be maintained; and (4) arbitration services can be purchased in a market without the costly delay that arises when scarce court time is allocated by waiting (Benson, 1997, 1998).

a "non-national and generally accepted rule or practice appropriate to the question at issue ... developed through the concerted efforts of those concerned with and participating in international commerce." Bernstein's (1992, p. 126) exploration of the systematic rejection of state-created law by the diamond industry in favor of its own internal rules (including arbitration institutions and privately produced sanctions) demonstrates that it is also possible to opt for a private jurisdiction within national boundaries: the New York diamond merchants' "Board of Arbitrators does not apply the New York law of contracts and damages, rather it resolves disputes on the basis of trade custom and usage," and the same is true for many other commercial groups. Indeed, while many contend that law is what judges say it is, this is only true to the extent that a judge is expected to have the last word on a dispute; when adjudication is not sought, perhaps due to the availability of ADR and the benefits it produces (and/or private sanctions to discourage adjudication, as discussed below), other behavioral rules can and often will control the involved parties' conduct.

C   Government Contracts with Private Providers of Legal Functions

Many local governments in the United States now contract with private firms for a wide array of traditional police functions, particularly in the area of "police-support" services such as accounting, maintenance, communications and dispatch, data processing, the towing of illegally parked cars, fingerprinting prisoners, crime labs, background checks on job applicants, school crossing guards, directing traffic, prisoner transport, and the guarding of prisoners in hospitals (Chaiken and Chaiken, 1987, pp. 1–3; Fixler and Poole, 1992, pp. 31–32).[3] Security firms also provide personnel to government units for general patrol, and for guarding ever-growing numbers of public buildings, sports

---

[3] In fact, of course, everything produced by "government" is actually produced by "private" inputs under contract. The difference between so-called contracting out and bureaucratic production is simply a matter of degree. In one case, some individuals who serve as management and decision-makers in a private enterprise are under contract with the government and they in turn contract with others in a privately organized hierarchy. In the other case, each private individual in the hierarchy is under direct contract with the government.

arenas, schools, public housing projects, convention centers, courts, and other public facilities (Fixler and Poole, 1992, p. 32). Chaiken and Chaiken (1987) suggest that "no jurisdiction [in the United States] has successfully transferred total police services to the private sector for any extended period of time," but this appears to reflect political forces more than an assessment of cost effectiveness (Benson, 1990, pp. 331–345). For instance, in 1975, Oro Valley, Arizona, contracted for police services with Rural/Metro Fire Department, Inc. (Gage, 1982, p. 25), but the arrangement was challenged by the Arizona Law Enforcement Officers Advisory Council, arguing that under Arizona law an employee of a private firm could not be a police officer. Rural/Metro could not bear the high court fees required to fight the challenge, so in 1977 the arrangement was ended. Several other contracts like this have been written elsewhere, however. Wackenhut had contracts with three Florida jurisdictions in 1980, for instance, and had proposals pending with 20 communities in 1985 (Cunningham and Taylor, 1985, p. 47). Reminderville, Ohio, contracted with Corporate Security for police services in 1981 (Gage, 1982, p. 24). Similarly, after the four-officer police force of Sussex, New Jersey, was dismissed due to a drug scandal, the community contracted for police services with Executive Security & Investigations Services (*New York Times*, July 13, 1993). Furthermore, contracting for police services is quite common in some other countries. In Switzerland, for example, one firm, Securitas, has contracts with more than 30 Swiss villages and townships (Reynolds, 1994).

Contracting for what might be called judicial support, such as public defender services, also has become the predominant system in some states, although contracting out for complete adjudication services including private judges is not widespread (interest arbitration for public employee contracts does involve private arbitrators). Instead, as noted above, the private sector provides a significant level of ADR directly to private parties. However, punishment services are being contracted out. In fact, perhaps the most visible aspect of contracting out in legal and administrative services is for corrections. There were no privatized secure adult facilities in 1980 in the U.S., and indeed, no state legislature had created expressed legal authority for such contracts. By the end of 1994, however, about half of the states had created the legal authority to contract for corrections. 1994 saw 80 contracts for adult facilities with 21 different firms in the United States (there were also four each in Great Britain and Australia) with 49,154 total beds (*Corrections Alert*, 1995, p. 1). Private entities also provide a vast array of other corrections services, such as halfway houses, juvenile facilities, and drug treatment centers, as well as subservices such as food, medical and drug treatment, and education (Logan, 1990).

II   Evaluating Market Provision of Policing Functions

Despite the ability to capture private benefits of many aspects of security and investigation, arguments against markets for such services abound. In general, these arguments are not valid, particularly when considered in light of the alternative—government production and the government failure that arises. To illustrate this, consider some common criticisms.

A   Poor Quality

Private security firms will presumably reduce quality and cut corners to raise profits, as evidenced by the "undertrained," "old," "high-school dropouts" that work as security personnel (*U.S. News and World Report*, 1983). First, the alleged evidence in support of this criticism is not true. Cunningham and Taylor's (1985, p. 89) survey of private security firms found that the average age of security personnel was between 31 and 35, for instance, and that 59% had at least some college education. Second, the premise upon which this criticism hinges is not valid, because the only circumstances under which the quality-cutting premise is likely to hold are when sellers have only short-term profit goals and/or the market is not competitive. There are con men in some markets who move into an area for a short period, defraud a number of consumers, and move on, of course, but no matter how uninformed consumers might be, it is unlikely that many of them would buy security services from such fly-by-night operations. A sense of permanence and a reputation for quality services should clearly be an important consideration. Furthermore, the number of private protection and detective agencies in the United States probably exceeds 13,000 today, and competition is fierce. When competitive firms have long-range profit goals, their incentives are to beat the competition by offering the same quality of service at lower prices or superior quality at comparable prices. After all, profits are *total revenues minus total costs*, so when reducing costs and quality means losing customers and revenue, profits fall.

The fact is, of course, that it would be foolish to employ a person with the training of an urban police officer as a night watchman, or to pay the $20,000 to $40,000 it would cost to hire that person. On the other hand, it would be foolish to hire someone to design and initiate a corporate security system who only has the training and skills of an urban police officer, and "virtually ignored [by the critics of private security] are the many thousands of well-qualified proprietary loss control personnel" (Bottom and Kostanoski, 1983, p. 31). In fact, as noted above, increasing technological sophistication in electronic detection equipment plays an important role in the increased demand for and proficiency of skilled private security personnel.

Most studies of crime control have examined the effects of public sector efforts, while ignoring potential market impacts. However, Clotfelter (1977, p. 874) considered the impact of private and public security services on the manufacturing, wholesaling, finance, insurance, and real estate sectors; his empirical results "indicate that private protective firms are more effective than public police at protecting firms in these industries" (the same is true for railroads, as noted below). He also found that private protection is more effective and more readily responsive in areas experiencing rapid population growth.

Donovan and Walsh (1986) performed what apparently is the only large-scale evaluation of a private policing system: the 54-person private security force in Starrett City, a 153-acre complex in a high-crime area of Brooklyn, with 56 residential buildings containing 5,881 apartment units and about 20,000 racially and ethnically diverse but largely middle-income residents. Starrett City also has eight parking garages and one outdoor parking lot, a shopping center with 35 businesses, a recreation complex, various open spaces and parks, and one elementary, one intermediate, and two nursery schools. The average age of the Starrett City security force was 39, 83.3% of the officers had at least high-school educations, 70.4% of them had prior security experience (over 25% had been either a public or a military police officer), and all of them had received prior security training, either from another security agency or from the New York City Police Academy. Of residents surveyed, 88.8% felt safe within Starrett City (Donovan and

Table 1. Reported Crimes per 1,000 Residents, 1984 and 1985

Crime	United States		New York State		75th Precinct		Starrett City	
	1984	1985	1984	1985	1984	1985	1984	1985
Murder/Mansl.	0.08	0.08	0.10	0.10	0.30	0.22	0.00	0.05
Rape	0.36	0.39	0.32	0.32	0.90	0.83	0.05	0.10
Robbery	2.05	2.14	5.07	4.56	16.00	15.51	3.60	2.57
Assault	2.90	3.20	3.66	3.86	6.10	6.88	1.90	1.05
Burglary	12.64	13.41	12.57	12.55	15.40	15.26	2.10	0.40
Larceny	27.91	30.49	27.55	28.41	12.10	11.65	2.90	1.30
Auto theft	4.37	7.27	6.51	5.90	10.10	9.51	1.80	1.10

Source: Donovan and Walsh (1986, p. 31).

Walsh, 1986, p. 56), and this perception was clearly warranted. Table 1 lists reported 1984 and 1985 crimes per 1,000 persons for Starrett City, for the 75th precinct in which Starrett City is located, for New York state, and for the United States as a whole. Furthermore, Starrett City's low crime rates do not reflect nonreporting (an issue addressed in more detail below). Residents are much more likely to report crimes than others in the 75th precinct, as evidenced by the fact that they report many more incidents of criminal mischief, trespass, petit larceny, reckless behavior, and disorderly conduct than are reported to public police. This may reflect recognition that the public police and courts will do very little in response to such reports, but it also suggests that private security will respond.

Railroad police have also compiled a remarkable record of effectiveness, particularly relative to public police. Between the end of World War I and 1929, for instance, freight claim payments for robberies fell by 94.5%, from $12,726,947 to $704,262 (Wooldridge, 1970, p. 116). With such success, it is not surprising that this private policing arrangement has survived for decades. In 1992, major railroads in the United States employed a 2,565-person security force which cleared about 30.9% of the crimes reported to it. Public police cleared about 21.4% of reported crimes that same year, but an estimated 75% of all crimes against railroads are reported to railroad police, whereas only 39% of all crimes against the public are reported to the public police. Therefore, clearance rates for railroad police (23.2) were 180% higher than for public police (8.3), adjusted for reporting (Reynolds, 1994, pp. 11–12). Furthermore, arrests by railroad police have resulted in an overall conviction rate at close to 98% over the years (Dewhurst, 1955, p. 4), roughly two to six times the convictions rates from public police arrests, depending on the type of crime and the jurisdiction. Wooldridge (1970, p. 117) suggests that the primary reason for this success is that through specialization, railroad police have developed "an expertise not realistically within the grasp of public forces." Similar specialization and consequent proficiency (and efficiency) often characterize private security and investigation services (e.g., see Reynolds' [1994, pp. 17–19] comparison of private bail bonding and public pre-trial release).

B   Abuses of Power

Another criticism of private security and policing is that without the constitutional due-process constraints that public police face, providers of private security and justice are likely to abuse their power. "Armed and dangerous" private security officers are expected to use excessive force, for instance, because most are "disgruntled people who want to be police officers but cannot make the grade." In reality, private police commit relatively little violence, and this is actually not very surprising. After all, less than 10% of the total private security force is armed (Cunningham and Taylor, 1985, p. 20). Security entrepreneurs report that while customers increasingly request armed guards, these requests are discouraged, both because they feel that weapons are generally not needed and because they face more liability and higher insurance costs when employees are armed (Cunningham and Taylor, 1985, p. 20). Most private police are also not disgruntled rejects from the public police. Cunningham and Taylor (1985, pp. 38–39) report, for example, that many senior public sector law enforcement personnel are actually attracted into private security because most security directors and many security managers now earn more than they do. More significantly, their extensive survey "tends to confirm other research indicating that (1) private security personnel are drawn from different labor pools than law enforcement officers, and (2) their personal characteristics are consistent with the functions they perform" (1985, p. 67; also see Donovan and Walsh, 1986). Thus, while security companies actively "discourage employees from detentions, searches, and the use of force" (Cunningham and Taylor, 1985, p. 34), they apparently go well beyond that by seeking employees inclined to be "service oriented" relative to public police (Donovan and Walsh, 1986, p. 49). And this pays off: for instance, the "concern shown by security personnel for care of property and prevention of disorder as well as the safety of residents and visitors" explains the high level of reporting in Starrett City (Donovan and Walsh, 1986, p. 36).

Actually, many individuals, whether publicly or privately employed, might abuse their positions by cutting costs, doing poor-quality work, and bullying *if they can*. Institutional arrangements within which people perform their tasks determine whether or not such abuses can be carried out, and competitive markets are one of the best (if not *the* best) institutional arrangements to discourage abusive, inefficient behavior. Beyond that, someone who is not fully responsible for the consequences of his actions is likely to be *relatively* unconcerned about those consequences. In this regard, however, private firms must satisfy customers to stay in business. Therefore, a security officer who abuses shopping-mall patrons, for instance, will not be an officer for long. Furthermore, even if a firm fails to respond to market incentives, a civil suit brought against an abusive private security firm can be very costly, perhaps even destroying the business. On the other hand, public police departments rarely go out of business, no matter how corrupt and abusive its members may be. Abuses investigated internally rarely lead to serious sanctions against public police (Benson, 1990, pp. 159–175), and a successful suit against a public law enforcement agency means that taxpayers pay the damage award, so the cost to the manager of that agency is relatively small. Furthermore, a public police officer cannot even be sued for false arrest in the United States unless the plaintiff can prove that he or she is innocent *and* that the police officer had no reason to suspect that individual. In addition, no legal claim against the government or its officials can be made by an innocent person who is wrongly imprisoned. It might be recognized that police made an error, but they have the *legal right* to make such errors and are not liable for them. Not surprisingly, tales of public police abusing suspects are quite common.

C   Public Goods or Common Pools?

Inputs to crime deterrence include private security that deters crimes for specific groups or locations, but both specific and general deterrence can also be produced by publicly employed resources like police and prisons. However, for effective public policing and prosecution, privately provided resources are also required. The fact is that people may not cooperate with the public police in pursuits and prosecution may appear to provide evidence of free riding. However, this characterization is misleading: given common access benefits of public law enforcement, crowding occurs (e.g., most reported crimes are never resolved because police do not have sufficient resources to investigate them, most convictions are achieved through plea bargaining in an effort to relieve court congestion, most convicted criminals cannot fit into crowded prisons so they are sentenced to probation) and there is an underinvestment by individuals in privately provided resources required to produce such services (Benson, 1994). This was not always the case.

Before England's kings began to concentrate and centralize power, individuals had rights to a very important private benefit arising from successfully apprehending and prosecuting law violators: victims received restitution (Benson 1994, 1996).[4] Effective collection of restitution required cooperation (e.g., of witnesses, of neighbors who could aid in pursuit, etc.) but anyone who did not cooperate with others would be ostracized. Policing was carried out by voluntary associations and free riding did not appear to be a problem. One consequence of the development of monarchical government was the creation of criminal law as a way to generate revenues and power for kings. Criminalization took away the private right to restitution and significantly reduced the incentives to voluntarily cooperate in law enforcement. The result is not a public good externality but a common pool problem. When most of the benefits of apprehending and prosecuting criminals involve common access rights rather than private rights, people have incentives to underinvest in the commons. Indeed, withdrawal of the positive incentives associated with restitution is actually what led kings to establish negative incentives (coercion) in an effort to remotivate cooperative policing (Benson, 1994).

Today, a huge portion of all crimes that come to the attention of public police are those reported by victims. Furthermore, without victim testimony, a very substantial portion of the crimes that are suc-

---

[4] Restitution still plays a major role in some societies. For instance, see the discussion of Japan in Benson (1996).

cessfully prosecuted would never be solved, but victimization surveys suggest that over 60% of all Index I crimes (murder/manslaughter, sexual assault, assault, robbery, burglary, larceny, and auto theft) are not reported in the United States (BJS, 1993). Clearly, victims cannot be described as free riders, since they have already born considerable cost. Nonreporting is a natural reaction to the high additional cost of victim involvement with the criminal justice system relative to the expected private benefits that might be obtained. Nonvictim witnesses, neighbors, and others who might be able to assist in prosecution also have to incur costs of involvement themselves and their personal benefits are virtually nonexistent. When the common-access benefits can be internalized, however, as in private developments and associations where contractual obligations to contribute are enforceable (e.g., as in Starrett City, or for members of the American Hotel-Motel Association), private investments are substantial, as suggested above.

The public good/free rider argument is really an ex post rationalization of public provision of policing rather than an ex ante explanation for its historical development (Benson, 1994). Of course, the close-knit families and neighborhoods that characterized historical voluntary policing associations (e.g., Anglo-Saxon tithings) and created the incentives to cooperate may not exist any more, but family and neighborhood stability are not the only ways to maintain reciprocal relationships. In fact, a wide variety of private contractual arrangements already exists when sufficient private benefits to crime control exist (e.g., prevention and protection), and with changes in property rights (e.g., creating a true right to restitution), many of the remaining underinvestment incentives associated with policing services can be eliminated. Even today, lack of cooperation in policing may not be an intrinsic problem that can only be resolved with coercion.

III Evaluating Alternative Dispute Resolution

As suggested above, some observers contend that precedents are external benefits for which private providers of ADR cannot charge. Thus, ADR presumably will not produce precedents. In support of this presumption, critics note that secrecy is often a characteristic of ADR, but this does not mean that precedents are never created. After all, as Fuller (1981, p. 90) explains, "Even if there is no statement by the tribunal of the reasons for its decision, some reason will be perceived or guessed at, and the parties will tend to govern their conduct accordingly." The parties to the dispute will probably consider the result in future dealings under similar circumstances, for instance, and explain them to trading partners. But information will also spread.

Consider that within the diamond industry "as long as judgments are complied with, the fact of the arbitration as well as its outcome are officially kept secret" (Bernstein, 1992, p. 124). Importantly, however, a diamond bourse (trading club) is "an information exchange as much as it is a commodities exchange. As one author put it, 'the bourse grapevine is the best in the world. It has been going for years and moves with the efficiency of a satellite communications network... Bourses are the fountainhead of this information and from them it is passed out along the tentacles that stretch around the world,'" as each local bourse is part of an umbrella organization that, among other things, arbitrates disputes between members of different bourses, enforces arbitration judgments from other bourses, and facilitates the establishment of uniform trading rules throughout the industry (Bernstein, 1992, p. 121). Under such a circumstance, "official" secrecy is probably not much of a constraint on the spread of important information about an arbitration ruling that might provide new precedent. It is clear that in the diamond industry arbitration results do "become known through gossip" (Bernstein, 1992, p. 126) at any rate. Furthermore, if external benefits are significant, there are strong incentives to internalize them, so when precedents are important, institutional adjustments are likely to be made. This actually provides incentives to form groups such as trade associations and diamond bourses. Within such an organization, it is easy to imagine a contractual arrangement that creates incentives to minimize disputes by setting clear precedents.[5] Thus, as Bernstein (1992, p. 150) explains,

---

[5] There are also a number of ways for new rules to evolve within a private legal order (e.g., through unilateral adoption of behavior that is observed and emulated, through bilateral negotiation and contracting, with resulting contract clauses spreading and becoming standardized), so when a particular ADR process does not appear to be designed to produce precedent it simply may mean that precedent is a relatively unimportant source of new rules for the relevant group, or that circumstances do not change often enough to require new rules (Benson, 1998).

diamond dealers have begun to recognize that "[t]he lack of written decisions and a tradition of stare decisis [decision according to precedent] makes it difficult to determine in advance the type of sanctioned behavior. In order to increase predictability, many bourses in the world federation have relaxed the norm of complete secrecy. Arbitrators publish written announcements of the principles used to decide novel cases while keeping the parties and other identifying facts secret." Clearly, flexible private dispute resolution mechanisms can adjust to accommodate the demands for precedent setting while still meeting demands for privacy. In fact, it appears that Landes and Posner's (1979, p. 240) contention that arbitrators "tend to promulgate vague standards which give each party to a dispute a fighting chance" does not hold. Instead, under the institutions that tend to evolve, incentives are exactly the opposite: "Being unbacked by state power ... the arbitrator must concern himself directly with the acceptability of his award. He may be at greater pains than a judge to get his facts straight, to state accurately the arguments of the parties, and generally to display in his award a full understanding of the case" (Fuller, 1981, pp. 110–111).

While the arguments made above are based on examples from commercial arbitration, they can also apply in other situations. For instance, both labor unions and corporate management are likely to recognize that repeated disputes over the same type of grievances are costly, and therefore that grievance arbitration which establishes clear precedent is desirable. In this light, consider the incident reported by Bloom and Cavanagh (1986, p. 412): "a system known as expedited arbitration was adopted by labor and management in the basic steel industry in 1971. Under this system, unresolved employee grievances that do not require precedent-setting rulings are arbitrated by a rotating panel of young, inexperienced arbitrators (mostly lawyers) who decide the case for a relatively small fee within two weeks of the decision to arbitrate." When a resolution is expected to be particularly valuable because it will set a precedent, more experienced, more expensive arbitrators are chosen. This system was established because of rising costs and increasing delays due to a relative shortage of experienced arbitrators, and it is spreading (Bloom and Cavanagh, 1986, p. 412). Clearly, employers and unions are in repeated dealing situations, so the benefits of precedent can be recognized and internalized within the "industry."

While custom, ADR precedents, and/or other rules determined within private organizations appear to be relatively important sources of "law" that at least some ADR providers consider, expectations about how judges will view these rules could significantly influence their content if, as is frequently claimed, a plaintiff must be willing and able to seek judicial enforcement in order to induce a defendant to accept ADR (e.g., Landes and Posner, 1979, p. 247). This implies that ADR's potential as a jurisdictional choice may be significantly limited even if judges never directly interpret the rules. After all, for the litigation threat to be credible, ADR rulings will have to be acceptable to judges, so they will have to correspond with expectations about how they will be viewed under judicial review. In contrast, Charny (1990, pp. 409–412) contends that "nonlegal sanctions" can induce the members of a "community of transactors" to accept ADR and comply with the resulting judgment, characterizing ADR and these nonlegal sanctions as "a perfect substitute for legal enforcement." Nonlegal sanctions are essentially the "private" sanctions discussed in that economics literature which explains how powerful sources of credibility can arise through "bond-posting" or "hostage-taking," including the potential loss of reputation or relation-specific reciprocities from repeated dealings. Viable private sanctions mean that ADR can escape the shadow of the law, but such sanctions vary considerably in strength. For instance, most businessmen expect to be active for a long time and value both reputations and ongoing reciprocities, and private sanctions clearly are strong enough to support widespread use of ADR in commercial areas (Benson, 1992, 1995). The same may be true of neighbors (Ellickson, 1991), at least in many cases, and for labor grievance disputes (Benson, 1997). The strength of these threats certainly may be too weak to back all potential ADR, of course, but even this fact does not necessarily imply market failure.

High levels of uncertainty tend to undermine the potential for private sanctions, but Rubin (1994, p. 32) explains that much of this uncertainty reflects political instability (government failure). When property rights are unstable due to potential opportunistic behavior by government (e.g., changes in tax policy to capture the quasi rents from investments in reputation and long-term relationships), threats of private sanctions are likely to be relatively weak, for instance. Under these circumstances, legal sanctions may induce arbitration (Rubin, 1994), but this presumes that a government which is too corrupt and/or inefficient to create stable property rights is sufficiently trustworthy and/ or efficient to create effective contract enforcement.

Even if an organized threat is necessary, it need not come from government, as both ex ante ADR commitments and reputation threats can be made more credible, in many instances, when individuals with mutual interests in long-term interaction form "contractual" organizations such as trade associations. The group can provide mechanisms to overcome many frictions in communication so information about refusal to accept ADR and/or ADR rulings can be spread quickly. These groups can also lower the transactions costs of ADR by establishing internal dispute resolution performed by individuals with considerable knowledge of the relevant transactions and rules, and this tribunal can be backed by a contractual obligation to boycott anyone who reneges on a promise to use it or accept its ruling.

Many people are almost never in a dispute that they cannot resolve through direct negotiation or exit, of course, and they may not belong to an organization wherein they can count on private sanctions or even observe ADR between other parties. Therefore, they may not be familiar with ADR options, or they may not understand them. If an unanticipated and apparently unsolvable dispute arises, advice may be sought from someone perceived to be an expert on dispute resolution, but the most likely source of such information is probably a lawyer. In this case, asymmetric information and lawyer self-interests suggest that principal-agent problems could lead to litigation rather than ADR (Benson, 1995). Perhaps the passage of statutes mandating court backing of ADR could resolve such "market failures" by creating information about alternatives along with a source of credibility for promises to use ADR (it also makes ADR more attractive to lawyers, as explained below). This suggests that such statutes are desirable unless they also have some adverse affects, but the fact is that they do.

Before several states passed statutes commanding judges to enforce arbitration agreements and rulings during the 1920s, these agreements and rulings were often not considered binding by state courts. The primary political impetus behind arbitration statutes came from bar associations rather than from business, however, as lawyers saw the growing use of arbitration without lawyers as a threat to their control over contract writing and dispute resolution (Auerbach, 1983; Benson, 1995). Lawyers offered "public interest" arguments for the statutes, of course, but a number of consequences clearly benefited the legal profession. For instance, businesses facing the prospect of judicial review had to make arbitration compatible with statute and precedent law, including public court procedure. To do so, they had to involve lawyers in arbitration. Not surprisingly, an enormous number of court cases were filed in states that passed such statutes, producing a "monumental tragicomedy" as individuals who arbitrated in order to avoid litigation found themselves litigating anyway, not over the merits of their disputes but over the merits and characteristics of arbitration (Isaacs, 1930, pp. 149–151).

If the wave of litigation was simply a response that often follows new legislation as individuals attempt to define the new legal margins, then ceteris paribus the level of litigation should have diminished over time. However, Ashe (1983, p. 42) explains that the early 1980s were still witnessing increasing litigation regarding arbitration awards, and he contends that this reflects the relatively strong tendency of losing attorneys to appeal an arbitrator's decision, compared with a business-man who loses in arbitration but without lawyer involvement. Of course, for this to be the case, the statutes must have created or exacerbated the principal-agent problem. A lawyer's advice could clearly be influenced by his own interests, and the increasing complexity of precedent law regarding arbitration makes asymmetric information between lawyers and their clients more likely, so Ashe may be correct. Increasing litigation of arbitration rulings is certainly correlated with the increasing involvement of lawyers in business decisions (Ashe, 1983, p. 42), supporting his hypothesis.

The potential for litigation to enforce promises that parties would be able to enforce with private sanctions may also "chill" commitment-making to the degree that parties expect that they will not be able to avoid litigation costs (Charny, 1990, p. 428). The possibility of appeal to litigation implies that arbitration rulings may be viewed as less decisive than they had been before the statutes were passed (Ashe, 1983, p. 42), implying weaker incentives to accept arbitration or abide by arbitrated settlements. Thus, these statutes may be a source of much of the alleged market failure limiting the use of ADR.

In a similar vein, Mentschikoffs (1961, p. 14) seminal research on arbitration, using American Arbitration Association (AAA) records as well as personal observations, concludes that lawyer participation significantly lengthens and complicates most arbitration cases without facilitating decisions. One reason for this is that lawyers do not understand relevant business usage and practice. Similarly, Lazarus, et al. (1965, p. 95) found, on the basis of their questionnaire distributed to arbitrators, that lawyers tend to be less than adequately prepared to represent clients in arbitration, and that they prefer to use practices that are valued in litigation rather than the informal procedures preferred by businessmen. In essence, a moral hazard has been created, as lawyers have relatively strong incentives to shirk during arbitration, which they often perceive as a procedural stage of dispute resolution rather than a jurisdictional alternative to litigation. Furthermore, as Lazarus et al. (1965, p. 102) stress, many of arbitration's procedural advantages arise because it differs from litigation, but some arbitration proceedings (e.g., by the AAA) have "been altered to accommodate lawyers" making them more like court proceedings. Thus, legal sanctions appear to have significantly increased the cost of arbitration and reduced its attractiveness.

In sum, the "business community" might be divided into three groups in an effort to consider the consequences of having legal sanctions to back up arbitration. First, a large portion of this community can use private sanctions to enforce contracts and to prevent both the use of lawyers and the appeal of arbitration rulings. Thus, availability of litigation threats probably has little impact on these businesses. Second, some portion of the business community may not be able to enforce arbitration agreements without legal sanctions. Reliance on the threat of legal sanctions leads them to use lawyers in such arbitration and principal-agent/moral-hazard problems may cause relatively large numbers of appeals of arbitration rulings. Therefore, their dispute resolution costs are higher on average than the first group's, but lower than they would be without legal sanctions. A third group may lie between the first two (indeed, a continuum may be more realistic than discrete groupings). Private sanctions may be relatively weak compared with the first group, but still sufficiently strong to induce compliance with arbitration under most circumstances in the absence of legal sanctions. However, with the advent of legal sanctions and the potential for appeal, transactions costs associated with arbitration rise for this group, as the potential use of litigation leads to lawyer representation in arbitration. How many businesses are actually worse off because they have been forced to include lawyers and consider the implications of appeal? There is really no way to tell, in part because efforts to bring arbitration under the shadow of the law may have significantly diverted the path of arbitration's evolution. Nonetheless, it does not follow that the level of commercial arbitration would be dramatically less in the absence of litigation threats, as stronger incentives would exist to use existing and develop more private sanctioning mechanisms.

What about noncommercial ADR? Numerous examples of ADR between neighbors, and between businesses and their employees or customers can also be cited, for instance, as noted above, but in some of these cases the role of private sanctions is less clear. Labor unions and private industry organizations may be able to institutionalize reciprocities and reputation effects for their own members, and institutionalized collective bargaining often establishes long-term repeating dealing relationships with one another. Such arrangements may provide sufficient stimuli for arbitration or mediation of many grievances between labor and private firms, perhaps backed by strike and lockout threats. Unfortunately, most of the economics literature has focused on compulsory interest arbitration, implying that it is a procedural alternative relying on statutory mandates of arbitration rather than strikes or lockouts. Compulsory interest arbitration is almost exclusively a public sector phenomenon, however (professional baseball being the major exception), and as such, it may have to rely on legal threats. After all, when laborers are protected by civil service "tenure," the potential for reciprocities and private sanctions influencing their behavior may be sharply limited. Private sanctions and expectations of reciprocities may be quite weak for their "employers" as well. Incentives of government decision-makers may be tied to particular constituencies who do not view an arbitrated outcome as desirable, for example.

It appears that repeated dealing and reputation sanctions can be quite effective inducements for using ADR in stable neighborhoods (Ellickson, 1991). The same is true of some consumer disputes, as evidenced by the long-term success of the New York Stock Exchange's arbitration of disputes between members and their customers (Lazarus et al., 1965, p. 27). On the other hand, while medical malpractice arbitration has been available since 1929, this alternative does not appear to be nearly as successful at preventing litigation. The current state of medical malpractice torts in the United States may explain why, however. When one dispute resolution forum appears to favor a category of litigants, they will attempt to avoid using an alternative unbiased forum, and there is a widespread perception that American juries tend to be biased in favor of patients in medical malpractice suits. Clearly, other patients are not likely to sanction a patient that litigates, since they also may be able to benefit from future malpractice litigation (collective action problems are also significant for consumer groups who might recognize unintended consequences such as reduced availability of some medical services and rising medical costs), and if doctors or hospitals attempt to boycott a litigious patient, the political fallout would be tremendous. Thus, in the current legal/political environment, medical malpractice arbitration is not likely to be attractive to patients without strong legal sanctions to back it. It still does not follow that such sanctions are necessarily desirable, of course. Tort reforms under consideration by many state legislatures could alter the incentives sufficiently to make malpractice arbitration attractive.

In general, a frequently interacting community of transactors can often offer private benefits and impose private sanctions that are sufficient to make ADR a jurisdictional choice. In the total absence of such a community, perhaps because biases in litigation undermine incentives to cooperate, ADR may still survive if the state sanctions it as a procedural option. Between these extremes are situations in which ADR lightens the "shadow of the law" without completely escaping its jurisdiction.

IV Government Failure and Contracting Out

A number of evaluation studies of contract prisons have been performed. They regularly find savings of 20% for construction costs and 5% to 15% from private management relative to the costs of comparable public facilities (Logan, 1990). Unfortunately, there are no independent evaluations of contract policing, although there is anecdotal evidence of similar savings (Benson, 1996), and in virtually every other area that has been evaluated (e.g., fire protection, refuse collection, data processing, maintenance), contracting out produces average savings of from 10 to 50% (Poole, 1978, p. 27). Thus, on average at least, contracting out appears to be an effective way to reduce costs. But critics contend that even if costs are cut through contracting out, it is achieved through quality reductions.

Profit-seeking firms have incentives to cut costs *if* the cost cutting *does not* result in offsetting revenue losses. However, this is an important "if" that critics generally overlook. After all, there may be several ways to cut costs. By more effectively monitoring employees, avoiding unnecessarily expensive means of production, and actively searching for technological advances, private firms can lower costs without lowering quality; in fact, such activity can simultaneously lower costs and enhance quality. Thus, the costs/quality tradeoff is not the only potential margin along which firms can adjust. In addition, private firms competing to sell services to government units have reputations to maintain so they can retain contracts and continue to attract new customers. After all, a survey of 89 municipal governments regarding contracting out found that the most frequently applied criteria used for awarding large contracts was *documented past performance* (Florestano and Gordon, 1980, p. 32). A record of past performance filled with evidence of or disputes over quality cutting will not attract many new customers or retain many old ones. On the other hand, a firm that offers better services than competitors at similar costs will be in a strong position for contract renewal and for obtaining new contracts elsewhere. Therefore, it should not be surprising to find that independent observers who monitor private prisons generally praise the quality of their operations (Logan, 1992). In a study of the privately managed Silverdale Detention Center in Chattanooga, for instance, Brakel (1992, p. 261) concluded that his findings "resoundingly disprove the trade-off assumption. The gains in efficiency yielded by privatizing the Silverdale facility were in fact found to be accompanied by significant quality improvements." Brakel examined several dimensions of quality, and found substantial improvements in upkeep and maintenance, safety and security, treatment of inmates, medical services, recreation programs and facilities, religious and other counseling, disciplinary procedures, inmate grievance and request procedures, and legal access. The same conclusion appears to apply for contract policing (Gage, 1982; Benson, 1996), although the evidence is more anecdotal.

In a competitive market, producers must compete for consumers by either offering a product of similar quality for a lower price than competitors offer, or offering a better quality product for the price that competitors are charging. In the market for contract services the consumer is the government agency letting the contract, so that agency is the most direct determinant of the quality of services. If the agency attempts to get a bargain by limiting payments too much (e.g., relative to production costs for a public bureau), a poor quality service may be provided. The agency is also likely to have considerable power to encourage, limit, or redirect competition. When competition is stifled or diverted to other dimensions, cost savings and quality enhancements need not arise.

Bureaucratic attitudes and incentives that influence government production in general can affect the level of competition for contracts. Consider the belief that "one efficient firm and a knowledgeable government official can reach an agreement to provide services at a cost no higher than it would be if ten suppliers were bidding" (Fisk, et al., 1978, p. 5). But when a private firm is given a contract with no fear of future competition it begins acting like a monopolist, and no government official is likely to be "knowledgeable" enough to determine true costs. For example, Fitzgerald (1988, p. 92) cites Pima County, Arizona, where for many years two firms had exclusive contracts to collect refuse: "When this policy was abandoned in favor of an open, free market, 15 private firms went into competition and prices to consumers were cut in half from what the monopoly holders had charged."

Governments have imposed a large number and variety of regulations, standards, and other requirements on the contracting process itself and on postcontract production, which makes "government contracting for the typical small firm, and for many large firms a chancy business. The risks impel many firms to limit the amount of government business they seek, and some now go after government contracts only because of ancillary advantages (such as access to information not otherwise available)" (Fitch, 1974, p. 518). The excuse for heavy monitoring is supposedly to prevent dishonest private firms from providing poor services. Of course, a competitive contracting process would do precisely that, as potential competitors monitor those providing services in hopes of spotting inefficiencies or abuses that will allow them to offer a superior contract. And furthermore, even with all the regulations, many critics remain "afraid that contract prisons will generate the same kinds of scandals as contract nursing homes, which despite numerous inspectors and standards have still frequently become substandard facilities" (Krajick, 1984, p. 27). Such concerns may be warranted. After all, as Fitch (1974, p. 517) notes, many of the regulations "have the effect of putting a greater strain on honest firms than on dishonest firms, which can often find some way of beating the regulation, if only by buying cooperation of government contracting officers." This brings us to another barrier to price/quality competition in contracting—corruption.

Political corruption becomes possible when government officials control the allocation of valuable property rights (Benson, 1990, pp. 159–175). Clearly, the right to act as exclusive supplier of some government service without fear of competition can be extremely valuable, particularly if a public official is willing to turn away when a producer cuts quality to increase profits. Thus, "contracts are one of the most common and lucrative sources of corruption in government" (Fitch, 1974, p. 517). When contracts are awarded by corrupt public officials, price/quality competition is replaced by a competition to "buy" contracts with bribe payments. In such cases, critics may be absolutely right when they argue that private firms reduce costs by cutting quality, but it is not because of market failure; it is because the incorruptible market regulator, price/quality competition, has been terminated and replaced by competition for the attention of and regulation by a corrupt public official. The level of corruption observed in criminal justice over the past decades (Benson, 1990, pp. 159–175) suggests that this could become a serious problem in the contractual arena as well, although there is no evidence to suggest that it is at this time, and as long as firms see the potential for large numbers of additional contracts with other government units, incentives to avoid a corruption scandal will be quite strong. Firms do not have to resort to illegal means in order to "purchase" contracts and other advantages from government, however. After all, the contracting decision is made in a political environment wherein "contractors are expected to make political contributions in order to be eligible for contracts," and they are "one of the principle sources of campaign funds" (Fitch, 1974, pp. 513, 516). Indeed, several respondents to the Florestano–Gordon survey (1980, p. 32) admit that an important "criterion" in awarding large contracts is "political considerations." Competition for political influence should push prices up, as the resulting costs are added to firms' production and contracting costs. Since expenditures are also diverted from productive inputs, quality could suffer as well.

V   Conclusions

In light of the preceding presentation, should markets in legal and administrative services be encouraged? A universal answer cannot be given. It is clear that at least many of the attributes of these services are not "public goods" and that changes in property rights can create private benefits that would provide incentives to demand and privately produce even more than are currently being produced (Benson, 1996). Scarce resources mean that there are always tradeoffs, of course, but the nature of the tradeoff depends on the institutional environment. When demand must filter through the political arena and supply is provided by public institutions, competitive forces are relatively weak and efficiency gains in the form of higher quality services at a lower cost are generally possible. When supply is privatized through contracting out, the incentives to compete for a contract are strong, but the competition can take many forms, including competition to bribe regulators, competition to win political favors, and competition to provide quality services at a low cost. Thus, contracting out can lead to efficiency gains, but it may not if bureaucratic rigidities, politics, or corruption stand in the way by creating an environment that shelters firms from price/quality competition. When property rights are such that private benefits can stimulate demand, and supply is also privatized, firms will have to compete on price and quality dimensions. Therefore, the greater the degree of privatization on both the demand and the supply sides of legal and administrative services, the greater is the potential for efficiency gains.

Bibliography

Ashe, B.F. 1983. "Arbitration Finality: Myth or Reality?" *Arbitration Journal* 38:42–51.

Auerbach, J.S. 1983. *Justice Without Law?* New York: Oxford University Press.

Benson, B.L. 1990. *The Enterprise of Law: Justice Without the State.* San Francisco: Pacific Research Institute.

Benson, B.L. 1992. "Customary Law as a Social Contract: International Commercial Law." *Constitutional Political Economy* 2:1–27.

Benson, B.L. 1994. "Are Public Goods Really Common Pools: Considerations of the Evolution of Policing and Highways in England." *Economic Inquiry* 32:249–271.

Benson, B.L. 1995. "An Exploration of the Impact of Modern Arbitration Statutes on the Development of Arbitration in the United States." *Journal of Law, Economics & Organization* 11:479–501.

Benson, B.L. 1996. "Restitution in Theory and in Practice." *Journal of Libertarian Studies* 12:75–98.

Benson, B.L. 1997. "Arbitration." In: B. Bouckaert and G. DeGeest (eds.), *The Encyclopedia of Law and Economics.* London: Elgar (forthcoming).

Benson, B.L. 1998a. "Arbitration in the Shadow of the Law." In: P. Newman (ed.), *The New Palgrave Dictionary of Economics and the Law.* London: Macmillan (forthcoming).

Benson, B.L. 1998b. *To Serve and Protect: Privatization and Community in Criminal Justice.* (forthcoming).

Bernstein, L. 1992. "Opting Out of the Legal System: Extralegal Contractual Relations in the Diamond Industry." *Journal of Legal Studies* 21:115–158.

BJS (Bureau of Justice Statistics). 1993. *Highlights from 20 Years of Surveying Crime Victims: The National Victimization Survey, 1973–1992.* Washington, D.C.: U.S. Department of Justice, Office of Justice Programs.

Bloom, D.E., and C.L. Cavanagh. 1986. "An Analysis of the Selection of Arbitrators." *American Economic Review* 76:408–422.

Bottom N.K., and J. Kostanoski. 1983. *Security and Loss Control.* New York: Macmillan.

Brakel, S.J. 1992. "Private Corrections." In: G.W. Bowman, S. Hakim and P. Seidenstat (eds.), *Privatizing the United States Justice System: Police Adjudication, and Corrections Services form the Private Sector*, pp. 254–274. Jefferson, N.C.: McFarland & Company.

Brunet, E. 1987. "Questioning the Quality of Alternative Dispute Resolution." *Tulane Law Review* 62:1–56.

Chaiken, M., and J. Chaiken. 1987. *Public Policing: Privately Provided.* Washington D.C.: U.S. Department of Justice, National Institute of Justice.

Charny, D. 1990. "Nonlegal Sanctions in Commercial Relationships." *Harvard Law Review* 104:373–467.

Clotfelter, C.T. 1977. "Public Services, Private Substitutes, and the Demand for Protection Against Crime." *American Economic Review* 67:867–877.

Corrections Alert. 1995. "Privatization Census Reveals Continued Expansion." *Corrections Alert* I:1–2.

Cunningham, W.C., and T.H. Taylor. 1985. *Crime and Protection in America: A Study of Private Security and Law Enforcement Resources and Relationships.* Washington D.C.: U.S. Department of Justice, National Institute of Justice.

Cunningham, W.C., J.J. Strauchs, and C.W. Van Meter. 1991. "Private Security: Patterns and Trends." *Research in Brief.* Washington D.C.: U.S. Department of Justice, National Institute of Justice.

Denenberg, T.S., and R.V. Denenberg. 1981. "Dispute Resolution: Settling Conflicts Without Legal Action." *Public Affairs Pamphlet* No. 597. New York: Public Affairs Committee.

Dewhurst, H.S. 1955. *The Railroad Police.* Springfield, Ill.: Charles C. Thomas.

Donovan, E.J., and W.F. Walsh. 1986. *An Evaluation of Starrett City Security Services.* University Park, Penn.: Pennsylvania State University.

Ellickson, R.C. 1991. *Order Without Law: How Neighbors Settle Disputes.* Cambridge, Mass.: Harvard University Press.

Fisk, D., H. Kiesling, and T. Muller. 1978. *Private Provision of Public Services: An Overview.* Washington D.C.: Urban Institute.

Fitch, L.C. 1974. "Increasing the Role of the Private Sector in Providing Public Services." *Urban Affairs Annual Review* 8:501–559.

Fitzgerald, R. 1988. *When Government Goes Private: Successful Alternatives to Public Services.* New York: Universe Books.

Fixler, P.E., Jr., and R.W. Poole, Jr. 1992. "Can Police be Privatized?" In: G.W. Bowman, S. Hakim, and P. Seidenstat (eds.), *Privatizing the United States Justice System: Police Adjudication, and Corrections Services form the Private Sector,* pp. 27–41. Jefferson, N.C.: McFarland & Company.

Florestano, P.S., and S.B. Gordon. 1980. "Public vs. Private: Small Government Contracting with the Private Sector." *Public Administration Review* 40: 29–34.

Fuller, L. 1981. *The Principles of Social Order.* Durham, N.C.: Duke University Press.

Gage, T.J. 1982. "Cops, Inc." *Reason* 14:23–28.

Isaacs, N. 1930. "Review of Wesley Sturges Treatise on Commercial Arbitration and Awards." *Yale Law Journal* 40:149–151.

Krajick, K. 1984. "Punishment for Profit." *Across the Board* 21:20–27.

Landes, W.M., and R.A. Posner. 1979. "Adjudication as a Private Good." *Journal of Legal Studies* 8:235–284.

Lazarus, S., J.J. Bray, Jr., L.L. Carter, K.H. Collins, B.A. Giedt, R.V. Holton, Jr., P.D. Matthews, and G.C. Willard. 1965. *Resolving Business Disputes: The Potential for Commercial Arbitration.* New York: American Management Association.

Lew, J.D.M. 1978. *Applicable Law in International Commercial Arbitration: A Study in Commercial Arbitration Awards.* Dobbs Ferry, N.Y.: Oceana Publications.

Logan, C.H. 1990. *Private Prisons: Cons and Pros.* New York: Oxford University Press.

Logan, C.H. 1992. "Well Kept: Comparing Quality of Confinement in Private and Public Prisons." *Journal of Criminal Law and Criminology* 83(Fall):577–613.

Mentschikoff, S. 1961. "Commercial Arbitration." *Columbia Law Review* 61: 846–869.

Phalon, R. 1992. "Privatizing Justice." *Forbes* 150:126–127.

Poole, R.W., Jr. 1978. *Cutting Back City Hall.* New York: Free Press.

Poole, R.W., Jr. 1980. "Can Justice be Privatized?" *Fiscal Watchdog* 49:1–2.

Pruitt, G. 1982. "California's Rent-a-Judge Justice." *Journal of Contemporary Studies* 5:49–57.

Reichman, N. 1987. "The Widening Webs of Surveillance: Private Police Unraveling Deceptive Claims." In: C.D. Shearing and P.C. Stenning (eds.), *Private Policing,* pp. 247–265. Newbury Park, Cal.: Sage.

Reynolds, M.O. 1994. *Using the Private Sector to Deter Crime.* Dallas: National Center for Policy Analysis.

Ricks, T.A., B.G. Tillett, and C.W. Van Meter. 1981. *Principles of Security.* Cincinnati: Anderson.

Rubin, E.L. 1995. "The Nonjudicial Life of Contract: Beyond the Shadow of the Law." *Northwestern University Law Review* 90:107–131.

Rubin, P.H. 1994. "Growing a Legal System in the Post-Communist Economies." *Cornell International Law Journal* 27:1–47.

Samuelson, P.A., and W.D. Nordhaus. 1985. *Economics.* New York: McGraw Hill.

Sherman, L.W. 1983. "Patrol Strategies for Police." In: J.Q. Wilson (ed.), *Crime and Public Policy*, pp. 145–164. San Francisco: Institute for Contemporary Studies.

Tullock, G. 1970. *Private Wants, Public Means: An Economic Analysis of the Desirable Scope of Government.* New York: Basic Books.

U.S. News and World Report. 1983, January 29. "Private Police Forces in Growing Demand."

Wooldridge, W.C. 1970. *Uncle Sam, The Monopoly Man.* New Rochelle, N.Y.: Arlington House.

Competition in the Market for Health Services and Insurance, with Special Reference to the United States

Mark V. Pauly

How do markets organize the production and financing of medical care? In most countries, governments play a dominant role in both functions, so little experience is available on which to judge the performance of the markets. An exception is the United States, which has permitted markets to furnish the bulk of services to the nonelderly population. However, as economists pointed out long ago (Kessel, 1959), medical markets in the United States were never an approximation of the economic concept of a competitive market; they contained both regulatory and monopoly elements. Recently, however, some changes have occurred in the U.S. system which may have made markets more competitive. What are these changes and what are the effects, good and bad, which they have had?

I Changes in the U.S. System

Greater "competition" in U.S. medical care and health insurance is largely associated with the rise of private health insurance plans using managed care. Rather than paying providers the market prices for whatever services they choose to provide, these plans control use and cost by paying providers lower prices for services, by using financial incentives to control volume (such as capitation), and by placing explicit managerial limits on what services will be reimbursed and which providers may be used. Some plans also own facilities and employ physicians. Figure 1 illustrates the rapid spread in recent years of several forms of managed care, relative to conventional ("indemnity") insurance. The health maintenance organization form of managed care typically uses both rules and incentives to hold down spending in its network of providers, and pays nothing for services outside the net-

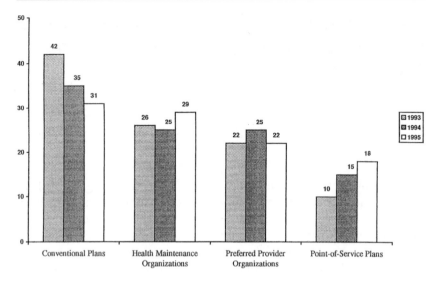

Figure 1. Percent of Employees Enrolled in Employer-Sponsored Health Insurance
Plans, by Type of Plan, 1993–1995
Source: KPMG (1994–1996).

work. The point-of-service plan is a health maintenance organization
which provides partial coverage if the consumer uses nonnetwork providers. The preferred provider organization also has differential coverage, but usually has fewer managerial limits on services in the network.

This transformation is most frequently given credit for the data on
growth of total expenditures shown in Table 1. Not only has the real
growth rate of national health expenditures (NHE) in the United
States slacked off dramatically beginning in 1993, but the reduction is
almost entirely concentrated in the private sector, where managed care
is growing rapidly, and is absent in the public Medicare and Medicaid
programs, where, until recently, managed care was uncommon. Official
1996 data is not yet available, but is expected to approximate the 1995
experience.

The unusual fact about the 1993–1995 downturn is not its uniqueness; there have been other two- or three-year periods for which the
drop in the rate of spending growth was nearly as large, though not to
as low a level. In both the period of the Nixon Administration price
controls and during the debate over President Carter's cost contain-

Table 1. Annual Rate of Growth in National (NHE) and Personal (PHE) Health Expenditures

Year	NHE Nominal	NHE Real[a]	PHE Nominal	PHE Real[b]	Real GDP Growth
1960–1970	10.6	6.2	10.5	6.1	4.4
1980	12.9	4.8	13.2	5.1	3.2
1985	11.6	6.3	11.8	6.4	2.6
1990	10.2	6.0	10.3	6.0	3.4
1991	9.2	5.1	10.1	5.7	−1.0
1992	9.5	6.6	9.5	6.6	2.7
1993	6.9	4.2	6.3	3.7	2.2
1994	5.1	2.5	5.2	2.6	3.5
1995	5.5	2.9	6.1	3.5	2.0

[a] Deflated by consumer price index less medical care.
[b] Deflated by GNP deflator.

ment bill, overall spending growth slowed. What makes the most recent period unique is that there is no obvious public policy influence on the fall in spending growth; rather, the cause appears in large part to be the rise of a more competitive market in private health insurance. The debate over health reform was largely over by early in 1994 (although it took longer for the political process to administer the last rites), while the slowdown in spending growth persisted even after any political pressures had evaporated.

From a public policy perspective, these are good times for private markets for medical services in the United States. After years of being the subject of criticism and the target for reform, the market is now getting some compliments. What is the basis for this more favorable opinion? In a word: control—of spending, of use, and (perhaps) of quality and outcome. In a development that has truly surprised almost everyone, this control has been exercised neither by government nor by private managers subject to strict public regulation, but rather by private managers trying to please their customers. In the process, the high-level organizational structure of this industry has been transformed. It can no longer be maintained that private markets are incapable of limiting the growth in medical services spending.

What caused this change? Is it all to the good? Is it a generalizable model for other countries? Will it last, or will either economic or political forces operate to displace current successes and frustrate future objectives? What impact, if any, does the transformation of a sector amounting to one-seventh of the economy have on the course of the economy?

A   What Really Has Changed?

In this section I first review empirical measures of public and private sector performance. As recently as 1993, private medical spending was rocketing ahead with a growth rate more than twice as great as the rate for all GDP. In 1994 and 1995, and probably in 1996, the growth rate of private sector spending dropped dramatically, to a rate about below that of the (relatively high) rate of growth of GDP per capita experienced in those years. The low growth for private spending contrasts strongly with the much higher growth rate for public spending, but, even so, total medical care spending grew at about the same rate as GDP.

However, while costs have been brought under control, two other, less positive developments have been occurring. First, the welfare of the uninsured has probably worsened. The proportion of the uninsured population has remained stubbornly high, despite increased public subsidies to insurance in both public and private sectors totaling nearly half of spending. Charity care has probably been falling. Secondly, a wholly new phenomenon has emerged: concern and criticism about the way managed care plans have been managing care.

In this essay, I briefly address the question of how these changes were affected by market competition and other influences. After that, I comment on two issues about future trends—whether cost growth is permanently slowed, and whether the political process will accept on a permanent basis the methods the market used to control costs.

Let us return to Table 1. It shows the most recent data available on the real (inflation-adjusted) rate of growth in national health expenditures (NHE) and personal health expenditures (PHE) in the United States. PHE differs from NHE primarily in excluding the administrative cost and underwriting profit or loss of private health insurers. Up to 1993, both measures show the same pattern: fluctuation of the real rate of growth in health spending in a range of 5% to a little over 6%, almost always higher than the approximately 3% growth in real GDP. (Subtract one percentage point to convert to per capita gains.)

Obviously, the share of GDP going to health care rose to reflect the difference in these two trends.

A number of factors contributed to the growth of real spending per capita. Least important has been aging of the population, accounting for 10% or less of the real growth. The great bulk of that growth is attributable to two causes: health care input prices (including profits) rising more rapidly than in the economy as a whole, and the use of more inputs per capita to provide health care. The last influence is usually labeled "technical (or technological) change."

Where is the current growth slowdown occurring, and what accounts for it? From an accounting perspective, the answer to the first question is clear: there has been a substantial drop in the growth of private sector spending on almost all categories of spending except for long-term care and pharmaceuticals. The most dramatic fall, however, has been in the administrative cost and profit of private insurers, which actually fell even in nominal terms in 1994 and 1995. This is indicated by the fact that in 1995, NHE (premiums) grew much less rapidly than PHE (benefits). Public sector spending for the elderly (Medicare) and the poor (and elderly) (Medicaid) showed a rate of growth substantially higher than that in the private sector. Medicare and Medicaid restrained the growth in their hospital and physician spending to some extent, but rising spending on long-term care (hospice, nursing home care, home health benefit) still drove their overall rates to the 8%–11% range.

In sweeping overview, these are the facts as we know them. No one can maintain, in the face of this data, that the private market is incapable of restraining the growth of spending. But is the change permanent? Has it improved economic efficiency? Will it be politically viable?

B The Causes of the Change

What is perhaps most surprising about the transformation of the American private health insurance market is that it has no easily identifiable cause. There was no national law that was passed, no defining conference or committee report. It is true that the movement toward managed care appeared to accelerate in California after that state removed previously existing bans on selective contracting—agreeing to pay for services from some doctors and hospitals but not others—by private insurers. However, the change was by no means limited to California.

Some observers attribute the transformation in insurance to a change in employer benefits provision, in which large employers ceased buying insurance from outside insurers and began self-insuring (Etheredge, 1996). The argument then is that, once employers experienced rising health care costs directly and individually, they conceived a desire to control those costs. While doing so might irritate hospitals and doctors, individual employers cared less about doctors' goodwill than did indemnity insurers who had to deal continuously with all of them.

The problem with this explanation is that the highly competitive insurance market would have had both the power and the incentives to achieve the same objectives much earlier. I believe that an easier, if less elegant, explanation for the change is suggested by Herbert Stein's famous dictum, "If things can't go on like this forever, they won't." Slightly more formally, as health benefits costs consumed larger and larger shares of workers' take-home pay, and as the price of health insurance rose substantially relative to other goods, employees became more willing to tolerate insurance that restricted their choice in providers. Once such a market began to develop, it then found it was able to extract substantial price concessions from hospitals with redundant capacity.

Another major contributing factor to the emergence of managed care, I would speculate, was the substantial increase in physician supply that has been occurring in the United States. While noneconomists deplored this expansion in the expectation that these new physicians would create demand for their services without limit, an alternative model, perhaps more consistent with recent developments, postulates limits to "induced demand" and a consequent greater willingness of physicians with time on their hands to contract with health maintenance organizations (HMOs) rather than join with other physicians to deplore them.

These hypotheses, taken together, may also help to explain why, to the present, competitive managed care has not yet emerged in most other countries. Their spending, while often high, was more under control in the late 1980s than in the United States, and the collective character of most systems precludes the U.S. piecemeal approach which could ignore the desires of organized medicine. It is, in short, unlikely that political choice will lead to a system of competitive health plans while full public financing remains in place. Something like the U.S. system (but so far without the dramatic effects on spending growth) has emerged in the Netherlands, but there, despite a larger private sector than in most other European countries, both public financing and public regulation are much more prominent.

II Some Definitions and Some Observations

Does this market-based change in the United States represent an improvement in market performance? The reduction in spending growth, to most noneconomist observers, is unequivocally desirable. However, economists, using a definition of market efficiency, might not be so sure. As I have noted elsewhere (Pauly, 1990), there is no necessarily intrinsic merit or benefit from a low health spending GDP share or low or zero growth in that share; to make a judgment about efficiency, even a speculative one, we would need to know the value of the alternative outputs from the inputs that were used or might have been used to produce medical care relative to the value of medical care. Increases in absolute spending on a particular service do not them- selves cause macroeconomic inflation (unless there is some conspiracy between doctors and central bankers), and no one in the medical sector really knows the value of the displaced output.

While even some economists object (Evans, 1997), I believe that the proper conclusion is that the ideal rate of growth in spending on health services is one that would occur if (contrary to fact) it were possible to satisfy all the assumptions (including optimal subsidization of exter- nalities) and have (a series of) perfectly competitive markets in medical services. A low rate of growth in spending could in theory be efficiency- reducing if it were below this ideal rate. To tell whether it is or not, we need some quantitative measures of the benefits from medical services that might be added if spending grew somewhat more rapidly and of the value of the resources represented by that spending in their next best use. Obviously, nobody knows these quantities for sure, so no one should as yet be unqualifiedly joyful about the slowdown in medical spending in the United States. Rather, the fundamental analytic ques- tion is whether we can make some educated guessses about the benefits and costs. In principle, it is possible to measure the benefits and costs of consumption goods independent of market arrangements, but so far no one has performed this exercise.

The other criterion economists propose in an evaluation of market change is equity. There are many interpretations of a society's equity objective, but the important proposition for us here is the unequivocal conclusion that a competitive market is not likely, except by a stroke of luck or tautologically, to be guaranteed to meet any social objective of greater equity. Government, not markets, must intervene if a particular distribution of consumption is felt to be undesirable, and this is true whether the concern is over the distribution of all items in the consumption package or just the distribution of medical services use or spending. Markets, in contrast, will tend to resist redistribution, even that desired by government. Competitive markets are not fair and they do not tolerate cross-subsidies.

III   Effects of Lower Cost Growth

To provide a concrete evaluation of the lower rate of growth of spending currently associated with greater competition, we need to know the form those spending growth reductions take. The data on this question is not completely conclusive, but two types of cuts seem surely to have occurred. One change is a slowdown in the growth of wages or profits for medical services suppliers. Real income of physicians has been flat or declining since the mid-1990s for the first time, and the rate of growth of health care workers' wages has been well below the high rates experienced in the late 1980s. The other phenomenon that has surely occurred is a reduction in the quantity of medical services. This reduction is especially pronounced in acute hospital bed days; there has been little reduction (and possibly an increase) in the use of prescription drugs and ambulatory care. However, since inpatient care is so expensive, the net effect is lower cost.

What is not yet settled is whether the movement to managed care has also reduced the rate of addition of new technology. It was primarily the addition of new more costly but beneficial technology that had driven spending upward in the United States for the last thirty years or more, but the most definitive (though now somewhat dated) evidence suggests that managed care does not add technology at a rate that differs from that for the old indemnity insurance (Newhouse, 1981). Some more recent research suggests that, with regard to some specific technologies, managed care has added them later and with less intensity (Ramsey, Hillman, and Pauly, 1996). On the other hand, there are also some technologies that were used earlier by managed care plans (Pauly and Ramsey, 1997). Moreover, as managed care directly reduces the level of cost associated with old technology, such as fewer inpatient days, it will need to reduce the amount of new technology to a disproportionately greater extent to generate a lower rate of growth in spending.

Unless such a reduction can be made to occur, the slowdown in cost growth will be temporary rather than permanent. Spending will still be lower, at any point in time in the future, than if there had been no change, but the rate of growth of spending may not itself be permanently lower. What drives the rate of addition of new technology? The extent (though not necessarily the form) of health insurance is one culprit (Peden and Freeland, 1995), but insurance coverage levels and changes cannot explain all of the growth. The notion that there is a supply-side technological imperative is a tautological but true explanation: new technology would not be added if it were not more beneficial than the old technology and, when it is added, it is more beneficial. However, I believe that the key to understanding new medical technology lies in two unexamined causes: the (permanent) rate of growth of real consumer income, and changes in the relative price per unit of health added. These causes remain to be investigated.

There are two other aspects of the recent changes to more competitive markets in the United States. One is illustrated in Figure 1, which shows the market shares of a variety of types of health insurance in the 1990s. Conventional insurance plans, which covered the cost of services from almost every provider with few restrictions, still remain a sizable minority presence vis-à-vis the set of all other types of health insurance; while this share may shrink a little more, this type of insurance is unlikely to disappear. Within the set of types of managed care, the pure HMO version is a minority and fairly slow-growing. The type of coverage which is growing most rapidly is the point-of-service type; it allows substantial coverage for unmanaged services provided by hospitals and doctors outside the managed care network.

The usual use of this chart is to illustrate the growth of managed care, and it does do so. But I would suggest that it illustrates another potential merit of competitive markets: the ability of such markets to supply a *variety* of different types of health plans, where "variety" primarily refers to the strictness with which cost is contained, which

Table 2. Alternative Health Insurance Plans

	Limited Network of Hospitals and Physician Providers	Any Insurance for Out-of-Network Providers	Restrictions or Incentives on Providers to Limit Volume and Intent of Service
Conventional Plans	No	Not Applicable	No
Managed Care			
Health Maintenance Organization	Yes	No	Yes
Point-of-Service Plans	Yes	Yes	Yes
Preferred Provider Organization	Yes	Yes	No

ranges from strict to weak (see Table 2). Some plans will allow use of almost all office-based doctors in the area, while others have a limited panel. Some plans offer strong incentives to doctors for cost containment, while others offer none at all. Variation in outcomes is yet to be documented, because our technology for measuring outcomes is so primitive and is biased toward finding no (significant) difference. However, the main clear message from this market so far (in contrast to national or heavily regulated systems, and in contrast to the American past when all but a tiny fraction of insurance was indemnity insurance), is that markets serve up diversity. It is too soon to say what the final mix will be, and there is some threat to diversity from insurer concentration in some cities. However, even when there are two or three dominant insurance companies, they almost always provide a number of different varieties of insurance plans for buyers to choose from.

IV Demerits of Markets

There are two potential problems with the emergence of more competitive markets: deterioration in cross-subsidies for indigent care, research and medical education, and risk segmentation.

On the first point, there is some evidence that increasing competition is associated with decreased subsidies to or availability of charity care, especially that provided by nonprofit hospitals that formerly possessed market power. Gruber (1994) discovered a modest decrease in charity care (primarily in the emergency room) associated with the emergence of more competitive markets in California. Apparently, at least in the time he studied, these hospitals were unable or unwilling to increase charitable contributions to make up for the lost cross-subsidies. There is less large-sample empirical evidence but much anecdotal complaining that academic medical centers are also finding smaller net revenues to use for research or subsiding the education of physicians as health insurance markets become more competitive.

Whether these changes represent reductions in efficiency depend on whether the benefits being provided through private cross-subsidization were greater than the cost imposed on paying customers. Provision of funding for public goods such as charity care and research (and perhaps medical education, although the case is less clear) has traditionally been assigned by economists to government, and by democratic governments to public choice. If government in the United States had been providing such funding at the efficient level, the loss of private supplements would not represent reduced efficiency (even though obviously some citizens would lose). Alternatively, there might perhaps be suboptimal public subsidization, in which case the demise of private cross-subsidies would make things worse. To say much more, one needs a theory that would predict whether there would be chronic public underfunding and whether private cross-subsides (generated by raising prices to paying customers above marginal cost) would be a more efficient and equitable source of funding than general revenue taxation. What is needed is both a private choice theory of charitable giving and a public choice theory of public expenditure, given private charity. One also needs to pay attention to the excess burden of private (nonprofit) monopoly as a way of raising funds relative to the excess burden of taxes governments can use.

Since there is widespread belief that the level of care for the uninsured and low-income people in general was and is insufficient in the United States, these problems of insufficient charity care in the United States appear to be the result of public sector deficiency. My own view is that, while we cannot rule out the possibility of efficient public subsidization and management of private charity, these problems ought primarily to be corrected by improving government's ability to identify and target subsidies, not by propping up private efforts which depend on provider market power as well as on the need for charity care or the benefits of research. In addition, public sector efforts can be the direct objects of public choice, whereas private sector efforts are only indirectly under public scrutiny. On balance, in pushing price closer to cost, greater competition actually improves the efficiency of private markets, but throws into starker focus the defects of government activity in this area.

The other potential defect of managed care has to do with the treatment of risk variation. The main thing that distinguishes a competitive market in managed care plans from the managed competition advocated by Enthoven (1979) is the presence or absence of regulations on competition intended to prevent both adverse selection and risk rating. Risk transfers between health plans, prohibitions on plans thought to be differentially attractive to lower risk, and rules forbidding risk rating are all part of Enthoven's scheme and the "semi-public" organization of competing health plans in the Netherlands and, to some extent, now in Germany.

The most striking empirical fact about the emergence of greater competition in the U.S. health care system in the mid-1990s is that it proceeded *without* the managed competition structures Enthoven advocated as essential. To my knowledge, there is little evidence in the private sector that the problems associated with risk variation have gotten worse in the process. In contrast, in the public Medicare program, risk selection has apparently gotten worse despite the presence of complete government financing and control.

A   What Should We Expect?

As already noted, the recent experience shows that competing private insurers can control medical services spending, to at least as great a degree as government has been able to do in the United States. Three good years do not prove that the long-term record will be as strong as in some European countries, and most forecasts are for continuing and modest increases in the rate of growth to a rate less than that which prevailed in the 1980s and early 1990s but still in excess of the growth rate of GDP. Since the marginal propensity to spend on medical services seems to be larger than the average propensity, especially when it comes to new technology, and since productivity improvements in American manufacturing and agriculture are large enough to accommodate this spending growth and still permit growing real income, it seems unlikely that the private sector will reenter a true "crisis" anytime soon.

What is most threatening as far as private markets are concerned is the combination of decreased cross-subsidy and government sloth in responding to the need for subsidies of lower income families. This may be an overstatement: there was an increase in generosity in the public Medicaid program in the early 1990s; there will be an additional increase in public funding for a relatively small number of poor children. Moreover, the erosion in private insurance coverage for workers appears to have halted, although we are still seeing some decline in coverage for children. On balance, however, while this sad situation has not gotten much worse, it has not gotten better either.

One issue that is now being and will continue to be debated is whether the demise of private cross-subsidies really does represent a market defect. To economists as economists, for the reasons mentioned above, I think the answer would be largely negative. To policymakers and ordinary citizens, things are not so clear, since the lost benefits are painfully apparent and the cost imposed in the form of higher prices is diffused by insurance. It is also true that the exit of some providers furnishing cross-subsidies may simply serve to even out the burden of providing a type of care which is to a large extent required by law (Pauly, 1997a).

B   Merit and Moral Hazard

One of the most frequently discussed aspects of health insurance of the conventional sort, whether furnished by the public or private sector, is the theoretical likelihood and empirical certainty that insurance will cause moral hazard, that is, that it will cause people to obtain medical care that is worth less to them than its cost (Pauly, 1971). Virtually all of the discussion of the merits and demerits of medical markets for middle class people can, I believe, be traced to moral hazard. The conventional method of dealing with this inevitable side effect of risk pooling is to use out-of-pocket payments, such as deductibles and cost sharing. We know from research that higher cost sharing for middle class people discourages medical spending to a substantial (though not overwhelming) extent and that it does not appear to adversely affect their health to any appreciable extent (Newhouse et al., 1995). We also know that consumers hate cost sharing, although they are willing to accept it if it saves enough money.

In an attempt to devise a more palatable method for controlling moral hazard, managed health care plans have turned to supply-side limits or incentives, arguing that such methods permit the person to be fully protected from financial risk and still have insurance which tries to pay for things that are worth the cost, and not for things that are not. After an initial period of acceptance of managed care by buyers (in the teeth of continued resistance by doctors and hospitals), the trend has now clearly switched to backlash, with managed care being criticized for refusing to pay for care consumers want.

This backlash appears to come from two market-related sources. First, actual managed care plans make mistakes. Through rules and incentives, they may induce providers to refuse to supply a service that is sometimes worth its cost. To be sure, the disgruntled patient could always buy the care directly out of pocket. The typical assertion that the patient did not do so because he could not "afford" the service is tantamount to asserting that the denied service, while unequivocally beneficial, is worth less than its cost to the patient. But the interruption of a course of treatment can deter use even if the cost were covered, and the purpose of insurance is to help consumers finance high-cost care. The net result is that managed care protects people from financial risk, but subjects them, to a greater extent than does conventional insurance, to a risk of not obtaining beneficial care.

One suspects, however, that the lion's share of the managed care backlash is not over the denial of certainly cost-beneficial care, but rather is over the denial of care whose expected benefit is positive with certainty but, with equal certainty, is less than its cost. People who might have accepted the explicit proviso that such care be limited to offer them a lower premium will, given human nature, profess to be greatly surprised when they are sick and the care is not delivered. And they will protest as well to the political system.

The cases so far discussed in which the political process has tried to overrule market forces—laws requiring an extra day of stay for a normal newborn, or an inpatient setting for breast surgery—have largely turned on the question of whether the evidence supports the conclusion that there are any positive health benefits—not whether benefits are greater than costs. However, some economists have pointed out that the cost savings may also have been overestimated by some health plans (Reinhardt, 1997).

Still, the main identified defect of managed care—that it rations care and that this may lead to lower quality—is not conclusive evidence for market failure. Quite the contrary: given the previous state of U.S. health care, the whole *purpose* of managed care was to reduce middle-class quality in at least some dimensions. Perhaps health outcomes might be left unaffected, but convenience and comfort were bound to suffer if costs were to be contained.

In my view, the greatest defect of the competitive market is not what it did—which was perfectly predictable—but rather how it explained what it did. To be specific, even now advocates for managed care plans are unwilling to admit that their plans have lower quality than can be achieved by knowledgeable patients under conventional indemnity plans. I would not argue that the average quality necessarily differed, since not all patients had sufficient knowledge to reject recommendations for care under overpriced indemnity insurance that may have done more harm than good, but I would argue that a knowledgeable but sick patient can surely do better under the old system than under the new. This is not, however, an indictment of managed care, any more than are assertions that a cheap computer will do less more slowly than an expensive one in expert hands or (perhaps a more apt analogy) that meals and rooms will be better on an expensive cruise than on a cheaper prepackaged, prearranged vacation. Inexpensive things are supposed to be of lower quality than expensive things. Nevertheless, the managed care plan with the marketing slogan, "Hurts a little, saves a lot," has yet to emerge.

While it is never possible to convince sick people that something beneficial to them should not be provided because it is too costly, public systems can make such statements and implement such policies more easily than can private systems. The public budget constraint is plain to see, and the nonprofit status of public bureaucracies means that there is no basis for the suspicion that someone else is profiting from the failure to provide care. (Of course, opposition politicians and patient advocates could still claim that the care could be provided were it not for waste, fraud, and abuse.)

In the case of a market insurer, however, there is more (legitimate) suspicion that the denial of care is intended to buttress the returns to owners of the plan, and appeals to politicians to regulate and require delivery of care are more effective for exactly the same reasons. Since it is difficult to show that a set of rules for any one procedure or diagnosis will raise break-even premiums appreciably, there emerges a process in which each illness has its "consumer advocate" and political champion, and limits on the plan's ability to control moral hazard accurate.

C   The Philosophical Struggle

No one would advocate that markets be allowed to provide medical care and medical insurance entirely free of government intervention. Subsidization for low-income or high-risk people, and some regulation of product quality (both in terms of the quality of care and the quality of health insurance) will obviously be required. What is most tendentious, however, is what the mix or balance should be between subsidies and regulation, on the one hand, and market competition, on the other. Some of the general principles that govern (or confuse) economic analysis of the role of government are salient here: we should not assume perfect governmental functioning, so the choice is between imperfect government and imperfect market; the political process is biased toward advocating government as a solution for market problems rather than markets as a solution for governmental problems; and the power to make choices is the power to make mistakes, but those who do make mistakes in market choices are likely to blame the markets rather than themselves, whereas those who make mistakes in political choice have no one but themselves to blame.

The discussion of how much medical insurance subsidy to offer can probably be handled as well as public expenditure issues are usually handled by the political process. The fact that government spending sometimes displaces private spending and that political entrepreneurs would prefer to have private money spent for public benefits (e.g., in the form of mandated employer coverage) are issues still to be resolved, although there are many good economic models of appropriate subsidy processes. The subsidy problem is primarily one of political choice and will, not analytic difficulty. The political durability of the current U.S. tax subsidy to employment-related insurance for high-wage heavily insured workers is evidence that efficient choice and will may be lacking in the political process.

There is perhaps a more serious debate now kindling on the question of regulation of markets that provide medical services and insurance to nonpoor people. At one level, the issue is whether government's proper role is primarily one of providing (or assuring) the flow of "adequate" amounts of good information, with consumers and buyers then free to make their choices of products of any quality, or, alternatively, whether government has a larger role to play in designing regulations that would make the buying and selling of certain allegedly low-quality services or plans illegal. The general principle of optimal product quality regulation says that it *is* desirable to forbid the offering of products that no well-informed consumer would purchase, but in medical services it is hard to identify what these products are (in large part because there is literally no one [physicians included] who is well-informed on many medical issues). When everyone is somewhat uncertain and knowledge of the relationship between inputs and outputs (how to produce health) is woefully incomplete, it is hard to design good binding regulations.

As if this were not bad enough, there is an even more difficult debate on how government should assist in the provision of information, if it is given that role. We know that, for the public Medicare insurance in the United States, government agencies have not as yet played an aggressive role in providing information that actually influences consumer choices, both because consumers of subsidized insurance are often not allowed choices and because providers disadvantaged by some information can lobby the government to suppress it (as happened with Medicare's measures of hospital outcomes). That the information is, as already noted, imperfect and "unreliable" (as an unequivocally accurate guide to best decisions) makes it easy to criticize and hard to come up with an alternative. The public good nature of information is also relevant here; at one level, this theory implies that government's role is in providing information that is not worth enough to people that they would buy it for themselves—but then it is difficult to take credit for providing that kind of information.

It is certainly fair to say that we have neither a professional nor a policy consensus on the role of government in furnishing information. There is always a strong temptation to require information to be better than it can be—and then either pretend that imperfect information is conclusive or that information which contains some signal but some noise is worthless.

D   Structural Reforms

Since it is difficult to fine tune medical markets on a day to day basis, an alternative strategy is to search for institutional structures which promote inefficiency, argue that they should be eliminated, and then the resulting outcome (whatever it is) be declared to be good. In the United States, there are some institutions which research says may be harmful. One is the system which excludes health insurance premiums paid as part of total compensation from worker taxable income. This "tax subsidy" is known to encourage the purchase of more costly insurance, and to discourage price sensitivity by buyers of insurance and medical care. A second defect in the U.S. system (to some extent related to the first) is that insurance is arranged and choices are made not by individuals but by employers. Not only may employers be inept in deciding which employees to please, there is considerable evidence that employers believe (for reasons which can be explained but which are contrary to economic theory) that they should be choosing benefits in ways which minimize insurance cost, rather than maximize worker (net) satisfaction (Pauly, 1997b).

V   Generalizable Messages and Conclusion

A   Generalizable Messages

It is too soon to render a definitive verdict on the merits of the American innovation in using competitive markets in medical insurance. Modest cost containment success may not last, and the political process is not comfortable with privately chosen rationing. One generalizable conclusion, obvious before in theory but doubted in practice, is that markets can lead to rates of cost growth which are moderate if a sufficient number of buyers demand low or moderate cost growth. Even if the pace picks up again as new technology is added, the primary conclusion of the managed care revolution—that buyers in medical markets can dominate suppliers—means that we should interpret such "inflation" differently. In a well-informed, competitive world, medical spending growth will be the consequence of buyer demand, not of seller imperatives or inefficiency. It is therefore no more of a problem than growth in any other kind of spending.

The other theoretically clear message for which we now have evidence is that competitive markets do not necessarily or even usually achieve ideal distributional objectives. Governmental action will be required if they are to be achieved. However, there are likely to be pressures from both myopic voters and vote-maximizing politicians to blame markets for their socially adverse outcomes, since the required political steps—increasing taxes, confronting physician and hospital lobbies—are distasteful and dangerous.

There is a third message, less obvious and less certain but possibly most important. The American market so far appears to suggest substantial diversity in consumer demand, related not so much to tastes about individual medical services but rather to varying preferences about the structures and the strength with which care is rationed. Moreover, these demands vary within as well as across income groups. For other populations and other countries, where there may be less variation in such tastes, markets may be less meritorious. However, the degree of variation is an empirical fact to be discovered, not a social characteristic to be postulated.

B Conclusion

Competitive medical markets have some merits, but government needs to do some things in order to maximize (or even make possible) those merits. We know what tasks we need government to do, but how it should do them and whether we can count on actual governments to do them and do them well are questions the answers to which remain unknown. We do not even have an appropriate measuring rod to evaluate what governments do, or to judge which tradeoffs they make. The market in the United States seems likely to proceed despite this public sector dithering, but the result is a continual state in which consumers and politicians alike love and hate medical markets at the same time. The same conflicts and confusion are cropping up all over the world as incomes rise enough that people have the means to care about and pay for their own health care. The debate is unlikely to end any time soon.

Bibliography

Enthoven, A.C. 1980. *Health Plan: The Only Practical Solution to the Soaring Cost of Medical Care.* Reading, Mass.: Addison-Wesley.

Etheredge, L., S.B. Jones, and L. Lewin. 1996. "What Is Driving Health System Change?" *Health Affairs* 15(4):93–104.

Evans, R.G. 1997. "Going for the Gold: The Redistributive Agenda Behind Market-Based Health Care Reform." *Journal of Health Politics Policy and Law* 22(2):427–466.

Gruber, J. 1994. "The Effect of Competitive Pressure on Charity: Hospital Responses to Price Shopping in California." *Journal of Health Economics* 13(2):183–211.

Kessel, R. 1958. "Price Discrimination in Medicine." *Journal of Law and Economics* 1:20–53.

KPMG (Peat Marwick). 1994–1996. "KPMG Survey of Employer Sponsored Health Benefits, 1997, 1995, 1993, 1991, 1984." New York: KPMG.

Newhouse J.P., W.B. Schwartz, A.P. Williams, and C. Witsberger. 1985. "Are Fee-for-Service Costs Increasing Faster than HMO Costs?" *Medical Care* 23:960–966.

Newhouse, J.P., W.G. Manning, N. Duan, E.B. Keeler, A. Leibowitz, and M.S. Marquis. 1987. "Health Insurance and the Demand for Medical Care: Evidence from a Randomized Experiment." *American Economic Review* 77(3):251–277.

Pauly, M.V. 1990. "Health Care Issues and American Economic Growth: Innovation in Financing Health Care." In: G. Libecap (ed.), *Advances in the Study of Entrepreneurship, Innovation, and Economic Growth,* pp. 97–125. Greenwich, CT: JAI Press.

Pauly, M.V. 1968. "The Economics of Moral Hazard." *American Economic Review* 58(3):533–539.

Pauly, M.V. 1997a. "Trading Cost, Quality and Coverage of the Uninsured." In: S. Altman, U. Reinhardt and A. Shields (eds.), *The Future US Health Care System: Who Will Care for the Poor and Uninsured?.* Chicago: Health Administration Press.

Pauly, M.V. 1997b. *Health Benefits at Work.* Ann Arbor: University of Michigan Press.

Pauly, M.V., and S.D. Ramsey. 1997. "Structural Incentives and Adoption of Medical Technologies in HMO and Fee-for-Service Health Insurance Plans." *Inquiry* 34(3):228–236.

Peden, E.A., and M.S. Freeland. 1995. "A Historical Analysis of Medical Spending Growth." *Health Affairs* 14(2):235–247.

Ramsey, S.D., A.L. Hillman, and M.V. Pauly. 1997. "The Effects of Health Insurance on Access to New Medical Technologies." *International Journal of Technology Assessment in Health Care* 13(2):357–367.

Reinhardt, U. 1996. "Perspective: Spending More Through 'Cost Control': Our Obsessive Quest to Gut the Hospital." *Health Affairs* 15(2):145–154.

Supplying and Financing Education: Options and Trends under Growing Fiscal Restraints

Edwin G. West

Research currently demonstrates that the supply of schooling in both developed and developing countries continues to be, on average, seriously inefficient. The problem is now accentuated by widespread fiscal constraints caused especially by government deficits. The pervasiveness of the inefficiency is usually demonstrated with figures showing growing public expenditure on schooling per head at a time when student achievement is stagnant or even in decline. This phenomenon will be taken as a point of departure in this paper, which will subsequently concentrate on trends and innovations in the finance of education that attempt to combat the inefficiencies.

I The Cost Disease

Before exploring the roots of the cost problem further, however, it is necessary first to respond to a well-known line of argument associated with Baumol (1967). The focus of his reasoning is upon the claim (or observation) that because, on average, government services are labor-intensive, it is in the private capital-intensive sectors that we normally look for dramatic productivity improvements over time. Once we recognize the differential rates of technological growth between the two sectors, it is only to be expected, Baumol argues, that the prices of the labor-intensive services will rise relative to others. Simply to find that government expenditure per student has risen, therefore, does not in itself indicate inefficiency. The reporting of increased costs in low-productivity growth sectors is often rationalized in terms of "Baumol's Disease" or the "Cost Disease." Such reasoning dominates explanations for cost growth not only in government services generally, but also in nonprofit activities such as the arts and recreation. It should be noticed, in passing, that the cost disease argument does not state that labor-intensive sectors suffer *decreasing* productivity; only that their rate of productivity increase is less than that of the typical capital-intensive sector.

Consider now the empirical studies of Hanushek (1996), who finds that educational productivity in the United States has been actually falling. The decrease has been nearly 3% per year in recent years. In his attempts at explanation, Hanushek observes (pp. 11, 12) that while the general Baumol arguments imply that external forces inexorably drive costs upwards, the data show that schools have been systematically choosing to hire more of increasingly expensive inputs. Collective bargaining has resulted in the salaries of teachers being a function of length of service (experience) and teachers' own education. Thus the percent of teachers with a master's degree increased from 23.1% in 1960–1961 to 52.6% in 1991. As well, the median years of teacher experience rose from 11% in 1960–1961 to 15% in 1990–1991. The pupil-teacher ratio, meanwhile, dropped from 25.6 to 17.3 (i.e. class size fell and cost per student increased).

If such increases in spending and resources had been accompanied by student achievement levels that improved at the same, or greater rate, there would have been less cause for concern. According to Hanushek (1996, p. 3), however, "the best available information suggests that the overall trend in student performance has been flat or falling."[1]

II   Rigid Supply Structures

As observed by Ferris and West (1996), the argument that external forces drive educational cost increases should not be accepted on its own terms. Privatization, for example, could lead to changes in the structure of supply that could result in "genuine" reductions in real costs. These reductions could be expected from the breakup of what is now a monopoly system of schooling. One aspect of this system is the

---

[1] Hanushek (1996) refers to data pertaining to the period 1970–1995 obtained from (a) the National Assessment of Student Progress (NAEP) for tests in mathematics, science, and reading, and (b) trends in the Scholastic Aptitude Test (SAT).

higher incidence of unionized labor. Recent econometric evidence has found that, compared with nonunionized districts, unionized districts are associated with increases in expenditures per student of between 7% and 15% (Eberts and Stone, 1986). Other evidence, moreover, shows that the size of the representative school district is growing, a phenomenon that increases the potential for the effective exercise of monopoly power (Kenny and Schmidt, 1994). One cause of the cost differential between the two systems therefore is the higher compensation of unionized teachers. Since private school teachers are less heavily unionized, full privatization can ultimately be expected to yield corresponding labor cost reductions.

Baumol warns that proposing an increasing switch to private enterprise will elicit determined opposition "which has shown itself, for example, whenever any measure is proposed that is perceived as even a minor threat to the public schools" (1993, pp. 26, 27). The "determined opposition" to privatization, however, is concentrated among those employed in the public school system and who have the most to lose through the erosion of their monopoly. This opposition, in other words, is itself a measure of the degree of monopoly power that exists. Gallup polls, meanwhile, show that around 50% of parents with school-age children favor education vouchers that would pave the way for competition. Being more dispersed than school employees, these parents certainly face higher costs of political lobbying. But this does not imply that their opposition to monopoly is less important in welfare terms than the opposition by the public education establishment to proposals for competitive supply.

III Traditional Input Analysis

The traditional (official) policy approach to the search for increased efficiency is based on a quest for optimal balance of measurable school inputs (the "production function" approach). In other words, some form of regression analysis is used to identify precise determinants of student achievement and to determine the relative importance of inputs such as the characteristics of schools, teachers, class size, and curricula. To date, the results of such analysis are disappointing. The evidence on teacher salaries in developing countries, for instance, "contain no compelling support for the notion that higher wages yield better teachers"

(Hanushek, 1995, p. 231). Evidence that smaller classes outperform large classes is also lacking, at least in the United States. Similarly the education and experience of teachers are not systematically related to student performance (Hanushek, 1995, p. 232). All these findings, to reiterate, strongly suggest that the authorities have been choosing to purchase more expensive inputs. The exercise of such choice is of course an administrative and/or political decision and the implication is that the policy should be reversed or canceled if the problem of educational cost escalation is to be tackled seriously.

Side by side with the evidence that measured inputs are not systematically related to student performance is the striking fact that schools differ considerably in quality in both developed and developing countries. This is a phenomenon that cannot be explained by aggregate input-centered analysis. Investigating variations in the quality of schools across a sample of primary schools in Egypt, Hanushek and Lavy (1994) found that the differences were enormous. The worst school showed an average student achievement gain that was 62% below the base school, while the best school was 30% above. Only 16% of the variance in school quality was related to teacher attributes (such as teacher education) and to school attributes (such as class size and facilities).

So far, attempts to provide additional measures of educational success have failed to explain a large portion of the systematic differences across schools. In other words, while the evidence reveals that schools differ in important ways, we cannot satisfactorily describe these differences. In the words of Hanushek (1995), "we cannot describe what makes a good or bad teacher, or a good or bad school. ... we should learn to live with that fact: living with it implies finding policies that acknowledge and work within this fundamental ignorance" (p. 236).

The logic of such discussion according to Hanushek, points to the need to shift emphasis from policies based on inputs to those based on outputs. And output policies imply the constant need for performance incentives and repeated testing. "Many countries do little systematic testing and evaluation of student performance" (Hanushek, 1995, p. 241). But if countries are backward in these respects, one must presumably search for alternatives to public schools in the form of private organizations that might act as "pacemakers."

It so happens that a variety of innovations claiming to introduce so-called market incentives into education have been introduced over the last 25 years. Such schemes have included tuition tax deductions, tax credits, open enrollment plans, charter schools, and education vouchers. Tax deductions and credits have hitherto been unsuccessful due to strong political opposition and because they fail to deliver assistance to low-income families that have little or no tax liability.

IV Open Enrollment

With regard to open enrollment, the state that has promoted it most vigorously in the United States is Minnesota. Bearing in mind that over $4,000 in state aid is *slated* to follow each child who transfers from one public school to another, the state governor has described the system as an example of "market forces at work." This proposition, however, contains five inaccuracies. First, real markets work with the use of full or near-full pricing. But prices (fees) have not been introduced into the Minnesota plan, since public schools must presumably remain "free." The second problem arises from the assertion that Minnesota school districts that fail under the new system will be forced to close. The proposition invites skepticism because there is little evidence that public schools have been allowed to go bankrupt. A third problem with characterizing Minnesota's plan as a market system is that, although the law envisages free choice of school districts across the state, the school boards are nevertheless free to elect not to accept students. Very little of such discretion, of course, occurs in free markets.

A fourth problem relates to Hanushek's call (above) for incentives. Open enrollment provides no clear incentives for teachers and administrators of particular schools. Incentives would be clear and obvious, for instance, if it were openly decreed that salaries of school principals as well as of teachers were to be related to a particular proportion of the enrollment they attract. Nothing is said on this score, however. Yet if the sponsors of the plan are really looking for market-like competition within the public schools, some such specification must be made. And it is interesting that such an incentive provision is included in the British Education Act of 1988.

When asked to accept out-of-district students without such incentives, several ways are open to a school board in Minnesota to refuse. For instance, a board is allowed to simply announce a blanket resolution that nonresident pupils outside the local "catchment area" may not attend any of the schools or programs. As well, any school can refuse to take on more students simply on the grounds that the school is "full" or is "overcrowded."

A full market system, in contrast, would oblige suppliers to use all possible improvisations and expedients to carry any increased load in the short term and to make all possible effort to expand in the long term. Suppose customers were transferring from a relatively inefficient retail store and were beginning to crowd the premises of a rival store. It would be an odd notion of efficiency that required the process to stop because it was encouraging "crowding." Any retreat to "catchment areas" to prevent crowding would remove the very pressure that was working to improve matters. Under such pressure the favored store would meet the crowding with temporary measures pending plans for expansion, while the unpopular store would be under constant pressure to try to match the superior services of its rival. Staff who were frustrated by their treatment by unimaginative managers in the failing store would be attracted by vacancies occurring in the successful crowded one.

The fact remains that clear and substantial individual incentives in general are largely absent from the public school system. Many of its teachers become disenchanted, not just with inefficient managers, but also with inflexible union rules. And the failure of many U.S. state legislatures to enact performance-related merit pay incentive programs because of the opposition of teacher unions is yet another conspicuous example.

Elementary economics tells us that the most crucial condition for competition is freedom of entry into a market. And this brings us to the fifth, and most important, problem trying to equate with open enrollment with a market system. Since neither the Minnesota plan nor any other public school open enrollment plan provides for free entry of new private and denominational schools, the conditions of full enrollment as "public schools for choice" is a misnomer, since choice that is constrained by the exclusion of private schools is no real choice at all.

Free entry is essential if we are to benefit from competition as described by classical economists such as Adam Smith. They envisaged competition as a dynamic process that promptly rewards those who introduce superior methods. Suppose that new lower-cost methods are available but have not yet been widely adopted. In a profit-driven free market system business entrepreneurs will seize the corresponding opportunities for entry. In the nonprofit world of public schools, in contrast, there are no such entrepreneurs, only administrators and decision-makers. The strongest incentives for prompt adoption of new ideas are therefore absent.

V Charter Schools

The next innovation to be examined is the charter school. Charter schools in the United States are public schools which operate under state-enabling legislation and receive pupil funding from taxpayers' dollars, usually by allocation of district-level education funding on a per-pupil basis. Sponsors must apply to local education districts or a state chartering authority for a charter under which they will function, stating educational objectives, curricula, and proposed methods of operating. Charter schools are governed locally by citizens, parents, teachers, and universities. Charter schools must admit all students under public admission rules and remain accountable to public authorities. The charging of tuition is not allowed. Charters are granted for a set period of time (3 to 15 years, depending upon the state legislation). Some significant incentive effects exist because a charter is in effect a performance-based contract: if the school does not perform up to the standard set in the charter, it can be revoked and the school shut down.

Several studies suggest that charter schools often receive less (sometimes significantly less) funding per student than comparable government schools, based on the state charter law funding mechanism formula. Charter school legislation, for instance, does not provide a specific reimbursement for capital costs to cover building or acquiring a facility, although some states provide modest initial start-up operating funds.

In the United States, 25 states now have charter laws, and by the end of 1997, about 500 charter schools will be in operation around the country. President Clinton has stated that the United States should set a goal of 3,000 charter schools by 2000.

Charter proponents generally classify state charter laws as "strong" or "weak", in accordance with the degree of operating autonomy, automatic exemption from laws and regulations, true fiscal and legal autonomy from the district school system, and sponsorship options other than local school boards. Elimination of most state laws and

Table 1. The Spread of Charter Schools

Year	Event
1988	Britain's Education Reform Act permits self-governing public schools. 1,116 direct "grant-maintained schools" (charters) now in place.
1989	New Zealand charters all of its 2,600 schools.
1991	Charter school legislation approved in Minnesota, USA. By 1997 close to 500 charter schools established in 26 states. President Clinton calls for 3,000 charters by year 2000.
1995	Alberta becomes the first Canadian province to adopt charter legislation. By 1996, 8 charter schools are approved.
1996	The Minister of Education in Ontario, Canada, announces that his government will consider charter proposals.

Source: Raham (1996, p. 4).

rules (except health, safety, and civil rights) governing conventional schools is a central feature of the charter concept. Although my account is focusing on the United States it must be recognized that the spread of charter schools involves several other countries. Table 1 gives a brief summary.

A   Charter Schools and For-Profit Organizations

If it is agreed that for-profit organizations experience the strongest incentives and disincentives, the main interest will be the United States, where "for-profits" are gaining ground. Canada, Britain and New Zealand, in contrast, are dominated by nonprofit private (charter) schools. It is true that American states have passed legislation that attempts to prohibit for-profit operators from chartering. This does not necessarily prevent for-profit companies from entering the market, however. Such companies may simply contract with the charter "holder" to operate a school. In the case of the successful for-profit school organization called SABIS,[2] for example, while it has not been

---

[2] The name SABIS was constructed from the abbreviated surnames of the founders Leila Saad and Ralph Bistany. SABIS is an international chain of for-profit private college prep schools with units in Lebanon, Pakistan, England, the United States, and five of the United Arab Emirates.

allowed to contract directly for a charter school in Chicago, it has got into the business indirectly by being hired as a charter school manager by a not-for-profit company. Elsewhere the for-profit mode is making a significant appearance. Of the 46 charter schools that began operation in Arizona in 1995–1996, 13 were being run by for-profit organizations.

B   The Springfield Massachusetts Venture

The example of SABIS is worth further comment since it appears increasingly successful at obtaining managements of new charter schools. Part of the explanation is its performance in its first entry into the "business" in Springfield, Massachusetts, in 1995. There, in one year, it transformed a below-average school in a "blighted" low-income neighborhood into the most sought after school in the district. Of the 600 students, 39% are white, 31% Hispanic, 29% black, and 1% Asian. The Iowa Test of Basic Skills results released in June 1997 show that the school, now known as the SABIS International Charter School (previously the Glickman Elementary School), has gone from nearly the lowest to among the highest in the city for student performance. Students progressed, on average, $1\frac{1}{2}$ years during a single school year.

The 1997 report by the state Department of Education contained the assessment of a team that visited the building in the fall of 1996. The team scrutinized nearly every classroom, meeting teachers, reviewing grades and test scores. The Department's general conclusion reads: "SABIS ... has assembled what appears to be a solid management team and fundamentally changed the second-worse performing school in the city into what appears to be a clean, well-equipped, safe and perhaps most impressive, one with high academic standards" (*Union News*, 1997, p. B2).

The chairman of the state Board of Education expressed approval of the focus on English and mathematics, the immersion in Spanish at all grade levels, and the position of an academic coordinator who works with the classroom teachers. The chairman pronounced the SABIS venture to be "the best charter school I have ever seen" (*Union News*, 1997, p. B2). This is high praise indeed coming from professional educators who are normally suspicious of for-profit organizations.

With such a growing reputation it is perhaps not surprising that the SABIS management is being appointed to more emerging charter schools. Besides Springfield it is now operating (or about to operate) in Chicago, Delaware, and Arizona.

C   The SABIS Approach

In this respect, it is pertinent that SABIS seems to have developed its teaching methods when facing the strong challenge of meeting education problems in developing countries in the 1960s. Accepting a contract to prepare students from underdeveloped Mideast nations, SABIS discovered that it had seriously underestimated the degree of adversity in the environment from which the pupils came. The primitive elementary schooling that they had typically received had left them further behind academically than was initially believed. It was from this exigency, indeed, that the school developed its characteristic system of incremented steps of academic achievement that are rigorously tested. The concept of incentives, indeed, is represented in this institution in all its aspects.

SABIS now divides its curriculum into concepts called "points." Teachers teach each point, pose questions about it, and check the answers of preselected senior students or "prefects." The "prefects" then check other students in a system that SABIS calls peer tutoring. Students earn points for their prefect work and they are listed on their report cards. It is open to each student in a school to apply to become a prefect of some sort. In addition to the traditional academic sphere, there are prefects in sports, in school management, and even in the supervision of garbage collection or the running of soda machines.

The concept of incentives is also demonstrated in the context of teacher remuneration. In contrast with the U.S. public school system, which, as shown above, remunerates in strict accordance with the length of teaching experience and the formal education (measured by diplomas or degrees) of the teachers, SABIS rewards teachers simply according to their success in the classroom. Such success is measured in terms of promoting gains (or "value added") in student achievement.[3]

---

[3] Peer tutoring plus payment of teachers by results was first developed systematically in 19th-century England and Wales. It eventually collapsed under the weight of strong opposition by the organized teacher/administrator profession. See Birchenough (1927).

D   Charter Schools in Perspective

As we have shown, not all charter schools are run by for-profit organizations. Indeed, several states do not welcome even indirect association with them. It has to be remembered meanwhile that charter
schools are public (government) schools, not private.

With few exceptions, and the SABIS school seems to be one such,
charter schools in most states are still hindered by a multitude of rules
and procedures. Many lack access to capital and start-up funding.
Some are forced to hand back significant portions of their budgets to
the local district as a rent or overhead payment. It is not clear therefore that the typical charter school will be able to continue to operate
with significantly less money than conventional public schools, and
simultaneously produce superior results. One should, in any case, keep
the situation in the following numerical perspective: even if the United
States reaches President Clinton's stated goal of 3,000 such schools by
the year 2000, there will still be some 80,000 public schools (over 96%
of the whole) that are not charter schools.[4]

VI   Vouchers

For governments to go a step further than the charter school arrangement in continued search for incentives, the next development
would presumably be that of education vouchers. An education
voucher system exists when governments make payments to families
that enable their children to enter public or private schools of their
choice. The tax-funded payments can be made directly to parents or
indirectly to the selected schools; their purpose is to increase parental
choice, to promote school competition, and to allow low-income families access to private schools. Vouchers can be of the *selective* variety
(as in Milwaukee, see below). In other words, they can be restricted to
families receiving less than a given income level. In so far as such
restricted vouchers caused efficiency in supply, such as with the SABIS
approach, the whole program could be judged unambiguously in terms
of equity as well as efficiency.

Some opponents argue that given the freedom to use vouchers, the

---

[4] This paragraph has drawn on Finn (1997).

families that are less motivated to exert themselves and take advantage of the new freedom will be left in gutted, underfunded, and decaying public schools. But this argument rests on the questionable assumption that the public system will refuse to adjust to competition in the face of private schools. Holmes (1990, p. 23) maintains that "there is no reason why inner-city schools of the future, where alternatives are available (with vouchers), will be worse than the ones at the moment where there is no choice."

It should be emphasized, that there are several forms of vouchers. The typical variety that appears to be developing around the world is one where "funds follow the child." With this method governments subsidize "schools of choice" in strict proportion to enrollment. This type of voucher has recently been adopted by developing countries such as Bangladesh, Belize, Chile, Colombia, Guatemala, and Lesotho, as well as by industrial countries such as Poland, Sweden, the United Kingdom, and the United States (West, 1997).

A   The Milwaukee Plan

One of the most striking examples of a successful voucher system for the poor is found in Milwaukee, Wisconsin. Pioneered largely by Democratic Representative "Polly" Williams in 1990, the plan permits a limited number of low-income Milwaukee students to use state funds to attend a private, nonsectarian school of their choice. The Milwaukee plan has been opposed by various educational establishment groups, including the State School Board Association and the Wisconsin Congress of Parents and Teachers, Inc. This opposition has probably influenced the administrative restrictions that have accumulated recently. Thus in 1994 the state legislature authorized a cap (ceiling) on the plan limiting it to 1.5% of Milwaukee's 100,000 school-age population, or 1,500 students. Schools participating in the plan must limit voucher students to 49% of their student body, so further limiting the number of places available. Since its inception, the plan's lack of space has resulted in more students being turned away than have been accepted into the plan. In consequence, spaces in over-subscribed schools are apportioned by lottery.

Despite its smallness, the Milwaukee scheme is the only source of hard evidence on the effects of vouchers in the United States. Comments hitherto on the success/failure of the scheme have depended on the annual reports of Professor John F. Witte, the state-selected outside evaluator. His first reports led some critics to complains that the participating schools suffered excessive attrition and that attainment tests were biased because the mothers of the families using vouchers have a higher average high-school completion rate. These complaints were later rebutted by McGroaty (1994).

The unambiguously positive parts of Witte's findings, meanwhile, appear to combat three popular fears or predications about the voucher program. The first is the suspicion that vouchers will help individuals such as the nonpoor, who need help least. Witte's evidence shows, on the contrary, that "choice families" are among the poorest of the poor. Their average income in fact, was about half the level of the average Milwaukee Public School family.

The second commonly expressed fear is that vouchers will lead to segregated and antisocial schools. Evidence supplied by Witte, however, shows that the Milwaukee program fosters *diversity* and that no participating school has been teaching cultural supremacy or separatism. "The student bodies of participating [voucher] schools vary from schools that are almost all one minority race, to racially integrated schools, to schools that have used the Choice program to diversify their almost all white student bodies" (quoted in McGroaty, 1994, p. 110).

The third fear is that voucher schools will draw the "cream" of the student "crop." From his evidence, however, Witte concludes: "One of the most striking and consistent conclusions from the first two years is that the program is offering opportunities for a private school alternative to poor families whose children were not succeeding in school. This is a positive outcome of the program" (quoted in McGroaty, 1994, p. 110).

Other positive conclusions from Witte's reports include the finding of high parental involvement, once in the system, and high parental satisfaction. "Respondents almost unanimously agreed the program should continue" (quoted in McGroaty, 1994, p. 110). In addition parents found that it increased learning and discipline.

Side by side with these positive findings is an intense controversy over whether the Milwaukee voucher schools do or do not generate student achievements (e.g., literacy attainments) that are greater than those in public schools. Witte finds that when students' socioeconomic backgrounds are properly accounted for, there are no significant differences.

I have three comments: First, the case for vouchers rests partly on argued needs for choice and diversity of schooling. Witte reports that in all five years of the Milwaukee program, parental satisfaction with choice (voucher) schools increased significantly over satisfaction with prior public schools. Such revealed preferences of education's customers should presumably receive appropriate weighting in any accounting of the total benefits of schooling. In other words, it is erroneous to confine attention to formal academic testing as the sole criterion when measuring total efficiency. When, for example, parents choose a voucher school partly to protect their child from violence in the officially allocated or zoned public school, their motives call for due evaluation in any overall measures of efficiency.

Second, the case for vouchers rests also on the argued need to weaken the public school monopoly or, in other words, to promote competition. But when competition is introduced, those suppliers who initially lose or expect to lose customers will, in self-defense, act to lift the quality of their services. Applied to our education context, six years of the Milwaukee plan is more than enough time for the threatened public schools to have improved under the pressure of new voucher competition. And insofar as vouchers can take some credit for inducing the improvements in tested achievement that have in fact occurred over the years 1990–1996 (in public and private schools), findings of no current difference in achievement growth between public and voucher (choice) schools do not unambiguously imply that vouchers have failed to improve efficiency. This is so even when we leave aside the new benefits of parental choice discussed in the previous paragraph.[5]

Third, in the first four years of the Milwaukee program, the value of the voucher was around $3000 while the public school costs per student were approximately $6000. (The voucher increased to $3,209 in 1994–1995, but this again was almost one-half of the public school costs per student in that period.) Economists speak in terms of benefit/cost (B/C) ratios such that, for instance, if one "firm" produces bene-

---

[5] New empirical evidence has been published in the 1990s showing that the introduction of competition via increased use of private schooling leads to improved public school performance. (See Couch et al., 1993; Minter-Hoxby, 1994; Rangazas, 1995; Borland and Howsen, 1996.)

fits worth $1,000 at a cost of $1,000 the B/C ratio is $1000/1000 = 1$ or unity. If a new competing firm produces the same benefits but at a cost of only $500, the B/C ratio increases to $1000/500 = 2$. The conclusion is that the new firm is twice as efficient as the first. A similar implication applies to education in Milwaukee. The benefit/cost ratio for private schools that accept vouchers is nearly twice that of the public schools. If we accept Witte's finding (reported in McGroaty, 1994) that private voucher schooling in Milwaukee is no worse than public schooling in terms of student achievement, then the voucher schools are overwhelmingly more efficient than public schooling per dollar spent.[6]

Milwaukee private schools are no exception to the finding that generally they are more economical than public schools, which, as we have seen, tend to purchase unnecessarily expensive inputs. Nationally in the United States, there are about 28,000 private schools, and they are, on average, low-cost institutions. In 1990, for example, average tuition non-Catholic private elementary schools was $1,780 and in secondary schools $4,395. This contrasts with average per-pupil expenditures in public schools in the same year of $5,177 (elementary) and $6,472 (secondary) (Catholic schools have even lower costs than non-Catholic private schools).

B   Privately Funded Scholarships

It should be noticed, finally, that in the United States there is a system of privately funded vouchers or scholarships which appears to be working well in the sense of competition and increased efficiency in education. Since the private funding of such vouchers is usually less than 100% there is considerable room for contributions also from parents.

Major examples of particular programs occur in Milwaukee, San Antonio, Atlanta, and Battle Creek. In Milwaukee, the largest pre-college scholarship program to date was launched with massive support

---

[6] Multiple regression research by Rouse (1996) finds that the Milwaukee Parental Choice Program has increased math scores in voucher schools by between 1.5 and 2 percentage points per year, while the results for reading scores were mixed.

from the Lynde and Harry Bradley Foundation and the Archdiocese of Milwaukee. In its first year, the Milwaukee program served more than 2,000 students. In the same year in San Antonio a group of business leaders, in conjunction with the Texas Publics Policy Foundation, launched a private voucher program serving over 900 students. As well, it made a concerted effort to replicate what is called the Golden Rule model in other cities with the offer of technical assistance and background materials to program organizers.

The Golden Rule model for awarding private scholarships for pre-college education includes a first-come, first-served admissions policy; income eligibility based on the formula for the Federal school lunch program; allowing the family or guardian to choose any nongovernment school; and awarding scholarships equal to one-half of tuition, subject to a dollar cap.

Programs vary widely in how they ensure that families match the scholarship amount in making tuition payments. Milwaukee, and Phoenix, for instance, do not require a match *per se*, and Indianapolis does not require an exact match but does insist that families pay something towards the cost of private schooling. Nine programs do require a match from families, and ensure the condition either by a certification from schools or an agreement with the school or family.

There is no doubt that the private voucher movement so far described is peculiar to the United States. One of the reasons is the more generous attitudes of American state governments towards tax deductions for charity donations. Most of the programs have had to apply for section 501(3)(3) tax-exempt status from the Internal Revenue Service, a process that takes on average between three and six months.

VII   The Increasing Intensity of the Voucher Debate

As the case for parental choice and competition has gained in popularity, the criticism of those antipathetic to vouchers has increased in fervor. This section summarizes the opposing arguments.

A   Intellectuals and the Market Place

When some intellectuals envisage the free market that vouchers would encourage, they think primarily of the abandonment of the pursuit of social welfare for the crude individual needs of "economic man," self-ishly pursuing his individual material gain. For a long time, however, economists have abandoned narrow assumptions about self-interest. As Gary Becker observes: "Behavior is driven by a much richer set of values and preferences. [My] analysis assumes that individuals maximize welfare *as they conceive it*, whether they be selfish, altruistic, loyal, spiteful, or masochistic" (Becker, 1993, pp. 385, 386). One pertinent example is the case of the members of the Polish Civic Educational Association in the late 1980s objecting to the national school system inherited from the collapsed Communist regime. Their position was that they wanted to maximize welfare as *they* as individuals saw it, and this was to be a welcome change from having welfare defined and imposed by totalitarian authorities or highly centralized bureaucracies (Glenn, 1995, p. 127).

Another common argument by intellectuals is that parents cannot be expected to make sound choices for their children (Carnegie Foundation, 1992; Levin, 1991; Bridge, 1978; Wells and Crain, 1992). One reply is that parents have hitherto been denied choice for too long but that after some initial experience with it they will become more adept. A second response is that if, in a democracy, there are serious impediments in decision-making by parents, they will show up also at the ballot box when they choose political representatives to make decisions on education. A third response is to quote empirical studies demonstrating rational choice for their children by parents who themselves have only modest amounts of education (Fossey, 1994).

A related argument by opponents is that a free market would lead to racial segregation (Krashinsky, 1986, p. 143). The usual reply here is to quote the work of Coleman (1990) which shows that segregation in the public school system is in fact greater than in private schools.

A further concern is that vouchers (or tax credits) for education might result in fraudulent practices. Murnane (1983) makes the analogy with food stamps in the United States. Experience there, he observes, shows that unscrupulous parties make claims for fictitious individuals. The work of Schmidt (1995), however, shows that the serious short-comings of fraud and dishonesty are already present in the public school system.

Shanker and Rosenberg (1992) argue that difficult-to-educate children would be rejected by profit-making schools under a voucher system. Lieberman (1991), however, found that the single largest U.S.

group of for-profit schools caters to the disabled. Evidence, meanwhile, that urban private schools maintain a higher level of discipline than do public schools is provided by Blum (1985).

B   Public versus Private Benefits from Education

Some economists emphasize that the education of one's child provides not only private benefits to the family (mainly by increasing income or the expectation thereof), but also public (or external) benefits (Krashinsky, 1986). Others point out that private schools are also direct producers of externalities (Hettich, 1969). But they also generate them *indirectly* (West, 1991). It is generally agreed that private schools are more efficient at producing private benefits, through more effective teaching of the "basics" such as literacy. This is so partly because public schools are monopolies, while private schools have greater output per dollar because they experience competition. But literacy is a necessary condition for communicating the common values and fostering economic growth. This indirect assistance by private schooling to the production of such public benefits is at least as important as the direct production.

C   Potential Damage to the Public School System

One of the most frequent arguments of government sector unions of teachers and administrators is that a voucher system will destroy the public school system. Krashinsky (1986), for example, argues that after the introduction of vouchers, middle- and upper-class parents would desert the public system in favor of private schools that discriminate in various ways against poor, disadvantaged, or minority applicants. The poor would be left in gutted, underfunded, and decaying public schools. But according to Wilkinson (1994) this kind of argument rests on the questionable assumption that the public system will refuse to adjust in the face of competition from private schools. Krashinsky's fear of middle-income parents deserting the public school system with the aid of vouchers has no basis, moreover, where they are allotted exclusively to low-income families, as in the case today in such widely different countries as Bangladesh, the United States, Puerto Rico, Chile,

Columbia, and the United Kingdom. By most reports, such systems are improving the condition of the poor relative to those in the rest of society.

D   Vouchers and Poverty Reduction

Krashinsky's implicit assumption is that the public school system benefits the poor in a way that is superior to any alternative. But low-income families are stratified residentially and their children are typically allocated to the schools nearest their homes. If they want to choose a better public school in a middle-class area they are obliged to purchase a home there. Usually, however, the house prices are so prohibitive as to prevent the move. Middle-class families, on the other hand, are more able to move because they are less restricted financially. In this way, the public school system becomes heterogeneous in provision, with the poor, on average, receiving the worst quality. Vouchers would help remove the barriers to mobility.

Friedman and Friedman (1980) insist that they, too, favor the reduction of poverty and the promotion of equal opportunity, but that in both respects the voucher system would unmistakenly improve things. They insist that liberty, equality of opportunity, and the reduction of poverty are complementary and not competitive goals of their voucher system. The main argument is that lower-income families, who are usually trapped in large-city ghetto schools, would benefit the most from vouchers: "Are the supermarkets available to different economic groups anything like so divergent in quality as the schools? Vouchers would improve the quality of the public schooling available to the rich hardly at all; to the middle class, moderately; to the low-income class, enormously" (p. 169).

E   The Middle-Class Windfall Gains Issue

Some voucher opponents focus on what they call the unequitable windfall gains for families (usually well-to-do) that customarily purchase private education. In other words, costs to governments would increase by the extension of vouchers (or tax credits) to rich private school clients not now financed by government (Gemello and Osman,

1983). West (1985) and Seldon (1986) point out, however, that *total* costs to government could fall depending on the value of the voucher as a proportion of per capita public school costs. The government *savings* would occur, according to Friedman, if the voucher value was 75% of public school costs. The implication of this reasoning is that, offsetting the cost of the windfall gain to accustomed users of private schools would be the economies caused by migrants from public to private schools, who would now cost the government 25% less than before. Notice, meanwhile, that because voucher supporters emphasize that private schools can deliver at lower costs than public schools, their case looks more consistent if they demand vouchers at values less than 100% of average per pupil costs in public schools.

The windfall gains problem could also be handled by making them subject to tax. Moreover, the choice of a *selective* voucher that was restricted to low-income families would be even more effective. In this case the high-income families now patronizing private schools would automatically be prevented from enjoying the windfall gains.

F   Regulatory Threats to Private School Identity

The remaining and latest aspect of the debate involves strong believers in the philosophy of freedom who want to see more competition in schooling but who are apprehensive that voucher systems would seriously threaten the autonomy of independent schools. Currently the most articulate and influential spokesman for this point of view in the United States is Richman (1994). In his words: "It is likely that before schools could accept vouchers, they would be required to meet a raft of standards that before long would make the private schools virtually indistinguishable from public schools" (p. 83). Voucher initiatives that insisted on zero regulation would stand no chance of acceptance because, "as the opposition would inevitably point out, the voucher plan would appear to authorize appropriation of 'public' money to institutions not accountable to 'public authorities'" (p. 84).

Expressing a similar opinion in the United States, North (1993) argues: "We will have federal guidelines operating in every voucher-using school, equal opportunity policies and quota systems of every kind, teaching hiring and firing policies, racially and religiously mixed student bodies. There will be a whole army of federal bureaucrats, not to mention state bureaucrats policing every 'private' school" (p. 149).

Friedman has always separated three levels of issues, first, whether schooling should be compulsory, second, whether it should be governmentally financed or privately financed, third, how it should be *organized*. His position has been that whatever may be one's answers on the first two levels, a voucher scheme would produce a better and a more effective organization than the present one; that is, vouchers remain a superior alternative to a system of governmentally run as well as governmentally financed schools. His most recent position indicates that, as do North (1993) and Richman (1994), he sees benefits also in eventually removing compulsion and government finance. But Friedman (1993) is concerned with the question of how to get there from here. Vouchers, he believes, are still a practical transitional measure.

As for the governments' regulatory takeover threat to private schools, Henderson (1994) points out that these institutions do not *have to* accept vouchers with all their tie-ins. Others argue also that the recipients of vouchers can and will lobby their government against heavy regulation. Lieberman (1991, p. 6), meanwhile, argues that the more likely cause of increased regulation will be the political objections to funding both public and private schools while closely regulating only the former. Consequently, Lieberman observes, supporters of vouchers must argue that to approach parity what is needed is the reduction of the regulation of public schools, not an increase in the regulation of private schools.

VIII   Conclusion

The quest for increased efficiency in public (government) school systems has been hindered by a lack of sound empirical analysis. The work of Hanushek, quoted at the beginning, appears to be doing much to fill this gap. He concludes that the traditional approach of seeking optimum aggregate combinations of *inputs* has largely been a failure. In consequence, he switches attention to the need to concentrate on *outputs*. The relationship between outputs and incentives, meanwhile, appears crucial.

This essay has offered, accordingly, a critical account of alternative patterns of finance and regulations that are claimed to be favorable to the incorporation of sensible incentives. Selected charter schools seem to be offering some partial solutions in this direction while, in the light of new experience with them, properly designed voucher systems seem to be even more promising. And while many remain adverse even to the mention of the incentive of profit seeking, an examination of the new achievements of for-profit organizations in education, as provided above, may well be salutary as well as surprising.

Bibliography

Baumol, W.J. 1967. "Macroeconomics of Unbalanced Growth." *American Economic Review* 51(June):415–426.

Baumol, W.J. 1993. "Health Care, Education and the Cost-Disease." *Public Choice* 77:17–28.

Becker, G.S. 1993. "The Economic Way of Looking at Behavior." Nobel Lecture. *Journal of Political Economy* 101(3):385–409.

Birchenough, C. 1927. *History of Elementary Education in England & Wales.* London: W.B. Clive.

Bistany, R., and L. Saad. 1994. "Bistany and Saad Earn High Marks in Business of Learning." *Star Tribune* (Minn.), January 16.

Blum, V.C. 1985. "Private Elementary Education in the Inner City." *Phi Delta Kappa* 66(9):645.

Borland, M.V., and R.M. Howsen. 1996. "Competition, Expenditures and Student Performance in Mathematics: A Comment on Couch et al." *Public Choice* 87:395–400.

Bridge, G. 1978. "Information Imperfections: The Achilles Heel of Entitlement Plans." *School Review* 86:504–529.

Carnegie Foundation for the Advancement of Teaching. 1992. "School Choice." Princeton: Carnegie Foundation.

Coleman, J. 1990. *Equality and Achievement in Education.* Boulder: Westview Press.

Couch, J.F., W.F. Shughart II, and A.L. Williams. 1993. "Private School Enrollment and Public School Performance." *Public Choice* 76(Aug.):301–312.

Eberts, R.W., and J.A. Stone. 1986. "Teacher Unions and the Cost of Public Education." *Economic Inquiry* 24(4):631–643.

Ferris, S., and E.G. West. 1996. "Cost Disease versus Leviathan Explanations of Government Growth." *Public Choice* 89:35–52.

Finn, C. 1997. Keynote Address to "Choosing Better Schools" Conference, Atlantic Institute for Market Studies, Fredericton, New Brunswick, May 4.

Fossey R. 1994. "Open Enrollment in Massachusetts: Why Families Choose." *Education Evaluation and Policy Analysis* 16(3):320–334.

Friedman, M. 1993. "Letter to the Editor of the *Freeman*." *Freeman* (July):306.

Friedman, M., and R. Friedman. 1980. *Free to Choose.* New York: Harcourt, Brace, Johanovich.

Gemello, J., and J. Osman. 1983. "The Choice for Public and Private Education: An Economist's View." In: T. James and H.M. Levin (eds.), *Public Dollars for Private Schools*, pp. 196–209. Philadelphia: Temple University Press.

Glenn, C.L. 1995. *Educational Freedom in Eastern Europe*. Washington, D.C.: CATO Institute.

Hanushek, E.A. 1995. "Interpreting Recent Research on Schooling in Developing Countries." *World Bank Research Observer* 10(2):227–246

Hanushek, E.A. 1996. "The Productivity Collapse in Schools." Allen Wallace Institute of Political Economy Working Paper No. 8, University of Rochester.

Hanushek, E.A., and V. Lavy. 1994. "School Quality, Achievement Bias and the Estimated Effects of School Resources." *World Bank Research Observer* 9:1–19.

Henderson, D.R. 1994. "Why We Need School Choice." *Insight*, January 10.

Hettich, W. 1969. "Mixed Public and Private Financing of Education: Comment." *American Economic Review* 59(March):210–212.

Holmes, M. 1990. "The Funding of Independent Schools." In: Y.L. Jack Lam (ed.), *The Canadian Public Education System*, pp. 62–78. Calgary: Detselig.

Kenny, L.W., and A.B. Schmidt. 1994. "The Decline in the Number of School Districts in the U.S. 1950–1980." *Public Choice* 29(April):1–18.

Krashinsky, M. 1986. "Why Educational Vouchers May be Bad Economics." *Teachers College Record* 88(2):139–151.

Levin, H.M. 1991. "The Economics of Educational Choice." *Economics of Education Review* 10(2):137–158.

Lieberman, M. 1991. "The Case for Voluntary Funding of Education." Policy Study No. 37. Chicago: Heartland Institute.

McGroaty, D. 1994. "School Choice Slandered." *Public Interest* 117(Fall):94–111.

Minter-Hoxby, C. 1994. "Do Private Schools Provide Competition for Public Schools?" Department of Economics, MIT (mimeo).

Murnane, R.J. 1983. "The Uncertain Consequences of Tuition Tax Credits: An Analysis of Student Achievement and Economic Incentives." In: T. James and H.M. Levin (eds.), *Public Dollars for Private Schools*, pp. 210–222. Philadelphia: Temple University Press.

North, G. 1993. "Education Vouchers: The Double Tax." *Freeman* (July):25–30.

Raham, H. 1996. "Revitalising Public Education in Canada: The Potential of Choice and Charter Schools." *Fraser Forum* (Aug.):1–16.

Rangazas, P. 1995. "Vouchers and Voting: An Initial Estimate Based on the Median Voter Model." *Public Choice* 82(March):261–279.

Richman, S. 1994. *Separating School and State*. Fairfax, Va.: Future of Freedom Foundation.

Rouse, C.E. 1996. "Private School Vouchers and Student Achievement: An Evaluation of the Milwaukee Parental Choice Program." Working Paper No. 371. Princeton: Princeton University, Industrial Relations Section.

Shanker, A., and B. Rosenberg. 1992. "Politics, Markets and American Schools: A Rejoinder." In: P.R. Kane (ed.), *Independent Schools, Independent Thinkers*, pp. 36–43. San Francisco: Jossey-Bass.

Union News. 1997. April 5, p. B2.

Wells, A.S., and R.L. Crain. 1992. "Do Parents Choose School Quality or School Status?: A Sociological Theory of Free Market Education." In: P.W. Cookson (ed.), *The Choice Controversy*, pp. 310–409. Newbury Park, NY: Corwin Press.

West, E.G. 1991. "Public Schools and Excess Burdens." *Economics of Education Review* 10(2).

West, E.G. 1985. "The Real Cost of Tuition Tax Credits." Public Choice 46(1).

West, E.G. 1997. "Education Vouchers in Principle & Practice: A Survey." *World Bank Research Observer* 12(1):83–103.

Wilkinson, B. 1994. *Educational Choice: Necessary But Not Sufficient*. Montreal: Institute for Research on Public Policy.

Subsidization and Promotion of the Arts

Alan Peacock

I Background

The definition of "culture" in this essay is a pragmatic one. It follows the Viner adage that "economics is what economists do," which in this case means studying cultural activities represented by the creative arts and their performance or presentation in the theater, concert hall, opera house, museum, or gallery, and even "en plein air" as heritage artifacts. In deriving satisfaction from these activities, consumers characteristically combine the artistic input with their own investment in artistic appreciation. As a consequence, consumers take seriously the judgments of *cognoscenti*, i.e., those involved in or particularly knowledgeable about the product, in arriving at decisions about purchase, e.g., by reading reviews, attending lectures, etc. They may gain insights from participation in amateur orchestras, play and painting groups, and as voluntary helpers in artistic ventures. Nothing in what has been said postulates some hierarchy of tastes and preferences or that more popular cultural activities are less worthy of the economists' attention.

Cultural economics is no longer a cult subject practiced by a few economists with artistic interests consulted by private and public bodies concerned with artistic policies. It is claimed by the editors of the reconstituted *Journal of Cultural Economics* that "we believe that cultural economics contributes to the discussion of fundamental issues in economics, particularly to the growing awareness of the role of information in explaining economic behaviour. Our field has insights to offer to the economics profession at large. It is also increasingly accepted by policymakers as an important aspect of cultural decision-making" (*The Culture of Cultural Economics*, 1994). As one of the editorial board of this journal, I suppose I must seek to justify this claim.

Cultural economists have identified some characteristics of the creative and performing arts that affect one's judgment of how far and in what form the government should support the arts, and at least some general account of these is a useful prelude to later analysis. These are:

(a) Creative artists fall into the category of those who derive satisfaction from work itself and not solely from the income it earns. Models of time allocation and career choice do take account of nonpecuniary influences, and have been adapted to the circumstances of artists and composers who are unable to earn a living wage solely from their artistic calling. One possible policy implication is that artists will be less inclined to use subsidies to increase rents or leisure but to substitute artistic activity for nonartistic activity (see, in particular, Throsby, 1994b).

(b) The utility function of creative and performing artists includes reputation with the peer group as an important argument. This translates into a denial of the proposition that their subsidized activities should be judged solely with reference to performance indicators designed to measure consumer satisfaction. "Quality" of output should be judged by artists themselves. (See III.C below.)

(c) There are particular difficulties in the creative arts in laying claim to property rights, as demonstrated in the long struggle of composers to exercise rights over performance. The dimension of these rights has become a thorny issue in public policy (see MacQueen and Peacock, 1996), but is not pursued here.

(d) It is claimed that the performing arts are beset by the impossibility of introducing process innovations that result in productivity gains —what is known in the trade as Baumol's disease. Indeed, Baumol and Bowen, in *The Performing Arts: The Economic Dilemma* (1966), can lay claim to be the inventors of cultural economics. In this context, one notes that the labor intensity of the performing arts has a bearing on the magnitude of cultural subsidies, *if* it is agreed that state support for them is necessary. (See Section IV below.)

(e) The presentation of works of art through performance and display has long been characterized by a complicated skein of transactions resulting from the fact that there is both public and private supply of them, with both the public and private sectors receiving finance from both government and private sources. It is far from easy to identity a satisfactory "flow of funds" system with numbers illustrating the relative importance of each sector (see Trimarchi, 1993), quite apart from the definitional problems associated with knowing what to and what not to include. Such calculations are carefully scrutinized by arts lobbies for evidence of "favoritism" (see Brosio, 1994).

(f) As a complement to (e), one notes that cultural production in both the public and private sectors is carried out predominantly by non-profit-making concerns. This entails the use of a developing area of economic analysis recognizing arguments in the firms' utility functions other than profit, and has an important bearing on how such firms are expected to react to methods of subsidization.

(g) While the apparent vulnerability of the creative and performing arts to economic forces beyond their control arouses the protective instincts of governments and patrons, it is noteworthy that at all stages of artistic production, there are well-organized pressure groups. A less tangible but important aspect of their pressure group activities is the comparative advantage that their leaders possess in the exploitation of histrionics!

Given this background, the next task is to consider how cultural economists approach the matter of justifying state support for the arts (Section II) as a prelude to appraising methods of subsidization (Section III). Sections III and IV draw attention to certain practical features of subsidization.

II Welfare Economics and State Support for the Arts: Market Failures

State support for the arts derived from conventional welfare economics turns out to be rather weak, although it offers a useful agenda for discussion. This follows directly from the assumption of consumer sovereignty. Market failure and hence prima facie evidence of the need for state intervention of some kind is alleged to occur in the following situations:

(i) "Spillover benefits to other producers." It is claimed that expenditure on performing arts benefits other producers through the creation of a cultural ambiance which attracts skilled factors of production and, as in the case of tourism, acts as a loss leader in attracting business from which other industries benefit. The benefits, it is held, cannot be captured other than by public subsidy. At the national level these benefits are largely pecuniary because an attempt to realize spillover effects, e.g., by subsidy, in one area or activity must be at the cost of taxpayers in all areas. We would have to introduce interpersonal or interregional comparisons of utility to push the argument any further. However, even if there were recognizable real benefits, in order to prove the necessity for state support, two further conditions would have to be fulfilled: (i) that extra inputs of "culture" were the most efficient way of obtaining the result; and (ii) that beneficiaries would have no incentive to negotiate agreements to support the cultural loss leaders themselves. Clearly in the latter case, the larger the numbers involved, the greater the likelihood of "free riding" and the stronger the case for an "imposed" solution.

(ii) "Spillover benefits to consumers." Here we distinguish between present and future generations. In the case of present generations, it is claimed that an option value can be attached to the arts, for even those who do not enjoy them derive satisfaction from the enjoyment of others, notably their nearest and dearest, and also from the prestige that the arts confer on their state or country. No less a luminary than Lionel Robbins deployed this argument in his defense of heritage as well as performing arts (see Robbins, 1963). However, the prestige case draws attention to a frequent omission in "externality" arguments. What if resources used to support the arts have alternative uses which produce the same result? The same argument could be used to support a whole range of options including space research, football teams, and fashion industries. The externality case cannot be made in absolute terms alone.

It will be noticed that already "standard" welfare economics has been modified by the introduction of interdependent utility functions. Economists have been more sympathetic to the proposition that individuals are concerned about the welfare of future generations who will be affected by decisions taken now about the preservation of the arts but have no say in them (see Baumol, 1987; Fullerton, 1991). One does not even have to invoke "altruism" in this context, for the welfare of *pres-*

ent generations may be affected by the worry that our grandchildren may curse us for letting particular art forms die out. This assumes that an art form, once destroyed, cannot be re-created, but this seems only plausible in the case of historical artifacts. There are other matters which make it fray at the edges. Future generations may not like what we choose to preserve for them, and if they are likely to be better off than ourselves, why give them a bounty at the cost of poorer present generations?

(iii) "Quality of choices." The application of the doctrine of consumer sovereignty presupposes that the problem of the distribution of opportunities for choosing by individuals is somehow solved. Such opportunities depend on the distribution of income and wealth, but I shall assume that this is a separate issue in the sense that the arts are not a mechanism for correcting distribution in line with public policies. A trickier problem is presented by the quality of choices, however we define these, because this entails considering how tastes and preferences are formed. Traditional welfare economics avoids this question by assuming tastes and preferences as given, whereas freedom of choice includes the freedom to subject oneself to experiences which may change them, the arts being a prominent medium for doing so. As Blaug (1976) puts it: "there is certainly nothing in economic theory that a competitive market will bring about an optimal level of investment in the formation of tastes."

The formation of the pattern of individual choices clearly depends on the education of which cultural education forms a part. Some libertarians might argue that taste formation is a family responsibility in the case of minors and an individual one if there is a personal desire as an adult to invest in self-education with a view to increase one's enjoyment in the arts. Scitovsky (1983) is much less pussyfooted, arguing that the human propensity for excitement and danger, if it is to avoid producing negative externalities in the form of violent behavior, may be satisfied by providing artistic outlets—"soothing the savage breast," as it were. The education system should then be assigned the task of teaching "new consumption skills" which channel the desire for excitement into appreciation of and participation in artistic pursuits. As with the previous arguments, there is some vagueness about how it is to

be translated into some form of public action—but more of this
anon.

(iv) "Trust the government rather than the market." Freedom of choice
in the final analysis includes freedom of choice over methods of
choice themselves (see Pommerehne et al., 1997), and individuals
may for a variety of reasons prefer a political to a market solution.
One reason may be that advanced by those who support "merit
goods" arguments. Individuals, while having different preference
scales, may support community values which can only be given
expression in collective action, Musgrave (1987) offering national
heritage as an example. Another might be that only the state can
be "trusted" to look after the interests of future generations, as
reflected in the voluntary bequests "to the nation" of art treasures
by their rich owners who insist that only public bodies can be
trusted not to sell this transfer of their patrimony. It will be noted
that the way I have formulated this approach does not require
that consumers cease to be rational economic agents in allowing
others to choose for them, but it does raise the awkward question
whether the political system performs an analogous function to
the market in the allocation of goods and services. If it is believed,
as some Chicago economists appear to believe (see Wittman [1989],
but cf. Tollison [1989]) that it does, then evaluation of the form
and content of public support for the arts becomes superfluous,
for expenditure on the arts would be as near optimal as it can be.
Economists would then be better employed trying to understand
the world of culture rather than judging how it might be organized.

Two obvious questions are raised by this survey of the arguments for
public support. The first is: what evidence is there that there is a willingness on the part of the public to sanction public expenditure on the
arts? A simpliste answer, which is at least consistent with the view that
the political system reflects individuals' choices, is to examine the data
on public expenditure. A more satisfactory answer can be derived from
surveys which indicate whether or not the public *approve* of such expenditures. Throsby (1994a) shows that opinion polls in several countries
indicate such approval. To go further than this to ascertain whether the
known levels of expenditure accord with what individuals are *willing* to
pay requires the use of sophisticated methods of inquiry. Contingent
valuation (CV) studies now abound in the field of the arts, notably in

regard to the preservation of heritage artifacts. As with other lines of inquiry designed to capture valuation of externalities, the public is asked to state its maximum willingness-to-pay to preserve a particular artifact or even for the support of the arts in general. Alternatively, it is faced with a "price" and asked whether or not it is willing to pay it. The limited evidence derived from CV also suggests that the public is willing to pay for the arts out of taxes (see Heilbrun and Gray, 1993). Of course, one is bound to be skeptical of surveys that rely on hypothetical answers rather than observed choices, for it costs individuals nothing to give strategic answers. Furthermore, evidence of approval can only in a very limited sense imply that individuals are obtaining "value for money." Any positive explanation of government expenditure on the arts cannot avoid considering the extent to which those art organizations subsidized by government, in common with subsidized concerns generally, are successful "rent-seekers." This is a question to which we are bound to return in considering subsidy measures in detail.

Once a case is made for state support, very few attempts are made to establish any connection between it and the forms of support. If reliance is placed on the doctrine of consumer sovereignty, then this would seem to point towards state *financing* but not state *provision* of arts ventures. It would suggest encouragement to individuals to attend artistic events and to enjoy heritage services, according to a pattern determined by themselves in the light of their changing knowledge and appreciation of the arts. This would minimize interference in the production of arts services and encourage competition between them. Hence the support for "arts vouchers" (see Section IV below).

This "*systemgerechte*" approach to financing, although derived from welfare propositions familiar to us all, does not penetrate actual financing and provision of the arts. The strength of the fourth proposition of "trusting the government" is clearly demonstrated in the presence of central and state government provision of heritage services (museums and galleries, historical monuments and sites), of theaters, opera houses, and concert halls with artistic personnel as government employees. These services are usually provided at less than cost and therefore require production subsidies, a method also applied on a wide scale in subsidizing private (normally non-profit-making) artistic ventures. In addition, governments influence the amount and composition of artistic services by *regulation*, notably in the control exercised over the preservation, restoration, and disposal of privately owned buildings and movable artifacts considered of historic importance.

The lack of correspondence between welfare economics (with a liberalist tinge!) and the widespread intervention of governments in arts provision offers a challenge to those of us who question the efficiency of governments in the management of the production of services which are not "pure" public goods and who seek to devise ways in which the market is made to play a larger part in their provision and financing. In the following section (III), I shall provide examples of "government failure" in subsidy policy which are complemented by discussion (Section IV) of some suggestions for policy reform which conform with the recent trend towards relying on market solutions to improve consumer welfare.

III Economic Analysis of Direct Subsidies: Government Failure

In this section, I illustrate the economists' contribution to the study of the arts with the purpose of shedding some light on the effects of direct subsidies to arts organizations, which, as already indicated, is the principal method of state support. Although there are major organizational differences between countries in which funding of arts companies is offered from government departments, state and local, and those countries who rely on an "arm's-length" system in which the task of funding is assigned to an independent body, as in the United Kingdom and Australia, the principal-agent relationship is similar and presents the same problems in trying to marry policies to practice.

A Artists' Behavior

As in other branches of economics, a significant amount of economic investigation of the arts is taken up today with models of the individual or group economic behavior and with testing hypotheses about that behavior. A common mistake perpetuated by arts pundits is that economists are only interested in materialistic behavior, whereas, as Frey (1994a) explains, economists postulate rational behavior which covers the study of how individuals with given preference scales act alone or in concert to maximize a welfare function, subject to constraints of resources and time. Empirically testable propositions may be derived from individual or group reactions to changes in the constraints.

Such an approach should be of interest, in principle, to policy-makers who, as is commonly the case, offer subsidies to individual artists and (usually) non-profit-making artistic ventures, such as theatrical companies, orchestras, and the like. The presumption is that both the amount and the form of the subsidy, representing the change in the constraints, will move the quantity and quality of "output" of individuals and companies in some desired direction.

Some very interesting examples of models of individual artist behavior now pepper the literature, notably in the work of Towse (1993) and Throsby (1994b). Both dispel the impression that economists need to assume, as is common in labor market models, that work is solely a means to income. Artists, in common with researchers and academics, are presumed to derive a positive pleasure from work to the extent that they will turn down better paid jobs rather than forego the pleasures of enjoyable work. However, as Throsby maintains, artists are characteristically constrained by the fact that they cannot earn enough at the work they enjoy doing in order to earn a living wage and so have to trade off time spent on artistic creation against time spent on work which provides them with a minimum income. His "work preference model" offers the interesting prediction that, suitably varied to take account of the differing constraints on artists, if the return to artistic work rises through time relatively to nonarts work, then artists will increase their supply of labor for arts work. This hypothesis receives a good deal of empirical support from his own and other investigations. He is therefore able to conclude that *if* there is a public interest in increasing artistic activity, artists in receipt of grants would increase their artistic output rather than use any improvement in their economic circumstances as rents or in order to increase leisure time.

Throsby's conclusion would certainly be popular with both providers and recipients of public funds. The former seek assurance that the costs of monitoring artistic performance will be low, including the awkwardness associated with detailed inquiry into the personal behavior of sensitive people. The latter's welfare is increased through a change in economic circumstances and the public recognition of his/ her contribution to the arts. This does not remove a bargaining situation between providers and recipients. Funding limitations will not allow all "deserving" artists to receive grants or provide the amounts which recipients would regard as reflecting their "true" worth.

B   Analysis of Producer Subsidies and Their Consequences

The situation may be markedly different when we look at the economist's contribution to the study of producer subsidies to large-scale arts companies. Analysis of the behavioral characteristics of providers and recipients of public funding and its results do not engender professional popularity, as it may demonstrate the possibility of "policy failure."

The point of departure of discussion of producer subsidies in cultural economics circles has been centered in the study of the reactions of cultural "firms" to the provision of either "lump sum" or "output" subsidies (see Throsby and Withers, 1979; West, 1985). In particular, attention has been concentrated on comparing the reactions of profit and non-profit-making firms, as a preliminary to evaluating the welfare effects in both cases. I assume that the analysis is sufficiently familiar so that I need only provide a summary of the results.

Throsby and Withers begin with a "no-subsidy" situation and a profit-making and non-profit-making firm with identical cost and demand curves. It can then easily be shown that output would be higher and price lower in the case of the non-profit firm. It follows that in both the case of a lump-sum or output subsidy, the non-profit-making firm would increase output most, whereas the profit-making firm, although it has an incentive to increase output, only does so to the extent that this is compatible with maximizing profits. If the objective of policy is to minimize the amount of subsidy to produce a given output, then subsidy should only be given to non-profit-making firms.

Throsby and Withers and West were well aware that the usefulness of this kind of exercise depends on the extent to which it reflects reality, and deserve credit for pioneering formal discussion of the subsidy problem.

There is bound to be friendly disagreement about how much "reality" to introduce at first approximation. My main caveat about the presentation of this analysis is that it assumes passive adjustment by the producer to the subsidizing agency. Unless some franchising provision is being assumed, with competition between firms seeking subsidies, then we have a classic "principal-agent" situation with asymmetric information, for the situation is not one of constrained maximization by the firm but of bargaining with the subsidizing authority. This is because the principal source of information on costs is the firm itself. Close scrutiny of the costs by the authority is itself a costly procedure. The point is recognized by West (1985) who draws attention to the "implicit assumption of zero interdependence between the granting of the subsidy and reported costs." This clearly muddies the waters of the analysis, because it can then be contended that non-profit-making organizations respond to producer subsidies, not by increasing output by moving along a minimum cost curve but by "capturing" rents obtained by raising the cost curve. Of course, such a proposition will be strongly denied by the subsidized firm, usually by claiming that whatever measure of output is used, an increase in costs per unit is reflected in increases in quality of performance!

This brings one to the heart of the problem of drawing up a contract between the grant-giving body and the client which at least clarifies the nature of the agreement between the parties. The grant-giving body (GGB) will wish to adhere to the principle of "additionality." It expects the client to "prove" that, in return for subsidy, it will provide a cultural benefit greater than would otherwise be the case if no subsidy were provided, and, in principle, one which would be greater than any alternative use of scarce resources available for supporting the arts. The client will always have a long list of "worthy" projects that "deserve" public support and will request finance which is likely to far exceed the funding likely to become available.

The first problem is how to draw up a contract which will minimize potential disagreement about its terms. One example is sufficient to illustrate the difficulties. The economic analysis presented above assumes that "output" can be precisely defined. Consider a symphony orchestra. Is the "output" the number of works played, the number of performances or the size of audience? Should the contract reflect "positive externalities" by specifying the content of programs (e.g., some minimum percentage of "new works"), or "reach-out" to new audiences defined in terms of "class" or "region"? How does one define and monitor "quality" of performance? How does one obtain consensus among members of the GGB about the "tradeoffs" between these various output indicators? (For further discussion of ex post measures of performance of orchestras, see Peacock [1993].) Even if

the contracting system induces bidders to provide as accurate information as possible about cost and output projections reflecting alternative performance "mixes"—a formidable undertaking—the scope for
disagreement about plan fulfillment between principal and agent is
bound to be wide.

The economic analysis of subsidy implies that it can tell us what
happens when the process is reversed and subsidy is reduced or with-
drawn—output may fall and cost rise, given the normal assumptions.
This static approach does not throw much light on subsidization as a
continuous process, as with the common practice of revenue funding
over a series of years. It is clearly not designed to illustrate the second
problem, that of the reactions of incumbents whose expectations
regarding the amount of continuing subsidy are disappointed. Incum-
bent recipients are usually well prepared for this situation. Their initial
strategy is likely to be to test the determination of the providers to
stick to their decisions. At the very least, it may be expected that the
providers will be willing, if only out of self-interest, to listen to repre-
sentations, and may be persuaded that the cost of time and energy and
the threat of further action are too high a price to pay for sticking to
its decisions.

This "further action" indicates that the outcome of the "subsidy
game" can be influenced by introducing players other than the GGB
and clients. Long-established incumbents with "national" or "regional"
status will not hesitate to try to outflank the GGB with media prop-
aganda and by lobbying politicians—particularly those who enjoy the
arts—and, of course, the funding government department.

Assuming the arts companies do not aim to maximize profits but
seek security of funding, they perceive that they can best achieve this
objective by appointing directors or trustees who can communicate
easily and effectively with suppliers of finance. In the United Kingdom,
the large national or regional companies have no difficulty in finding
public figures who derive utility from being associated with artistic
events, either because it enhances their prestige or caters to their cultural
preferences. In my experience they are a mixed blessing when it comes
to their representation of the arts companies' interests. A fair proportion, noted for their acute commercial sense in their own line of business, become completely captured by communities of creative and performing artists. They begin to argue that corporate planning and
management accounting have no relevance in arts organizations and

even try to emulate the artists themselves in making emotional appeals to the public authorities!

C   The Utility-Maximizing Museum Curator

Identified in most countries as a significant element in the presentation of the cultural heritage, the activities of museum and gallery curators have become subject to close scrutiny by economists (see, for example, Frey and Pommerehne, 1989; Feldstein, 1991).

Frey and Pommerehne introduce the analysis by employing a useful "back door" method. They ask the question: why is it that in museums and galleries, we observe that the ratio of displayed artifacts to the total stock is characteristically as low as 1 to 4, and, in important instances, such as the Prado, 1 to 10? Further, why do curators resist proposals for changing the composition of stock by sale and purchase —in other words, why is de-accessioning "*streng verboten*"? The answer lies, so it would appear, in the welfare function of the "curators" who perceive their duties as only partly that of providing a service to the museum and gallery visitors but more as guardians of a repository of heritage goods which must be preserved for posterity and whose importance is determined, not by common perceptions of their value to future generations, but by the "expert" opinions of art historians and archaeologists—their professional confrères. In order to maximize their objective function, they must therefore resist attempts to have them derive their income primarily from admission charges and to encourage inquiry into whether they take proper account of the opportunity cost of capital stock. The main, permanent, source of funding must therefore be the state (see impassioned argument in Cannon-Brooks [1996]).

Glancing at the common methods of financing of museums and galleries would confirm the influence of the "professional" view, but, in so doing, we once again observe that the specification of the "contract" between the providers and recipients of funding runs into the principal-agent problem. However, I would draw attention to a much more fundamental source of disagreement between economists and museologists. The former frequently argue that aesthetic values are purely subjective and therefore that there are no "experts" in heritage preservation, though that is not to say that those who pay for heritage services, either through being taxed to preserve artifacts or by paying admission charges to view them, will not derive benefits from an investment in information which only these experts can provide. Even if one were to get around this problem by relying on "merit goods" arguments as a way of justifying vicarious choices by experts, one has to point out that the "experts" rarely agree among themselves on the rank-ordering of heritage items, and not infrequently change their minds. There is no guarantee that their prediction of what future generations will value in the form of heritage goods will be superior to that of nonexperts. Economists and the self-styled guardians of heritage must clearly agree to differ (see, further, Peacock, 1995).

The use of production subsidies on a major scale invites the speculation that major clients are well placed to "capture" GGBs. Certainly, as GGBs rely on professional advice from creative and performing artists themselves—poachers turned gamekeepers—there are strong inhibitions at work to prevent GGB council members from giving offense to those on whom they may have to rely for future employment, notably the more prestigious clients with artistic and political "clout." Additionally, lay members of GGBs and supporting senior bureaucrats are sensitive about being branded as philistines who may be made unwelcome at gala occasions, once they demit office. Of course, capture can be resisted, simply by the need to work within normally strict budget constraints so that controversy about the allocation of funds can be diverted towards disagreements among the clients themselves about their relative artistic "worth." Alternatively, as is common in bargaining situations, the two sides can make common cause against the funding authorities. The annual reports of the Arts Council of England (formerly of Great Britain), although a government agency entrusted with the allocation of central government funding for the creative and performing arts slipped into its Mission Statement a few years back the achievement of its aims by "pressing the case for the arts and public funding" (ACGB, 1991/1992)! It may also be of interest to note that in 1994, when the funding available for the capital expenditure on the arts was substantially increased by the allocation of 28% of the proceeds of the new National Lottery, the immediate beneficiaries were the highly influential and well-established national companies in London, noted for their lobbying skills, who creamed off a major share.

IV   Markets and Consumer Choice in the Arts

Before considering specific proposals for building a closer relationship between consumer sovereignty and the provision of cultural services, as defined above, it may be useful to summarize the debate about the future prospects for the arts in "rich" countries. In the case of the performing arts, this is particularly associated with the Baumol–Bowen thesis (see I[d] above). In its more general context, as an explanation of the lagging productivity in service industries, the thesis is well known (e.g., Baumol, 1996). The performing arts and heritage services are examples of service industries in which productivity gains through the substitution of capital for labor are difficult to obtain, whereas the general characteristic of economic growth must be increases in the productivity per head of population. Thus once a piece of music or a play is written, the labor input is fixed, and reducing the input destroys the product. (Removing the horns from Mahler's *IVth Symphony* to shed labor does precisely that. Also speeding up production has the same effect—if you still have an LP, try playing Wagner's *Wesendonck Lieder* on a 33 LP on the 78 speed!). However, through competition in the market for labor services, the remuneration of performing artists is likely to keep pace with earnings in general, so that costs of performances cannot be kept down by paying performing arts relatively less. Finally, it is questioned whether the rise in relative costs will be offset by income elasticity effects as incomes grow. If the time input for cultural activities remains relatively fixed, and the price of leisure rises with growing incomes, then consumers will switch to less time-intensive forms of artistic experiences. (For a simple formulation of the "cost disease," see Peacock [1996].)

Broadly speaking, the existence of a "cost disease" seems fairly well established, but the growth of costs does not preclude its offset by an increase in value productivity, although this raises further awkward questions about suitable measures of "output." Also one must account for the fact that performing arts organizations do survive without an increase in the proportion of income derived from subsidy or patronage. Companies may be able to shift demand curves to the right by skillful marketing, but, over time, Baumol and others would claim that survival is only possible by reducing the quality of the product, e.g., attracting mass audiences by offering only popular "classics," film music, and participation in TV drama and music shows. The edge is taken off artistic endeavor, concerts and plays become matters of routine performance and barriers of entry are raised against contemporary composers and playwrights seeking to differentiate their product from those of the past. Cynics might add that any attempt to remove the "artistic deficit" could be an open invitation to modern composers and playwrights to add to the stock of works that will never survive after their first performance!

In the case of heritage, current discussion centers less on the cost disease and more on the major difficulty of squaring the growth in the official inventories of buildings, monuments, historic sites, etc., with the resources available to preserve and to restore them. These inventories are compiled largely on the advice of art historians and archeologists (see, Benhamou, 1996) whose enthusiasm for listing historical artifacts, from pebbles to palaces, is comparable with that of environmentalists concerned about the dying out of every species of beetle. They are equally vociferous about the "underfunding" of preservation either by the public authorities or by private owners of historic properties. The exploitation to the full of the "underfunding" argument, in my view, is a way of masking major differences between experts about what is "worth" preserving. The admission that a resource constraint on preservation is reasonable, would reveal that informed judgments about what to preserve for the satisfaction of present and future generations would not result in a consensus. Bitter and protracted disputes about what to and what not to preserve weaken professional bargaining positions, adding to doubts as to whether historical, architectural, or artistic qualifications are sufficient conditions for the occupation of senior managerial posts in museums, galleries, and historic buildings. I suffer no discomfort from adopting an anthropocentric view which denies that historical artifacts have inalienable rights to preservation, and have proposed that government policy should be directed towards outlining a "sustainable" heritage position by identifying what one might call "representative" artifacts by period and type, and that one should not give into the magpie-like proclivities of those who would preserve almost every physical manifestation of the past. This would both recognize the existence of resources constraints and permit sufficient flexibility in policy to take account of our lack of knowledge of future generations' perceptions of the importance of heritage to them and of uncertainty about how present generations' tastes may change and develop. (For fuller development of this argument, see Peacock [1997].)

With this general background, I look at the prospects for moving towards a cultural policy which embodies measures which better reflect the consumer interest, while recognizing the educational and interpretive role of the experts.

I shall consider three such proposals: (i) vouchers, (ii) pricing of cultural services, and (iii) public participation in decision-making.

(i) Vouchers

The assumption of consumer sovereignty immediately suggests that provision of funding to represent the "publicness" element in cultural goods should be in the form of consumer subsidies (see Peacock, [1969] 1994; West, 1985). These vouchers would entitle recipients to a reduction in the price of a range of cultural goods which are in some way "certified" by the advisers to the public authorities (but see [iii] below). The producers of the cultural goods would then present the vouchers to the funding authorities in exchange for credits. The voucher would be divisible so that individuals could allocate the expenditure that it represents according to their tastes and preferences, and arts companies would be induced to compete for voucher income.

It would be foolish not to recognize right away that such a scheme faces technical difficulties. An initial comparison with educational vouchers makes this clear. Schemes for educational vouchers presuppose that education is compulsorily consumed and that the voucher is for the purchase of a single item, a school place and is nontransferable. It is inconceivable that cultural vouchers would entail compulsory consumption and it would defeat their purpose if recipients were only allowed to exchange their money's-worth for a single event or art form. Too much bureaucracy would be involved in trying to make them nontransferable. If made transferable, the likelihood is that those with a relatively strong preference for cultural goods—generally speaking the well-educated and well-off—would obtain a windfall increase in consumer rent by entering the voucher market and, although the poor and ignorant would be compensated by cash, this hardly commends itself as an efficient way of redistributing income. There is also the additional problem of other direct costs falling on the culturally starved customer, notably differential transport costs and opportunity cost of time that are not unimportant if cultural centers are some distance away. This reinforces the difficulty of matching a wide distribution of the benefits of subsidization by class and region with a simple system which does not require detailed calculation of the differing costs to individuals of attendance at cultural events. It is not surprising that GGBs sympathetic to the general idea of helping individuals to help themselves have tended to target particular groups who can be clearly identified, notably "future generations" represented by the school and college population, with transport subsidies being a widely used method.

These and other difficulties of marrying practice to principle would exist in designing any system from scratch. However, any attempt to use them to modify existing systems of art funding must encounter strong resistance from interest groups. My only evidence is anecdotal, being based on my experience as chairman of the Scottish Arts Council responsible for the disbursement of public funds, mainly to the performing arts. The major proportion of members of the council were appointed because of their expertise or commitment to a particular art form. Understandably, though obliged to agree to decisions on the allocation of funds available, they faced professional obloquy if they did not manifestly fight for their own art form. Their rejection of my proposals to move even some way towards channeling funding through consumers, while given respectful attention, were totally at odds with their perception of their role. Consumer subsidies would diffuse support for a particular art form by promotion of free choice, and therefore restrict individual members' influence, as well as get them into trouble with their professional confrères. Likewise, administrators would lose their discretionary power if a fair proportion of funding went directly to consumers. Companies used to continuous revenue funding were understandably appalled at the prospect of having to compete for voucher income, with the prospect that a voucher scheme might be used to encourage new entrants into their business. Politicians, too, could be easily persuaded that reallocation of spending to consumers might result in arts organizations in their constituencies having to lose custom and to shed labor (see Peacock, 1993). My experience may be unique, but only in the sense that even discussion of the idea of channeling funding through consumers is not likely to be found on the agenda of GGBs.

(ii) Pricing and Related Issues

I proceed here to give a brief account of some of the proposals that have emanated from cultural economics studies and which offer policy suggestions compatible with a shift towards voucher-type funding:

(a) Cultural services should be privatized as far as practicable. This need not take the form of a shift from heavily state-run services to profit-making private enterprises. It could take the form of private non-profit-making institutions, like the English and Scottish National Trusts, which are funded by individual and corporate subscriptions, interest and dividends from assets, and from rents of property, though, it will be noted they rely heavily on donations which attract tax relief.

(b) Although it is conceivable that governments could cease to be owner-occupiers of property and could rent or lease all necessary accommodation, one has to assume that important items of national heritage, such as palaces and national monuments, will continue in state ownership. However, in this case, too, it should be possible to turn over the running of such institutions to private agencies, who would have competed for the franchise.

(c) Cultural producers would be self-financing and would have freedom to price these services to attain that end, given also that finance from governmental sources would be available through voucher schemes. This would not preclude state support which reflected externalities, notably in regard to research and training.

(d) Within the guidelines on "sustainable heritage" (see Section III above), boards of management of galleries and museums should be allowed much more freedom over the accession and de-accession of artifacts (see Frey, 1994b). Consistent with these guidelines, the listing and scheduling of historical buildings and artifacts should be less restricted, allowing an easing of export controls and also giving the opportunity for modern architects to exploit their talents in modifying and extending old buildings. (There are copious examples of famous historical artifacts—the English cathedrals, Venetian Palazzi come to mind—which are valued artistically for their mixture of styles. Present-day planning restrictions in heritage-minded countries would make this artistic evolution difficult if not impossible today!)

This list is no more than an agenda for reform and the acceptability of individual suggestions will depend on the state of debate and official practice in individual countries. Thus (a) would be more of an issue in

European countries such as France, where the concept of culture is closely bound up with national prestige assumed by government-run arts and education institutions of all kinds. In the United Kingdom, the farming out of a large part of the built heritage administration in England and Scotland to nondepartmental public bodies and to executive agencies, which is at least compatible with (b), though looking rather unadventurous alongside the privatization revolution in the United Kingdom, but is far in advance of any similar developments in other EC countries. In contrast, while admission charges (cf. [c]) for state-supported museums and galleries are taken for granted in many countries, with exceptions for targeted groups such as children and pensioners, they have been violently opposed by museum directors of the older school, particularly from the British Museum, and their professional supporters (see Cannon-Brooks, 1996; Sewell, 1997). In contrast, well-known "national" theater, orchestral, and opera companies in the United Kingdom cast envious eyes at the relatively generous state subsidies in other EC countries and this reinforces their attempts to resist any move to make them more self-financing and emboldens them to seek "top-slice" funding from government expenditure on the performing arts.

It is proposal (d) that has already become the source of controversy in which conservationists, following the environmentalists' example, could seek to impose rules for identifying and preserving historical artifacts that imply both that they have the exclusive right to do so and assume that their judgments must prevail in measuring the social costs and benefits of heritage investment. A striking example is to be found in the acceleration in the discovery of movable artifacts and immovable sites through the growing use of the metal detector. Archeologists have sold the idea to national governments and even international cultural agencies, such as UNESCO, that "treasure trove" belongs to the nation, that compensation need not be paid to the finders, and that owners of land on which archeologists have identified sites of historical interest, even if these consist of a small pile of stones, may face restriction in their property rights. Even if one avoids the obvious question concerning the growing opportunity costs of the heritage policy underlying such measures, they have to be increasingly draconian if their objectives are to be achieved because they encourage widespread looting and illegal international trade in movable artifacts. They also cause friction between countries, national governments, and regional governments, not to speak of private individuals, about the access to the benefits of discovery (see, e.g., Giardina and Rizzo, 1994; Selkirk, 1997).

(iii) Public Participation in Decision-Making

The elaborate processes necessary to elicit public opinion on willingness to pay for cultural activities are designed, it would seem, to act as a substitute for referenda. Therefore, it has been asked, why not subject the government arts budget, or specific items of it, to the referendum process? Referenda could circumvent the principal-agent problem and restrict the discretionary power of arts bureaucrats. Referenda procedures require the public authorities to supply information, so reducing the costs to voters of participation in sensible and intelligent debate of the issues, and politicians and public officials can be forced to defend their proposals. Frey and Pommerehne (1989) elaborated this argument and have pointed to Swiss experience in Basel, where referenda were held on the purchase of Picasso paintings and on increases in subsidies to the municipal theater.

This proposal deserves more attention than given here, but I rule it out of practical consideration for two reasons. The first is that a case would have to be made for singling out the arts component of government budgets for special consideration. The second is that response to voter/taxpayer pressures, including the use of referenda, are likely to be more successful in confederations of the Swiss type than in centralized democracies and federations in which individual states are highly dependent on central government finance. Given the structure of government as a constraint, referenda might work in only a restricted form, for example, as a method of deciding on whether or not large individual projects should go ahead.

An alternative suggestion (Peacock, 1995) requires that there be direct public participation in the governance of those bodies that are publicly financed and are directly responsible to government for their operations. This is not simply an endorsement of the common arrangement by which "lay" persons are nominated to the boards of such bodies as well as co-opted as directors of government-financed performing arts companies and the like. There is no guarantee that nominees will be representative of public opinion. What I have in mind is an extension of the system by which heritage administrations, as in the United Kingdom, identify the public directly with their activities by calling upon it to subscribe to their support. This support should bring with it the right to elect representatives to the governing bodies, allowing the interested public to sensitize the experts to the views of those who are taxed or charged to publicly fund the arts, and to remind them that, while recognition of artistic quality may be reasonably assigned to them, aesthetic judgments are ultimately, by their very nature, subjective. This would hardly be a perfect solution, because the subscribing public may simply be a special set of "ax grinders," and may not perceive positive benefits to them from taking account of "option demand" and a view of the interests of future generations. But it is wholly compatible with the agenda for reform put forward in (ii) above.

V Concluding Remarks

An attempt to derive a case for subsidizing the arts from conventional welfare economics, assuming the objective of maximizing consumer satisfaction, is fraught with difficulties. Even if the analysis is extended to take account of choices which can only be expressed through the political system, and even leaving aside the difficulties of devising such a system to reflect individual choices completely, there can be no guarantee that there will be correspondence between what voters are prepared to pay by way of taxes to finance cultural activities and what those who claim to know about the benefits of cultural activities would consider to be the minimum expenditure obligations of government. The conventional view of welfare economics would imply that a government that accepted the latter position would be promoting a reduction in welfare, as well as adopting a patrician stance. However, a liberalist position is not bound by such a restrictive view. Liberals who firmly believe, as I do, that society would be worse off if the creative and performing arts languished under the threat of Baumol's disease, while accepting the judgment of the market and ballot box, are not obliged to like their verdict. Nor are they obliged to accept that they should subscribe to a welfare analysis that assumes away the possibility of changing preference structures. On the contrary, an essential element in a liberal society is that individuals should be free to adapt their tastes and preferences in the light of their cultural development and to allow those who believe that the arts are good for us to use reasonable means of persuasion. Of course, this view would be subscribed to by *cognoscenti* holding very different political positions, but the liberalist position is distinguished from others, as I have tried to demonstrate, by the emphasis placed on the strengthening of the direct link between artists and their public. The general aim of public subsidy should then be to achieve its own demise, so that the public becomes willing to support the arts from its own resources.

Bibliography

ACGB (Arts Council of Great Britain). 1991/1992. *Annual Report*. London: ACGB.

Baumol, W.J. 1996. "'Children of Performing Arts'—The Economic Dilemma: The Climbing Costs of Health Care and Education." *Journal of Cultural Economics* 20(3):183–206.

Baumol, W.J., and W.G. Bowen. 1966. *Performing Arts: The Economic Dilemma*. New York: Twentieth Century Fund.

Benhamou, F. 1996. "Is Increased Public Spending for the Preservation of Historic Monuments Inevitable: The French Case." *Journal of Cultural Economics* 20(2):115–132.

Brosio, G. 1994. "The Arts Industry: Problems of Measurement." In: A.T. Peacock and I. Rizzo (eds.), *Cultural Economics and Cultural Policies*, pp. 17–22. Dordrecht: Kluwer.

Cannon-Brooks, P. 1996. "Cultural-Economic Analyses of Art Museums: A British Curator's Viewpoint." In: V.A. Ginsburgh and P.-M. Menger (eds.), *Economics of the Arts*, pp. 255–274. Amsterdam: Elsevier.

"The Culture of Cultural Economics." 1994. Editorial of the *Journal of Cultural Economics* 18:1–2.

Feldstein, M. (ed.). 1991. *The Economics of Art Museums*. Chicago: University of Chicago Press.

Frey, B. 1994a. "Art: The Economic Point of View." In: A.T. Peacock and I. Rizzo (eds.), *Cultural Economics and Cultural Policies*, pp. 3–16. Dordrecht: Kluwer.

Frey, B. 1994b. "Cultural Economics and Museum Behaviour." *Scottish Journal of Political Economy* 41(3):325–335.

Frey, B., and W. Pommerehne. 1989. *Muses and Markets*. Oxford: Blackwell.

Fullerton, D. 1991. "On Public Justifications for Public Support of the Arts." *Journal of Cultural Economics* 15(2):67–82.

Giardina, E., and I. Rizzo. 1994. "Regulation in the Cultural Sector." In: A.T. Peacock and I. Rizzo (eds.), *Cultural Economics and Cultural Policies*, pp. 125–142. Dordrecht: Kluwer.

Heilbrun, J., and C.M. Gray. 1993. *The Economics of Art and Culture: An American Perspective*. Cambridge: Cambridge University Press.

MacQueen, H.L., and A.T. Peacock. 1995. "Implementing Performance Rights." *Journal of Cultural Economics* 19(2):157–175.

Musgrave, R.A. 1987. "Merit Goods." In: J. Eatwell, M. Milgate and P. Newman (eds.), *The New Palgrave Dictionary of Economics*. Volume 3, pp. 452–453. London: Macmillan.

Peacock, A.T. [1969] 1994. "Welfare Economics and Public Subsidies to the Arts." *Journal of Cultural Economics* 1(2):151–161.

Peacock, A.T. 1993. *Paying the Piper: Culture, Music and Money*. Edinburgh: Edinburgh University Press.

Peacock, A.T. 1995. "A Future for the Past: The Political Economy of Heritage." British Academy Keynes Lecture. In: *Proceedings of the British Academy*, Volume 87, pp. 187–243. Oxford: Oxford University Press.

Peacock, A.T. 1996. "The 'Manifest Destiny' of the Performing Arts." *Journal of Cultural Economics* 20(3):214–215.

Peacock, A.T. 1997. "Towards a Workable Heritage Policy." In: M. Hutter and I. Rizzo (eds.), *Economic Perspectives on Heritage*, pp. 225–235. London: Macmillan.

Peacock, A.T., and I. Rizzo (eds.). 1994. *Cultural Economics and Cultural Policies*. Dordrecht: Kluwer.

Pommerehne, W., A. Hart, and F. Schneider. 1997. "Tragic Choices and Collective Decision-Making: An Empirical Study of Voter Preferences for Alternative Collective Decision-Making Mechanisms." *Economic Journal* 107(May):618–635.

Robbins, L. 1993. *Politics and Economics: Papers in Political Economy*. London: Macmillan.

Scitovsky, T. 1983. "Subsidies for the Arts: The Economic Argument." In: W.S. Hendon and J.L. Shanahan (eds.), *Economics of Cultural Decisions*, pp. 6–15. Cambridge, Mass.: Abt Books.

Selkirk, A. 1997. *Who Owns the Past?* London: Adam Smith Insitute.

Sewell, B. 1997. "Admission Charges: An Argument Against." *Art Quarterly* (30):15–16.

Throsby, C.D. 1994a. "The Production and Consumption of the Arts: A View of Cultural Economics." *Journal of Economic Literature* 32(March):1–29.

Throsby, C.D. 1994b. "A Work-Preference Model of Artist Behaviour." In: A.T. Peacock and I. Rizzo (eds.), *Cultural Economics and Cultural Policies*, pp. 69–80. Dordrecht: Kluwer.

Throsby, C.D., and G.A. Withers. 1979. *The Economics of the Performing Arts*. London: Edward Arnold.

Tollison, R.D. 1989. "Chicago Political Economy." *Public Choice* 63(3):75–89.

Towse, R. 1993. *Singers in the Marketplace*. Oxford: Oxford University Press.

Trimarchi, M. 1993. *Economia e Cultura*. Milano: Franco Angeli.

West, E.G. 1985. *Subsidizing the Performing Arts*. Toronto: Ontario Economic Council.

Wittman, D. 1989. "Why Democracies Produce Efficient Results." *Journal of Political Economy* 97(Dec.):325–341.

Part III
Normative Issues of Global Trade

A Global Competition Policy for a Global Economy

Dennis C. Mueller

The growth of world trade since World War II and the decline in restrictions on international trade contained first in the GATT agreements, and now promulgated by the World Trade Organization (WTO), have produced what truly can be called "a global economy." The main targets of GATT and the WTO have been *government* restrictions on trade, however. As these have fallen and trade has expanded, the importance of *private* restrictions on trade has grown. What gain is there to a country that reduces a tariff on a product by 20%, if an export cartel promptly raises the price of the product by 20%?

The European Union recognized that its program of freeing trade across the borders of its member states had to be combined with an effective competition policy, just as the United States eventually recognized that its internal "free trade" policy needed an effective competition (antitrust) policy. An obvious parallel question given the rise of the global economy is whether we now need a global competition policy.

Scherer (1994) has recently answered this question in the affirmative, and proposed the creation of an International Competition Policy Office (ICPO) within the WTO, and a set of policies along with a timetable for implementing them. In this paper I shall not discuss the specific proposals Scherer made nor the exact timetable he proposed. I shall assume that an ICPO has been created, and that it can enforce a set of competition policies that resemble those of the European Union or the U.S. antitrust laws. The questions I wish to consider concern the extent to which the logic underlying national competition policies can

The financial support that the Ludwig Boltzmann Institut provided for this research is gratefully acknowledged.

be extended to defend an international competition policy, and some general issues that arise in the latter context that do not arise under national competition policies. In the first section, I take up the general goals of competition policy. The next four sections discuss the likely need for an international competition policy in each of its four, main traditional areas: collusion, monopolization, vertical restraints, and mergers. Section VI briefly draws some conclusions.

I   The Goals of Competition Policy

Bork (1978, pp. 61–66) has argued that the intent of the Sherman Act from its first passage was the promotion of consumer welfare, what we might now express as the maximization of consumers' surplus. More recently, however, Libecap (1992) has claimed that the driving force behind the passage of the Sherman Act was a coalition of businesses hurt by the rise of the great trusts. Regardless of which explanation best accounts for the adoption of the act, it is certainly the case that the issue of whether the antitrust laws *ought* to protect competitors or competition has been long debated in the United States (Bork, 1978, chs. 2, 3, 7). Any international competition policy would also need to resolve this fundamental question if it were to be implemented coherently.

The disappearance of unsuccessful competitors is a normal and healthy characteristic of the competitive process. Any set of policies designed to protect and promote competition will inevitably lead to the disappearance of firms unable to compete in the market. Such disappearances can cause considerable personal hardship, of course, and the state has a legitimate role to play in reducing these hardships. Unemployment insurance is an example of one such policy. Others would include tax deductions for expenses incurred searching for a new job, moving to take up a new job, and so on. Retraining programs and in extreme cases state subsidies for firms in situations in which a firm's departure would impose large losses on a community are still others. A coherent set of policies to promote competition would prohibit all private and governmental actions that harmed the competitive process, while allowing individuals and governments the freedom to mitigate the risks from competition through private and public insurance schemes. The "costs of competition" would be borne by private citizens through their savings and purchases of insurance, or by the taxpayers. They would not be borne by consumers in the form of higher prices to subsidize inefficient firms.[1]

Compared with most other countries, it can be said that U.S. anti-trust policy has been geared more closely toward protecting competi-tion than toward protecting competitors. Even in this country, how-ever, exceptions have been made with respect to cartels or workers (labor unions), farmers, oddly enough baseball team owners, and most significantly exporters. In Europe, national policies protect workers and farmers from competition, and EU competition policy exempts small and medium size firms from its anticartel provisions. Many other laws, like those regarding shop opening hours, are clearly intended to protect some groups from competition. The same can be said for most other countries. An international competition policy that sought to protect competition but not competitors would run against the domes-tic policies of many countries.

Many national policies to protect competitors are harmful to con-sumers only in the countries implementing them, however. Austrian consumers suffer from high shop prices and inconvenient shopping hours, because of its laws, but these do not affect consumers in other countries. Thus, many domestic policies could be left to stand, and much conflict between ICPO and WTO member governments avoided, if the ICPO's goal were clearly defined as that of promoting *inter-national* competition, and any national policies that harmed only the consumers or taxpayers of the nation implementing them were ignored. A strict interpretation of protecting international competition would logically condemn some worker and farmer cartels, but political prudence would suggest not requiring an ICPO to take on these. With these exceptions, the simplest and easiest goal to defend for an ICPO would be the protection of international competition against those practices by private parties and governments that harm international buyers. These practices can be conveniently grouped into four main categories. I begin with cartel arrangements.

---

[1] In this regard, current European Union policy that forbids member countries and regional governments from subsidizing their local firms is mistaken, and forces these governments to try to protect their firms in other ways that are det-rimental to the competitive process. For a discussion of when and why subsidies for firms can be justified, see Mueller (1997b).

II   Collusion

No components of the U.S. antitrust laws enjoys broader and more unequivocal support among economists than Section I of the Sherman Act prohibiting collusive agreements. Cartels are such blatant devices to benefit producers at buyers' expense that the courts in the United States have come to regard collusive agreements as *per se* illegal. The plaintiff need not prove that the collusive agreement harms consumers or the competitive process. The mere existence of the agreement suffices to condemn it. Although Article 85 of the Treaty of Rome that defines the European Union's policy with respect to collusion does not impose a *per se* criterion on the Commission, this article has nevertheless been vigorously enforced against collusive agreements, *at least against such agreements between larger companies.* European competition policy, like U.S. antitrust policy from time to time, has failed to condemn collusive practices when they have been adopted by small and medium size firms (George and Jacquemin, 1990, pp. 209–222). Indeed, it explicitly allows for such exemptions (Martin, 1994, p. 555). Since it is difficult to contemplate a meaningful world competition policy that would not include and strictly enforce an anticartel provision, I shall assume that this would be the overriding goal of a global competition policy.

Most obviously an anticartel rule would have to apply to companies based in different countries. But equally obviously, it should also apply to companies based in a single country if their anticompetitive actions harm consumers in other countries. *Thus, all export cartels would have to be challengeable.*

In many cases, international cartels have been aided or even organized by the governments of the main producing nations; the OPEC cartel was perhaps the most dramatic and for a while the most successful of these. Once again, it seems obvious that an agency charged with the task of breaking up international cartels must have the authority to challenge international agreements to set prices, regardless of whether they are initiated by private firms or by the governments of their countries. If an ICPO did not have this power, any private firms that wanted to form a cartel would be able to do so, so long as their government(s) was (were) willing to sponsor the cartel. Such an arrangement, in turn, would favor those countries whose governments are more closely entwined with their "private" sectors, which in general would be the less democratic and less capitalistic countries. Such an arrangement would not encourage developing countries to speed up their adoption of democratic and market institutions. It is difficult to see, therefore, how an international anticartel policy could effectively protect competition if it could not attack both privately and publicly constituted cartels.

III Monopolization

What several autonomous organizations cannot achieve in concert, a single organization can sometimes achieve on its own. A single overwhelmingly dominant firm in a market would almost certainly charge a price far above the potential competitive price, even if it fell short of the pure monopoly price.[2] The mere existence of an overwhelmingly dominant firm in a market would therefore seem to demand intervention in the form of either regulation or dissolution.

Although Learned Hand's decision in *Alcoa* (1945) might be interpreted as declaring the mere existence of overwhelming market dominance as a violation of Section II of the Sherman Act,[3] subsequent court decisions have not condemned the possession of market power per se (e.g., *Berkey Photo Inc. v. Eastman Kodak Company*, 1979). Some *action* by the dominant firm to create or *preserve* market power in a way which is harmful to competition has been demanded. Such reluctance to attack dominant firms can be consistent with the advancement of consumer interests if one assumes that the firm achieved its dominance by superior efficiency or innovative activity (Bork, 1978, pp, 67–69).

The creation of a monopoly through the acquisition of one's competitors is, perhaps, the most transparent act of monopolization that is unlikely to advance consumer interests. Indeed, mergers falling well short of producing a monopoly are likely to run counter to the goal of advancing efficiency and social welfare. These shall be left for Section V, however.

---

[2] An exception would be a monopolist in a perfectly contestable market (Baumol, Panzer, and Willig, 1982). Where dominant firms are found, however, their markets do not seem to meet the criteria for perfect contestability.

[3] Hand's famous utterance that "no monopolist monopolizes unconscious of what it is doing" would seem to make every conscious action of a monopolist a willful monopolization, and thus be in violation of a literal reading of the statute.

Table 1. Market Shares and Profits of Dominant U.S. Companies

Company	M_{50}	π_{50}	π_p	π_{94}
Campbell Soup	63.2	0.05	0.56	0.67
Caterpillar	48.2	0.05	0.72	0.29
Coca Cola	30.2	0.34	0.98	2.24
Gillette	43.4	1.41	1.58	0.85
Hershey Foods	38.1	0.64	0.72	0.63
IBM	47.9	0.01	1.10	−1.40
Kellogg	20.5	0.82	1.20	1.77
Procter & Gamble	29.9	0.37	0.86	0.05
Tecumseh Products	38.7	0.78	0.93	0.39
Wm. Wrigley, Jr.	52.8	0.44	0.63	2.67

Source: Mueller (1986, pp. 34–35; 1997a).

Other than mergers, the most transparent acts of monopolization fall under the heading of *predation*, efforts by a dominant firm to drive its competitors from the market. Such actions are likely to be particularly contentious in an international environment. If a dominant international firm must predate to maintain its position, the targets of its predation will often be competitors in other countries. Natural empathy for the underdog combines with chauvinistic sentiment for domestic over foreign producers to produce a potentially explosive situation. If local competition policy proscribes predation, one can expect considerable pressure on local authorities to try the dominant, international firm. Although it would not be able to dissolve a company outside of its borders, it could presumably introduce fines and proscribe particular actions deemed to be predatory. If many countries initiated actions against the dominant firm, it would find itself embroiled in countless legal struggles which could dissipate its resources and divert its management's attention from the important task of running the company efficiently.

The history of dominant firms in the United States leads one to the following observations: (1) Dominant firms often do charge prices substantially above their marginal and average costs, and thus earn substantially higher profits than other companies. The first column of Table 1, labeled M_{50}, reports the market shares in 1950 for a set of dominant firms in the 1950s and 1960s. Although no single source exists that reports the market shares of these companies in later years, it is known that they maintained or increased their market positions following 1950. Column 3, labeled π_p, lists the long-run projected returns on capital for these companies. These projections were made using data for the 1950–1972 period, and are projections to time equals infinity measured as a deviation from the sample mean. Thus, based on its 1950–1972 profits record, I projected that IBM would earn an after-tax return on its total assets that was 110% greater than that of the average manufacturing firm into the indefinite future.[4] The columns labeled π_{50} and π_{94} list the deviations from the sample mean for returns on capital for these firms in the initial years of the earlier study (1950–1952) and for two recent years (1993–1994). Although IBM lost its dominant position in computers and thus by the 1990s was no longer one of the most profitable U.S. companies, other market leaders like Caterpillar, Campbell Soup, Gillette, and Wm. Wrigley did succeed in maintaining both their positions of market dominance and their high profitability.

Observation number two is that the inordinate profits of dominant firms often lead to efforts by other companies to capture these profits. Observation 3 is that the dominant firm often puts up a fight to avoid losing its market position and the profits that go with it. So it was with IBM in the late 1960s as new entrants into the "peripherals markets" for equipment that attached to computer mainframes brought out clones of IBM products, and sold them at substantial discounts below IBM's prices. IBM responded with vigor, and the peripherals manufacturers were driven from the market into the court room, where they accused IBM of predatory behavior.

Whether one judges IBM to have been guilty of predation or not depends on the definition of predation one adopts, the interpretation one gives to the facts, and perhaps the weight one places on the arguments put forward by the economists IBM hired, versus those of the economists who worked on the government's side (Brock, [1989] 1994; Fisher, McGowan, and Greenwood, 1983). Regardless of how one views the facts and outcomes of the IBM cases, however, one must conclude that such cases raise extremely difficult issues of fact and

---

[4] The average was based on my sample of 551 manufacturing companies. This sample was drawn from the largest companies in the economy and thus should have approximated the average for all of manufacturing companies fairly closely.

interpretation, and are likely to be particularly difficult to arbitrate in an international context.

IBM was able to win all of the private antitrust suits filed against it, in large part because the courts accepted the definition of predatory action put forward by two law professors hired to testify on IBM's behalf. Areeda and Turner (1975) recommended that a firm be presumed not to have engaged in predatory behavior, so long as it did not charge a price less than either its short-run marginal costs or its short-run average costs. Such a definition of predation places exclusive weight on allowing welfare-enhancing transactions in the short run. While buyers are clearly better off in the short run if dominant firms are allowed to cut their prices below their and their smaller rivals' long-run average costs, buyers may be worse off in the long run if the small firms disappear and the dominant firm returns to a high price/ high profit strategy.

The adoption of the Areeda–Turner definition of predation by a global competition policy authority would result in few successful convictions of dominant firms. Countries would see local firms arise and offer cheaper versions of the products sold by giant international companies, and then would have to standby and watch their local heroes driven into oblivion by the international companies. The wisdom of such a lax standard for predation is likely to escape the recognition of the countries whose local firms have departed if the large international firm subsequently chooses to raise its prices. In an international context, therefore, a rather tough attitude toward predatory behavior would seem to be warranted. One such approach has been outlined by Joskow and Klevorick (1979). They would allow firms to be convicted even when they charged prices above their short-run marginal or average costs, so long as these prices were below their long-run average costs and it appeared that the dominant firm was purposefully pursuing a policy of driving its competitors from the market, and that this policy was likely to succeed in both this objective and to result in higher prices in the long run.

The approach to predation advocated by Joskow and Klevorick is more in line with the language of the Sherman Act and its enforcement since 1890 than that of Areeda and Turner. It also probably provides greater scope for conviction. Nevertheless, convictions would likely be rare in an international context. Proving the existence of high entry barriers in a global economy should be more difficult than doing so at the domestic level. Moreover, any future rise to world dominance by a company is likely to be based largely on technological leadership. In such instances a predatory strategy of a dominant firm will typically not be restricted to charging lower prices than its rivals, but will involve combinations of changes in technology, product design, and pricing formula—as was alleged in the cases brought against IBM, and has been alleged against IBM's heir to dominance in computer products, Microsoft.

Gazing forward during the closing days of the Johnson Administration in the late 1960s, one might well have predicted that, left alone, IBM would continue or even extend its dominance over the computer industry, and that only the dissolution of this giant through a successful Sherman Act case would restore competition in this industry. Anyone who made that prediction was proved wrong. IBM missed the onset of the personal computer revolution, and has yet to make up for this mistake. Indeed, one might argue that if the U.S. government had pressed its case against IBM, and won a quick dissolution, one of the ensuing parts of IBM would have probably recognized the potential of the PC, and the antitrust suit would have had the opposite effect of what was intended.[5] Be that as it may, the history of the computer industry suggests that projections of future performance in technologically progressive industries are far more difficult to make than in the soft drinks and chewing gum industries. He who bets on Microsoft being a dominant firm with supernormal profits 25 years from now faces big odds.

This being the case it is tempting to conclude that there would be no need for a global policy with respect to dominant firm predatory practices. The forces of technological change and Schumpeterian competition will suffice to eliminate positions of dominance before the force of a global competition policy could reasonably be expected to have an effect. Such an attitude toward predation would be further justified to the extent that one accepts the argument, put forward by some, that

---

[5] Comanor and Scherer (1995) have made such an argument with respect to the breakup of Standard Oil of New Jersey's monopoly in 1911. The resulting components proved much more successful at growing and generating profits than did the United States Steel company, which avoided dissolution with a 1920 victory against the government.

predation is seldom a rational policy on the part of a dominant firm.[6] If a dominant firm is unlikely to succeed in maintaining or extending its dominance in a single country, how could it hope to do so across the world?

To ignore predation in a global competition policy would, however, be a mistake for several reasons. (1) Because future dominance in world markets is likely to rest on technological superiority, any firms achieving such dominance can be expected to be based in one of the technologically progressive, highly developed countries. The products it sells will be very highly priced relative to income levels in some developing countries. The incentive for local firms to copy the dominant firm's products, and sell them at a fraction of the price of the foreign firm will be strong. A policy of benign neglect to any attempts by the dominant firm to stomp out such competition is likely to be interpreted as politically motivated. Developing countries would deem global competition policy to be stacked in favor of the global economic powers.

(2) Efforts by local firms to copy the products of a dominant international company often involve infringements on patents and/or trademarks. Both technologically progressive firms and their host countries have a strong incentive to curtail such infringements. Having a strong antimonopoly/antipredation component of a global competition should help in getting the governments of developing countries to police international patent and copyright laws.

(3) The most important reason for having a strong antipredation policy as part of an international competition policy, however, would be that it would allow, *indeed logically compel*, the repeal of all antidumping laws (Scherer, 1994, pp. 78–87). Although the exclusive focus of Areeda and Turner on the short-run pricing behavior of a dominant

---

[6] See, McGee (1958), Bork (1978, pp. 144–160), and Elzinga ([1989] 1994). These arguments are based on calculations of likely losses in the short run and gains in the long run from predation through price cutting, under the assumption that the dominant firm must reduce its price on all of the units it sells. As already noted, price reductions are typically only part of the predatory policy of a firm that owes its dominance to technological leadership. It also often faces competition in only some of its markets. Substantial losses in these may be a cost effective way to signal to potential entrants into other markets that such entry would be a mistake.

firm cannot be defended, if one wants an effective policy against predation, the intuition behind their proposal—that low prices are *ceteris paribus* to be welcomed—is definitely right. If the dominant firm cannot achieve a monopoly and subsequently raise prices, then consumer welfare is advanced by the competitive struggle between the dominant firm and its rivals. Antidumping cases often resemble predation cases in that they revolve around comparisons of prices and costs. As with predation cases, the basic complaint is that prices are too low. But the goal of international trade and an international competition policy is low prices. Antidumping laws are inevitably intended to protect *competitors* rather than consumers or competition and thus are antithetical to the fundamental goals of free trade and an international competition policy. If this competition policy contained a strong antipredation component, one would be assured that any alleged dumping by foreign firms would benefit domestic consumers in the short run, and would not harm them in the long run. Any harm done to domestic competitors should either be ignored as part of the normal competitive process, or offset by subsidies for the domestic producers (Mueller, 1997b).

IV Vertical Restraints

Various vertical restrictions on trade have been proscribed by both the U.S. antitrust laws and the EU competition policy. A large literature has now evolved that argues that these practices are benign if not beneficial with respect to the competitive process (Bork, 1978, chs. 14, 15, 19, 20; Klein and Saft, 1985; Marvel, 1982; Marvel and McCafferty, 1984, 1985; Warren-Boulton, [1989] 1994), and Posner (1976) and Bork (1978) have, on the basis of this literature, argued that the relevant sections of the Clayton Act should be repealed. I shall not go deeply into this debate, but rather focus on some of the issues that come up in an international context.

A Price Discrimination

A firm that has any market power will maximize its profits by setting prices for its products that satisfy the following equation:

$$(P_i - C_i)/P_i = 1/e_i,$$

where P_i is the price charged for the product, C_i the marginal cost of producing it, and e_i is the price elasticity of the firm's demand schedule for this product. This equation is, of course, the familiar Lerner index of monopoly power with the exception that the elasticity of *the firm's demand schedule* replaces that of the industry's demand schedule. Any firm that possesses some market power and can divide its customers into separate groups and charge them different prices will try to do so if the groups have different demand elasticities or there are different costs in supplying them. Not surprisingly, one finds that price discrimination is ubiquitous, ranging from theaters charging different prices for seats, to liquor companies charging significantly different prices for brands of liquor that have only modest differences in production costs.

International firms with market power can be expected to engage in considerable price discrimination also. Markets are geographically and legally separated, and demand elasticities can be expected to differ greatly across countries with tastes and incomes. The costs of supplying different countries may also differ. One should not be surprised to find large differences in both the prices that international firms charge for their products in different countries, and in their price-cost margins. Differences in price-cost margins would constitute price discrimination under an *economic* definition of this action.

Both U.S. and European competition policies do not employ an economic definition of price discrimination, however, but rather define price discrimination as charging different prices for the same product. In the United States a firm can defend itself against a charge of price discrimination if it can justify its prices on the basis of differences in the costs of supplying the different customers. Experience with the U.S. policy has revealed that it is often very difficult to establish such a cost-based defense.[7]

The cases that have been brought against firms accused of price discrimination either under the 1914 Clayton Act or the 1938 Robinson–Patman Act amendment form the least edifying and least economically defensible chapter in the U.S. antitrust history (Edwards, 1959; Scherer and Ross, 1990, pp. 508–516). In this area of antitrust, more than in any other, the enforcement of the antitrust laws have

---

[7] The second line of defense, "meeting an equally low price of a competitor," has been the more successful of the two options allowed under the law.

worked to protect competitors rather than competition. Where competition *is* protected by protecting competitors, as in predation cases and mergers, other policies can be effectively employed. A global competition policy should not include special provisions against price discrimination.

B   Resale Price Maintenance

It is common practice in many industries for a manufacturer to demand a promise from the retailers selling its product that they charge the price for it set by the manufacturer. Such policies often arise as part of a cartel arrangement among the retailers. Being large in number, they require that someone run the cartel for them. A large manufacturer is an obvious choice. Manufacturers may also stand to benefit from such cartels in that vigorous competition at the retail level sometimes works its way back to the manufacturing level. Retailers complain to the manufacturer that they cannot survive in the face of the competition occurring at the retail level unless the manufacturer cuts its price to the retailer. By fixing the price charged by all of its retailers, the manufacturer averts the possibility that competition at the retail level gets "out of hand" and forces retailers to cut prices.

Since retail price maintenance involves a cartel among retailers, it can in principle be challenged under an anticartel policy. In fact, many countries that have competition policies, like France and Germany, sanction resale price maintenance agreements in some areas, like book sales, and France has recently introduced additional legislation to protect its small retailers from competition from large retailers (*Economist*, 1996). Such measures are obviously harmful to consumers, as is retail price maintenance when it exists to protect retailers from competition (Marvel and McCafferty, 1984, 1985; Warren-Boulton, [1989] 1994). But the costs of these restrictions on competition fall entirely on the consumers of the country that introduces them. They do not directly harm international competition. Any attempts by retailers to form cross-border cartels and to require that resale price maintenance agreements be implemented multinationally should be easy to observe, and could be challenged under the anticartel provisions of a global competition policy. There is no compelling reason for a global competition policy to concern itself with resale price maintenance as such.

C   Territorial Restrictions

In addition to setting prices at the retail level to protect its retailers, manufacturers have also placed geographic restrictions on where retailers can locate and even to whom they can sell. Thus, automobile manufacturers have forbidden their Belgium dealers to sell cars to citizens of other European Union countries. As with resale price maintenance, an efficiency rationale can be given for some forms of territorial constraints, but they may also be intended to protect both retailers and manufacturers from competition. Both car manufacturers and their retailers probably have benefited from the higher prices that have existed in some EU countries.

To achieve the benefits of free trade, manufacturers should be allowed to sell their products in different countries without restrictions. These benefits may also be forthcoming if retailers are free to make cross-border sales, and consumers can cross borders to take advantage of lower prices. Territorial restrictions on sales imposed by manufacturers, when defined along national lines, restrict the free flow of goods and services precisely as do restrictions imposed by governments. A competition policy which banned cross-national territorial restrictions by manufacturers would be a natural complement to reductions in tariffs, quotas, and other governmental restrictions on international trade.

D   Exclusive Dealing and Tying Agreements

Tying agreements have been most frequently employed as a means for engaging in price discrimination. For example, IBM originally required that users of its computers purchase from IBM the cards used to read in data. By overpricing its cards, IBM was able to charge large users of its computers higher prices than small users. A firm cannot successfully employ a tying arrangement unless it has considerable market power in the tied product's market, otherwise consumers will simply purchase the products of rivals which do not require tie-ins. Thus, these sorts of tying arrangements raise the same issue as other forms of price discrimination raise. For the same reason, they are probably best ignored. None of the other possible anticompetitive effects of tying arrangements arise frequently enough, or have sufficient anticompetitive effects to warrant an ICPO's attention. Tying arrangements can also safely be neglected by such a global competition authority.

Exclusive dealing contracts between manufacturers and retailers are harmful to competition only to the extent that they *foreclose* distribution outlets to new entrants into a market, thereby raising entry barriers. For example, if all existing automobile retailers in a country are contractually tied to particular automobile manufacturers, an automobile manufacturer that wishes to begin selling in this country will not be able to find an existing retailer to handle its cars. It will have to develop its own network of retailers, which raises the cost of its entering this country considerably.

Exclusive dealing arrangements are only profitable for firms that can generate large sales volume through single outlets to allow the retailers to survive by selling only the products of the manufacturer, as for example, automobile and farm machinery manufacturers, petroleum companies, and the like. On an international level, such companies are quite large. In the long run, the costs of running one dealer network are the same as for another. Thus, if it is profitable in the long run for one of these large international firms to enter the market of a particular country, the need to make up front investments to establish a dealer network should not constitute a significant entry barrier. Exclusive dealing arrangements are also not prime candidates for inclusion in a global competition policy.

E   Refusals to Deal

In a vertical production chain in which the output of industry A is used in the production of B which is distributed by firms in C, competition can be hurt by a dominant firm in A refusing to sell to firms in B, and by firms in C refusing to buy from B. In an international context, these possibilities are of interest if A, B, and C are located in different countries.

In general, a firm is not going to make more profits by *refusing to* sell its product in some countries than by selling it. An upstream firm's refusal to sell to buyers in other countries could only be part of a profit-maximizing strategy, therefore, if the upstream firm was attempting to drive downstream firms out of business and thereby create a monopoly for itself over several parts or all of the vertical chain. Such a strategy would be an obvious attempt to monopolize and could be challenged as predatory behavior. Special rules regarding refusals to sell are not necessary in a global competition policy.

Refusals to *buy* are quite another matter, however. Such actions can create significant barriers to entry in countries where companies adopt refusal-to-deal policies, and thereby constitute a barrier to trade. One example of this would be the refusal of retailers in *C* to handle products from manufacturers in *B*. There are good normal business reasons why some retailers refuse to handle some manufacturers' goods. For example, a retailer that specializes in upmarket cosmetics might refuse to stock cheaper brands out of the belief that its customers would be unlikely to purchase them, and that its image as an upmarket store would be adversely affected if it did sell these products. A refusal by *all* of the retailers in a country to carry the products of a foreign firm is unlikely to be the result of independent, profit-maximizing behavior, assuming of course that the quality and prices of the products would make them competitive in this country. Concerted refusals to deal of this type would seem possible only as part of an agreement that included all retailers and perhaps also domestic manufacturers seeking to avoid competition from foreign producers. Since domestic competition policies will not always proscribe such agreements, and domestic competition policy authorities might for obvious reasons be reluctant to attack them even if they could, such refusals to deal must be subject to challenge by an ICPO. They would certainly fall under an anticartel rule, but might be explicitly prohibited to facilitate the ICPO's ability to challenge them.

An explicit prohibition against refusals to deal could also be used to challenge the policies of single, large monopsonistic buyers, like a country's telephone company, major utilities and railroads, and even the government itself. In these instances, no cartel as such exists, but a *conspiracy* of sorts is suspected between the buyer and the domestic suppliers of competing products. Such conspiracies are equally harmful to competition when they are politically motivated as when they are economically motivated. As with resale price maintenance agreements, the prime losers from these sorts of refusals to deal are the consumers and taxpayers in the country engaged in these practices, however. Unlike international cartels, the adverse effects do not spread across countries. The extent to which a global competition authority should concern itself with refusals to buy depends, therefore, very much on whether its mission is only to protect *international* competition from the practices of international firms, or whether it is also charged with the task of protecting consumers within a country from its domestic firms and even from its own government.[8]

V Mergers

The passage of the Sherman Antitrust Act in 1890 and the subsequent enforcement of its anticartel provisions arguably contributed to the first great merger wave in the United States (Bittlingmayer, 1985). The more stringently cartels are policed, the greater the incentives firms have to merge. An effective global competition policy will need to prevent anticompetitive mergers. In addition to their adverse effects on competition, mergers can harm social welfare by *reducing* the efficiency of the merging firms.[9] Since these two effects of mergers raise somewhat different issues with respect to a global competition policy, I will discuss them separately. I begin with anticompetitive mergers, broken down into the customary three categories of horizontal, vertical, and conglomerate mergers.

A Horizontal Mergers

Just as a cartel among exporters can benefit not only the companies which are members of the cartel, but also their countries of origin, a merger between companies that control a large fraction of a world market can lead to higher prices harming buyers in the importing countries while perhaps benefiting the exporting countries. Any hori-

---

[8] For a skeptical review of the significance of these sorts of vertical restraints to trade with respect to automobiles and film in Japan, see Scherer (1997).

[9] Although some studies have found small increases in profits for merging firms, most have found that the profits of merging companies either do not change or decline, on average, after the mergers. The significant gains in wealth to shareholders of acquired companies at the time of the mergers are subsequently offset, or more than offset by losses borne by the shareholders of the acquiring companies. The growth rates and market shares of merging firms decline after the mergers. This literature is reviewed in Mueller ([1977] 1991, 1996), Caves (1989), and Ross and Scherer (1990, pp. 167–174).

zontal merger involving companies that account for a large fraction of a world market should be challengeable under a global competition policy. In a recent paper, I have proposed that any domestic merger between a company with 20% or more of a market, and a second firm with 5% or more of the market should be presumed in violation of an antimerger statute, *subject to an efficiency defense* (Mueller, 1996). A reasonable global policy toward mergers would look similar, but would calculate market shares relative to world production.[10] Such a policy would ban all mergers between firms possessing the designated market shares, but would allow them to go forward if the merging firms could demonstrate that the merger promised a net welfare gain because the cost savings due to greater efficiency more than offset any consumer surplus losses from higher prices.

The most obvious efficiency to expect from a horizontal merger is through the realization of scale economies. While such economies might be sufficiently large to justify mergers between companies serving a domestic market, where market shares are measured relative to this market, few if any industries have such gigantic scale economies that they need large shares of world production to obtain minimum efficient size.[11] Thus, few if any horizontal mergers that exceeded the market share limits of the regulation would be likely to present a successful efficiencies defense based on economies of scale if the market shares were measured relative to world production. Although market share thresholds like 20% and 5% are somewhat arbitrary, when measured relative to the size of world markets they certainly do not seem excessive.

A merger that did not pass a market share test like the one above would be expected to have the same adverse effect on world competition when the merging firms are located in the same country as when they are in different countries. Thus, a global competition policy would

---

[10] In some cases, a domestic market might be so large relative to world production that a purely domestic merger would violate the global standard. A company's world market share should then be calculated as its total sales less its domestic sales divided by world production in this market less domestic production. For companies producing in more than one country, this adjustment could only be made for its largest domestic market.

[11] For evidence of the magnitude of scale economies relative to market sizes, see Scherer et al. (1975).

have to be capable of blocking "domestic" mergers when the merging firms account for sufficiently high shares of world sales. A good example of a merger that might result in a sufficient increase in market power to benefit not only the merging companies, but also their home country, is the recent Boeing/McDonnell–Douglas merger.

B   Vertical Mergers

Vertical mergers can have anticompetitive consequences by raising entry barriers into vertically integrated markets. The possibility of achieving such dominance in a world market is unlikely to arise in any industries other than those linked to minerals and other natural resources. An antimerger regulation like the one discussed in the previous subsection would effectively deal with vertical mergers, where the market shares would now pertain to firms vertically linked in a production chain.

C   Conglomerate Mergers

Several studies have found that companies that compete against one another in several separate markets tend to have higher profit rates and higher prices than one would predict based on their market shares and industry concentration levels (Scott, 1982, 1993; Evans and Kessides, 1994). *Multimarket contact* appears to facilitate collusion and cooperation between rivals. These results based on diversification within national boundaries imply that international diversification might also have anticompetitive effects if the multinational companies were diversified into similar markets in the same set of countries.

One way to deal with the adverse consequences of multimarket contact would be to treat it as a form of collusion, and challenge it under the regulations dealing with cartel behavior. If, however, multimarket contact only facilitates *tacit* collusion between firms, as the empirical evidence suggests may be true, a global competition policy authority which found a group of multinationals guilty of collusion would have to do so on the basis of evidence suggesting higher prices or price-cost margins in some countries than in others. As discussed in connection with price discrimination, such evidence is costly to come by, and decisions to fine or break up international firms based on such evidence would likely be highly controversial.

A simpler approach would be to prevent multimarket contact from arising in the first place by prohibiting the mergers that bring it about. Such an approach would also be fraught with difficulties, however, if the ICPO had to prove that a particular diversification merger was likely to have substantial anticompetitive effects. For such a demonstration, the ICPO would have to be able to determine the number of markets and countries in which a set of multinationals must jointly compete for multimarket contact to be raised to an undesirable level. Any policy that prevented some companies from undertaking mergers that would "merely" allow them to duplicate the international diversification patterns of their chief rivals would appear arbitrary to the companies prevented from merging, and most likely to the governments of their countries of origin. Such a policy would again be likely to embroil an ICPO in considerable controversy.

An alternative way to prevent those diversification mergers that lead to anticompetitive increases in multimarket contact would be simply to ban all mergers between firms above some absolute size, again subject to an efficiencies defense. I have proposed such a ban as part of a domestic antimerger policy (Mueller, 1996). Since only very large multinationals could achieve significant multimarket contact, a size-related ban would prevent those mergers that were most likely to achieve significant multimarket contact.

Although such a policy would obviously target the mergers of large multinationals, it would not prevent firms from becoming large multinationals *if significant economies can be achieved from running large, diversified international firms.* If significant economies of scope can be achieved, let us say, from jointly producing and marketing cigarettes, beer, coffee, and chocolate, then a firm could achieve these economies through either internal expansion or merger in its domestic market. It would also not be prevented from achieving these economies on an international basis, if it chose to do so by building breweries, chocolate factories, and the like in other countries. It would only be prevented from growing as a multinational by *buying* existing breweries and chocolate manufacturers, *unless* it could demonstrate that such mergers were likely to result in significantly lower costs and prices. If significant economies of scope could be achieved by combining these activities, then the would-be multinational would presumably already be experiencing them in its diversified operations in its home country. All it would have to do to justify a similar international diversification effort would be to show that it had lower costs and prices than its rivals in its home market.

D Efficiency-Reducing Mergers

Efficiency-reducing mergers can occur for a variety of reasons: to fulfill the empire-building desires of managers, to fill the pockets of promoters and speculators, out of managerial hubris, etc. (Markham, 1955; Mueller, [1969] 1991, 1996; Roll, 1986). Even when the speculators and managers gain from the mergers, the shareholders of the acquiring companies lose. Society loses also, because the efforts of managers of acquisition-oriented firms are diverted from creating assets to transferring them, and because the mergers often go awry destroying the assets of once healthy companies. The many studies that find that mergers reduce profits, market shares, and shareholder wealth imply that society would gain from the prevention of these mergers.[12]

A ban of all mergers between firms above some absolute size, subject to an efficiencies defense, would also prevent those efficiency-reducing mergers that occur across borders. These might be many or few, depending on where one drew the size threshold. Should it prove difficult to meet the efficiencies defense, conceivably some mergers that would have been socially beneficial would not occur. But so, too, would many that would have reduced efficiency and harmed most likely those living in the country of the target firm. Given that internal expansion is always an alternative to merger, and one which is *sure to create* assets and jobs in the short run, whereas a merger merely *transfers* assets and jobs in the short run and may or may not create them in the long run, society would not lose from a ban of large international mergers.

VI Conclusions

The challenges in establishing and enforcing a global competition policy are at once considerably greater and smaller than for an individual country. They are greater in that for an individual country the winners and losers from the application of a competition policy are both gen-

---

[12] See again the references in fn. 9.

erally located within the country. Any protest about the application of the policy by those who are harmed by it will to some extent be drowned out by the applause of the gainers. Politicians can deflect the protests of the losers to some extent by eliciting the support of the gainers. Since the net gains to a community from the enforcement of competition policies are positive in the long run, popular support for such policies may reasonably be expected to develop over time, even though particular policy decisions may become the focus of much controversy.

On the other hand, even within countries, a political imbalance between the gainers and losers from competition policy often exists, because the losers are typically the owners and possibly the employees of companies that are prevented from enjoying the rents engendered by monopolistic practices, while the immediate or ultimate beneficiaries are consumers. Thus, the losses are concentrated upon relatively small and well-organized groups, while the gains are spread widely and thinly over a politically poorly organized group. This political disparity helps explain the strength and venerability of laws and regulations protecting workers and workers' cartels in Europe relative to European competition policies and other forms of consumer protection.

This political disparity is even more pronounced with respect to international trade and competition. In the international arena the gains from anticompetitive policies accrue to firms and workers in one set of countries, the losses they generate fall mainly on those in other countries. Thus, not surprisingly one finds countries like the United States, which has relatively consistently and vigorously enforced a domestic anticartel policy, simultaneously allowing domestic firms to form cartels when the victims are buyers in other countries.

The growth in prosperity that has accompanied the liberalization and expansion of world trade over the last 50 years should be ample proof that "free trade" causes, or at least is compatible with, economic prosperity. As the process of liberalization continues to expand with more countries entering the WTO and additional barriers to trade falling, the need for an effective global competition policy grows. Little is to be gained from falling tariffs if cartels are free to substitute their restrictive practices for those of the state.

Up to the present, states have generally allowed their firms to participate in internationally oriented cartels, often encouraged and supported such participation, and sometimes have even organized and run the cartels. The most conspicuous example of the latter has been, of course, the OPEC cartel. The increases in the price of oil that this cartel brought about in the 1970s helped precipitate a major world recession from which Western Europe arguably has never fully recovered. Billions of dollars of assets were destroyed or failed to be created as unemployment rose and investment fell around the world. The value of the assets destroyed by the cartel was undoubtedly far greater than the participating countries could have destroyed had they gone to war against the rest of the world. So long as countries and companies are free to form cartels and engage in other sorts of anti-competitive practices, the growth in wealth of the nations of the world will be hindered. The most difficult challenge facing a global competition policy is to convince governmental leaders of the advantages of such a policy.

This challenge is made somewhat easier by the fact that the full panoply of competition policies that have been tried and are perhaps warranted in the context of an individual country is not required to preserve competition on a global level. I have identified three major components of such a policy: (1) an anticartel policy that can be applied to international cartels, domestic export and import cartels, and government operated cartels; (2) an antimonopolization policy with effective protection against the predatory practices of internationally dominant firms; and (3) an effective antimerger policy. Although refusals to deal (buy) and cross-national territorial restrictions are likely to involve cartel or monopoly abuses and thus be challengeable under the first two policies, additional regulations might also be useful in these areas.

An anticartel policy would eliminate the most important source of restrictions on trade other than those directly raised by governments. An effective antipredation policy would eliminate the only legitimate reason for concern about *low* import prices, and thus would *allow* the repeal or international prohibition of all antidumping regulations. An effective antimerger policy would prevent all firms from achieving market advantages through merger that they could not achieve through the quality of their products and efficiency of their operations. Until an enforceable global competition policy with these elements exists, global trade can never truly be free, and citizens everywhere will be partially held hostage by those who can manipulate "the terms of trade" to their advantage.

Bibliography

Areeda, P., and D.F. Turner. 1975. "Predatory Pricing and Related Practices Under Section 2 of the Sherman Act." *Harvard Law Review* 88:697–733.

Baumol, W.J., J.C. Panzer, and R.D. Willig. 1982. *Contestable Markets and the Theory of Industry Structure*. New York: Harcourt, Brace, Jovanovich.

Bittlingmayer, G. 1985. "Did Antitrust Policy Cause the Great Merger Wave?" *Journal of Law and Economics* 28:77–118.

Bork, R. 1978. *The Antitrust Paradox*. New York: Basic Books.

Brock, G.W. [1989] 1994. "Dominant Firm Response to Competitive Challenge: Peripheral Equipment Manufacturers' Suits Against IBM (1979–1983)." In: J.E. Kwoka, Jr., and L.J. White (eds.), *The Antitrust Revolution*, pp. 160–182. Glenview, Ill.: Scott, Foresman & Co.

Caves, R.E. 1989. "Mergers, Takeovers and Economic Efficiency: Foresight vs. Hindsight." *International Journal of Industrial Organization* 7:151–174.

Comanor, W.S., and F.M. Scherer. 1995. "Rewriting History: the Early Sherman Act Monopolization Cases." *International Journal of the Economics of Business* 2:263–289.

Economist. April 6, 1996, pp. 81–82.

Edwards, C.D. 1959. *The Price Discrimination Law*. Washington: Brookings Institution.

Elzinga, K.G. [1989] 1994. "Collusive Predation: Matsushita v. Zenith (1986)." In: J.E. Kwoka, Jr., and L.J. White (eds.), *The Antitrust Revolution*, Second Edition, pp. 238–259, Glenview, Ill.: Scott, Foresman & Co.

Evans, W.N., and I.N. Kessides. 1994. "Living by the 'Golden Rule': Multimarket Contact in the US Airline Industry." *Quarterly Journal of Economics* 109:341–366.

Fisher, F.M., J.J. McGowan, and J.E. Greenwood. 1983. *Folded, Spindled, and Multilated: Economic Analysis and U.S. vs. IBM*. Cambridge, Mass.: MIT Press.

George, K., and A. Jacquemin. 1990. "Competition Policy in the European Community." In W.S. Comanor et al. (eds.), *Competition Policy in Europe and North America: Economic Issues and Institutions*, pp. 206–245. Chur: Harwood Academic Publishers.

Joskow, P., and A.K. Klevorick. 1979. "A Framework for Analyzing Predatory Pricing Policy." *Yale Law Journal* 89:213–270.

Klein, B., and L.F. Saft. 1985. "The Law and Economics of Franchise Tying Contracts." *Journal of Law and Economics* 28:345–361.

Libecap, G.D. 1992. "The Rise of the Chicago Packers and the Origins of Meat Inspection and Antitrust." *Economic Inquiry* 30:242–262.

Markham, J.W. 1955. "Survey of the Evidence and Findings on Mergers." In: *Business Concentration and Price Policy*. Princeton: Princeton University Press.

Martin, S. 1994. *Industrial Economics*. Second Edition. Englewood Cliffs, N.J.: Prentice-Hall.

Marvel, H.P. 1982. "Exclusive Dealing." *Journal of Law and Economics* 25:1–25.

Marvel, H.P., and S. McCafferty. 1984. "Resale Price Maintenance and Quality Certification." *Rand Journal of Economics* 15:346–359.

Marvel, H.P., and S. McCafferty. 1985. "The Welfare Effects of Resale Price Maintenance." *Journal of Law and Economics* 28:363–379.

McGee, J.S. 1958. "Predatory Price Cutting: The Standard Oil (N.J.) Case." *Journal of Law and Economics* 1:137–169.

Mueller, D.C. [1969] 1991. "A Theory of Conglomerate Mergers." In: G. Marchildon (ed.), *Mergers and Acquisitions*, pp. 496–512. London: Elgar.

Mueller, D.C. [1977] 1991. "The Effects of Conglomerate Mergers: A Survey of the Empirical Evidence." In: G. Marchildon (ed.), *Mergers and Acquisitions*, pp. 349–381. London: Elgar.

Mueller, D.C. 1986. *Profits in the Long Run*. Cambridge: Cambridge University Press.

Mueller, D.C. 1996. "Antimerger Policy in the United States: History and Lessons." *Empirica* 23:229–253.

Mueller, D.C. 1997a. "First-Mover Advantages and Path Dependence." *International Journal of Industrial Organization* 15:827–850.

Mueller, D.C. 1997b. "The Public Economics of Public Subsidies for Private Firms." Forschungsbericht N. 9713. Vienna: Ludwig Boltzmann Institut.

Posner, R.A. 1976. *Antitrust Law: An Economic Perspective*. Chicago: University of Chicago Press.

Roll, R. 1986. "The Hubris Hypothesis of Corporate Takeovers." *Journal of Business* 59:197–216.

Scherer, F.M. 1994. *Competition Policies for an Integrated World Economy*. Washington, D.C.: Brookings Institution.

Scherer, F.M. 1997. "Retail Distribution Channel Barriers to International Trade." ESRC Working Paper No. 55. Cambridge: University of Cambridge.

Scherer, F.M., A. Beckenstein, E. Kaufer, and R.D. Murphy. 1975. *The Economics of Multi-Plant Operation: An International Comparisons Study*. Cambridge, Mass.: Harvard University Press.

Scherer, F.M., and D. Ross. 1990. *Industrial Market Structure and Economic Performance*. Third Edition. Boston: Houghton Mifflin.

Scott, J.T. 1982. "Multimarket Contact and Economic Performance." *Review of Economics and Statistics* 64:368–375.

Scott, J.T. 1993. *Purposive Diversification and Economic Performance*. Cambridge: Cambridge University Press.

Warren-Boulton, F.R. [1989] 1994. "Resale Price Maintenance Reexamined: Monsanto v. Spray-Rite (1984)." In: J.E. Kwoka, Jr., and L.J. White (eds.), *The Antitrust Revolution*, Second Edition, pp. 400–431. Glenview, Ill.: Scott, Foresman & Co.

International Trade in "Bads"

Anne O. Krueger and Chonira E. Aturupane

Our assignment is to survey the literature on trade in "bads." To do so requires three steps. A first is to define "bads," at least for purposes of this paper. A second is then to attempt to set forth an analytical framework against which trade in "bads" can be evaluated and the optimal policy with respect to trade in "bads" can be addressed. It is important to note that it is trade policy, not overall policy, and trade policy from an international viewpoint, not from a domestic perspective, that is discussed here. The third step is to survey what is known about trade in "bads." These tasks are tackled in that order in what follows.

I What Are "Bads"?

A moment's thought as to what is "bad" immediately conjures up visions of drug cartels smuggling their wares across international borders. But other things can be "bad," too: weapons, alcohol, cigarettes, environmental waste, and slaves are a few that come to mind. There is also trade in goods that are made in a "bad" way: this might include environmental degradation, use of prison labor, use of child labor, hiring workers in unsafe (or at least not safe by industrialized country standards) workplaces, and so on.

But these examples come from widely different forms of trade: trade in drugs takes place by smuggling precisely because it is mostly illegal. Trade in alcohol and in cigarettes is legal, although usually subject to taxation (and there is sometimes smuggling to evade taxes). Environmental waste is different yet again, in that, unlike drugs, alcohol, and cigarettes, it provides no positive utility to anyone—people have to be paid to accept it.[1] And the last group of items is considered "bad," not because of properties of the goods in the group per se, but because of the ways in which the goods are made. One can thus think of "bads" that are bad because of some undesirable aspect of consumption and others that are bad because of the process by which they are produced. The second group, the "process bads" have led to calls for "labor standards," environmental agreements, and a variety of other measures. Fortunately, another paper in this volume is devoted to environmental and labor standards, so trade in commodities produced in a "bad" way are not further considered here.[2]

The other examples[3] fall into two categories. In the first, individuals attach positive utility to the "bad" in question, while society as a whole or some significant portion of it suffers a negative externality. In the second, there is no positive utility attached to private consumption of the good, but its very existence generates some negative externalities.

With drugs, individual users derive utility but it is at least in part offset by negative externalities imposed on others. These are presumably the societal losses associated with addiction, including the increased incidence of crime. So drugs, alcohol, and cigarettes clearly fall into the first category (as do such things as pornography if society's views as to the negative externalities are strong enough). The arms trade is

---

[1] One could, however, argue that the "good" that generates utility is the resources that are received in compensation for accepting the waste, while the negative externality is generated by the waste itself.

[2] See Brander and Taylor (1997) for a straightforward model of trade between two countries when one has a stronger "taste" for environmental protection than the other.

[3] There are also a number of other items not mentioned here, which might be considered "bads." One would include such things as pornography which would, by some, be placed in the class of bads, presumably on the argument that one person's consumption of pornography negatively affects the rest of society. Without evaluating the "badness" of pornography and similar cases, the argument presented below covers them if they truly provide negative externalities. Another interesting case concerns trade in such things as rare tropical birds, where the concern is not that ownership of a rare bird is generating negative externalities, but that the bird is, or is becoming, an endangered species. The considerations governing that trade are the same as those governing trade in ivory, whale products, and fishing. Since concern is about the environment, the negative externality is in production, rather than in consumption of the item. Therefore, those issues are not dealt with in this paper.

interesting: most of it is to governments and legal, but there is also illegal trade either because exporting nations have banned arms shipments on foreign policy grounds or other grounds, or because importing countries want to cut off arms to guerrillas and insurgents and/or to private citizens.

Toxic waste is an example of the second type, in which the negative externality is the health hazard (or the costs of disposal in ways that prevent the hazard) imposed on those in the vicinity of the disposal site. People therefore charge for taking the waste, and, assuming that the compensation is deemed adequate to offset or more than offset the negative externalities, a net welfare gain can accrue to those accepting the waste.

For purposes of analysis, it would at first sight appear that public policy toward the consumption of "bads" falls into three classes: (1) bads where taxes or other regulations are imposed on consumption (as with alcohol and tobacco), (2) bads where consumption of the good is illegal (as with drugs and arms shipments to insurgents), and (3) bads where governments themselves may be a consuming agent (weapons, toxic waste).

In fact, however, it seems reasonable to categorize "bads" into two classes. For, if negative externalities are large enough (or if enforcement of taxes is sufficiently costly), it may prove cost-effective to prohibit consumption of the goods in question.

If, for example, taxes on consumption of a particular item are very high, smuggling of that item may occur in any event; a sufficiently high tax is equivalent to an import (or even consumption) prohibition, and can induce smuggling in the same way as can a prohibition.[4]

Once it is recognized that prohibition is simply a form of extremely high taxation, then the types of "bads" may be broadly grouped into two groups: those where there is positive utility to individuals in consumption but negative externalities to the rest of society; and those

---

[4] One way in which prohibition of consumption and imports may make enforcement cheaper is that law enforcement agencies no longer need to prove the illegal origin of the item, but only its existence. With a high tax and *any* positive legal level of consumption, law enforcement agencies would have to prove that the item was obtained illegally. A smuggler might purchase one unit of the item at the tax-inclusive price and be able to show his receipt whenever challenged with regard to possession of the item.

where there is no individual positive utility but where there are negative or positive externalities accruing to society as a whole. This is partly the case with the weapons trade (weapons purchased by a government may be regarded as an instance of a positive externality, or public good, accruing to society; weapons smuggled into a country presumably generate private utility to the consumers, so the arms trade has aspects of both), and probably entirely the case with toxic waste.

II What Is Optimal Policy with Respect to Trade in "Bads"?

The categorization of trade in "bads" into two types provides a relatively simple basis for a welfare criterion, which is the same as that for virtually all analyses of trade policy. A situation is Pareto-optimal if there is no way of achieving greater welfare for some individual or group without making someone else or some other group worse off.

Using this criterion, from a world welfare viewpoint, anything that is produced should be produced where it is produced most cheaply, and a world welfare optimum will obtain when the marginal rate of transformation between goods that are produced is the same wherever they are produced. This, in turn, implies that whenever externalities are in consumption (and not in production), production of anything that is produced in the world should take place where there is comparative advantage. If, for example, the United States were the low-cost supplier of opium, but Congress deemed negative externalities so large that domestic consumption were prohibited (or taxed at a sufficiently high level such that there was no legal domestic consumption), while use of opium was legal elsewhere, world welfare would be maximized (U.S enforcement costs aside) if the United States produced and exported opium.[5]

In practice, however, the policy issue seems to arise the other way around: countries are asked to prohibit or limit domestic production and to prevent exports of various drugs to countries where consumption is illegal. Especially if there is not universal agreement as to the negative externalities (or if the demand for these items exists only in some countries), the practice of demanding that low-cost producers

---

[5] In fact, there are some low-cost producers of opium, such as Turkey, where domestic residents do not seem to choose to use it.

refrain from production seems questionable, especially for "bads" which seem to be in almost perfectly elastic supply.

Similarly, world welfare is maximized when the marginal rates of substitution in consumption (taking into account externalities) are equalized. Evidently, when consumption of a good is illegal (because of negative externalities), it is difficult to see why domestically produced and foreign-produced "bads" should be treated differently.[6] If it is illegal to produce the "bad" domestically for domestic consumption, then clearly national treatment would suggest that imports of the good should also be banned, although not necessarily production for export!

In considering trade in drugs (see below), however, it is evident that the social costs of smuggling may be sufficiently high—in terms of the breakdown of legal processes and the weakening of the state—and the benefits sufficiently low to warrant reconsideration of legal prohibition.

Similarly, when domestic consumption is taxed, taxation in like proportion on the imported item is warranted. Clearly, if the negative externality is attached to the consumption of the good, taxing consumption is appropriate, and there is no case for interfering with production in the country or countries with comparative advantages. There is no case, therefore, for taxing imports differently from domestic production.

The final case—where government is the consumer—is also fairly straightforward. When negative externalities (as with toxic waste) are experienced by those within the importing country, the receiving government should charge an amount sufficient to compensate those adversely affected (or, more likely, to incur the costs necessary to avoid the harmful effects on the local population).

When governments themselves are consumers, as with weapons, the case for obtaining the items at the cheapest source remains valid.[7]

---

[6] The question as to whether prohibition is a desirable policy instrument is dealt with briefly below. In the case of drugs, see Wolf (1997) for arguments that prohibition is an inefficient way to control drug use.

[7] Of course, protection of domestic industries has been rationalized in many instances because of the "national defense" rationale. In those instances, however, it is not trade in "bads" that is at issue, and many of the items protected have had both civilian and military uses. A famous (and ludicrous) case in the United States was the infamous oil import quotas, imposed until the 1960s on "national defense" grounds. See Dam (1971) for an analysis.

An interesting problem arises, of course, when other governments believe that exports of weapons to the would-be importing country are harmful and have negative effects on the exporting country. This has been the case, of course, with U.S export controls on high-technology items, where it has been believed that these would enhance military capabilities of governments in countries where the United States had security concerns.[8]

III   What Do We Know about Trade in "Bads"?

In fact, none of the literature we located evaluates trade in "bads" according to the criteria suggested above. In part, this is because the criteria are straightforward to apply but too little is known about trade in "bads," except those in government-to-government trade, such as trade in arms. And that part is exceptionally difficult to evaluate using any clear-cut welfare criterion.

Not only is there no significant analysis of trade in bads according to standard analysis of commercial policy, but there is virtually no analysis except at the level of individual bads. In what follows, therefore, the chief items are treated individually.

As will be seen, if estimates can be relied upon, the value of illegal trade in drugs probably exceeds that of the other "bads" for which estimates are available put together. Before turning to drugs, however, it is useful to examine a "bad" which is subject to a different regime than drugs, one in which high taxes and some social controls are used to regulate consumption.

A   Alcohol and Cigarettes

The regime used for these two "bads" represents a possible alternative regime for drugs. Alcohol and cigarettes are generally thought to have

---

[8] Even here, questions can be raised as to the effectiveness of these export prohibitions if other countries are able to export similar items. In this case, the United States may be, or may have been, harming its own producers without affecting the military capability of would-be importers significantly. U.S. export controls have been significantly relaxed because of this concern.

negative externalities in consumption, and consequently their purchase is taxed. There have been efforts at prohibition, as in the United States with alcohol in the interwar period, and these were largely ineffective.

Currently, almost all countries tax alcohol and cigarettes fairly heavily. Smuggling does occur and there are enforcement costs. But consumption is not illegal, although it is restricted to the adult population and there are restrictions on places in which there may be public consumption in many countries.

The values of world exports of alcoholic beverages and of tobacco in 1994 are reported by the United Nations (1995) to have been $23.5 billion and $16.6 billion, respectively. Interestingly, in the case of tobacco, reported world imports were $12.6 billion. This would suggest that considerable smuggling does take place as there are few countries with export taxes on tobacco. Nonetheless, the control regime for tobacco and alcohol stand as an alternative to that employed for drugs.

B Drugs

As already stated, the trade in illegal drugs is by far the largest trade in bads. Precisely because it is mostly illegal, estimates of the volume of such trade are subject to wide margins of error.

There is general agreement that the international drug trade was a relatively small industry in the 1950s. Moreover, drug trade was apparently conducted by a large number of relatively small traders.

By the 1990s, it had become a much larger industry, absolutely and relatively. Furthermore, drug traders had become considerably larger in size and the industry was apparently more concentrated.[9] The impetus to this seems to have come primarily from the demand side, with the upsurge in demand in the 1960s and 1970s. However, the costs

---

[9] Despite this, it seems to remain the case that entry into the drug trade costs very little. Anyone with a small amount of resources can obtain a drug in a producing country, buy a plane ticket (or arrange another mode of transport) and bring the good into a consuming country. Risks of detection must, of course, be accepted.

It should be noted, however, that once an activity (the drug trade) is illegal, the costs of attempting to form and enforce a cartel are greatly reduced, since activities must in any event be covert.

of many illegal supply endeavors may have fallen, as the increased volume of passenger and cargo traffic between countries has rendered the task of enforcement of prohibition difficult, if not impossible.[10]

The OECD estimated in 1990 that consumers in the United States and Europe may have spent about $122 billion annually on heroin, cocaine, and cannabis. Other estimates at about that same time ranged from $50 billion to $150 billion (Stares, 1996, p. 123). Stares (1996, p. 2) puts the numbers for the mid-1990s for global retail sales of illicit psychoactive substances at $180 to $300 billion. He estimates that the illegal money then laundered from these sales probably amounts to around $85 billion annually.[11] In 1997, the *Economist* reported that the drug trade had risen to a $400 billion dollar industry (*Economist*, 1997, p. 19). These numbers suggest that the trade in illicit drugs is far greater than that in the other bads considered here combined. Moreover, for 1996 the value of world exports reported by the International Monetary Fund was around $5 trillion. That would make illicit drug traffic equal to approximately 8% of the value of (legal) world trade.

The transformation of the drug trade took place as new suppliers entered the market, and different countries and groups of countries specialized more in particular types of trade. Stares (1996) regards opium growing and processing as concentrated in the "Golden Triangle" countries of Laos, Thailand, and Myanmar, and the "Golden Crescent" countries of Afghanistan, Pakistan, and Iran. Meanwhile, coca cultivation is concentrated in Peru, Bolivia, and Colombia, with Colombia accounting for around 70% of all processing.[12] The production and distribution of cannabis (which is the raw material for marijuana and hashish) is much more geographically dispersed. Also

---

[10] Efforts at enforcement have increased, although analysts take changes in the quantity of illegal drugs captured as an indicator of the rate of change in total drug activity. It could, of course, be the case that the additional costs of avoiding detection (or the increased risk of detection) offset the declining direct costs of smuggling. See below for estimates of the cost paid in the United States in efforts at drug enforcement.

[11] The estimates are, of course, subject to wide margins of error. Estimates as to the rate of growth of drug trafficking are at least as problematic. One estimate put the annual rate of increase of opium production between 1990 and 1991 at 33% and hashish production at 65%. See Flynn (1993).

[12] Stares also reports (p. 3) that there are rumors of new sources of supply in the Central Asian Republics.

during the 1970s and 1980s, some groups emerged and greatly expanded their operations: Colombia and the cocaine cartel (apparently now challenged at least in part by Mexican drug lords), a Turkish heroin syndicate, and ethnic Nigerian "organizations."[13]

The profits from the drug trade are huge, as can be seen from estimates reported by Stares (1996, p. 53).[14] A kilogram of cocaine base in Bolivia or Peru sells for about $650 to $1000 and it can be processed into cocaine hydrochloride for export at about $900–1,200. That same quantity then sells wholesale in the United States for $13,000 to $40,000 and then yields between $17,000 to $172,000 at the retail level. Heroin from Burma also has astronomical markups: from $70 a kilogram it goes to $3,000 a kilogram in Thailand, and is sold for export in Bangkok at $6,000 to $10,000. In the U.S. at wholesale, it would sell at $90,000 to $200,000, and at retail would yield about $1 million.[15]

On the supply side, the basic products are typically grown in areas where alternative uses of land and of peasants' labor yield poor returns. Moreover, the economic impact of the production of those basic products is highly significant in a number of countries. Giusti (1991) estimates that direct employment generated by the narcotics industry in Bolivia, Colombia, and Peru is between 600,000 and 1,500,000 persons, with a much greater number indirectly employed. Given the size of those countries' labor forces (5, 28, and 17 million, respectively) these numbers are in themselves very large, especially when it is recognized that this employment is all in rural areas where alternatives have very low returns.

---

[13] Based on a reading of Stares's (1996) history of the drug trade, it would appear that individual countries can fairly effectively suppress production of the raw material for drugs. But those countries that have done so have been rapidly replaced by new sources of supply. Moreover, to reduce or eliminate production requires the ability of the state to carry out a mandate: one of the side effects of the drug trade is clearly a weakening of that mandate and of the state, especially in producing countries.

[14] Giusti (1991) cites a figure of profits of the Medellin Cartel at $4–$5 billion annually in the early 1990s. That was significantly higher than Colombia's coffee exports and about equal to the value of *all* legal exports. Peruvian export earnings from drugs are estimated to be twice those of copper.

[15] The immense profits in the drug trade have greatly increased international money laundering. See the *Economist* (1997) for an analysis of the major concerns that arise with respect to the growing volume of internationally laundered money.

Thoumi (1992, 1993) has produced an interesting argument as to the determinants, or properties, of the countries that have a comparative advantage in the drug trade. He argues that the ability to organize activities outside the protection of the law has been fostered in some countries more than in others, and that it is characteristic of the people in those countries (acquired through their past history of extralegal and illegal activity) that then enables them to compete more successfully in illegal trade. He thus attributes much of the success of the Colombian drug traders to the earlier conditions prevailing in Colombia.

Expenditures on attempting to enforce prohibition are also large. In the early 1990s, the consolidated federal, state, and local expenditures on enforcement in the United States were reported at more than $20 billion (cited by Miron and Zwiebel, 1995, p. 176). While these include expenditures aimed at reducing U.S. consumption, they also include a considerable measure of expenditures geared to prevent importation of drugs. And, of course, other countries also spend resources on preventing the drug trade.

Whenever there has been a relatively effective program for suppressing production in a particular country, other sources of supply have rapidly sprung up (Stares, 1996, ch. 2). Based on economic history, a working hypothesis should be that the supply of the basic agricultural products that constitute the raw material for drugs is close to perfectly elastic. As real incomes rise with economic development, the supply price of these crops may rise; but until that time, there are enough impoverished peasants in the Andes, Central Asia, South and Southeast Asia, and Africa to provide alternatives for very large swings in supply from current producers.

Little needs to be said about the demand side. Most demand seems to originate in Western Europe and the United States, and the trade is almost entirely illegal. The large upward shift in demand in the 1960s and 1970s has already been noted.

The fact that efforts to prohibit drug trade have proved ineffective naturally raises questions as to the costs of prohibition policies. While much attention has focused on issues of crime[16] and of diseases

---

[16] An unanswered question is whether crime is high because of the high cost of drugs (in which case measures which raise the cost of drugs may increase crime rates) or because drugs induce psychic states in which normal psychic controls are relaxed.

acquired through shared needles, there are also serious issues concerning the undermining of the state.

There are constant newspaper reports about the breakdown of the authority of the state in many countries, perhaps most notably Colombia. Given the reported orders of magnitude of profits derived from the drug trade in that country, it is certainly plausible that the state authorities are not able to maintain control.

Thus, in addition to national problems associated with crime and the societal costs of disease and other externalities, problems arise in the individual exporting states.

In addition, the volume of transactions in the drug trade has grown so large that there are now growing concerns about the magnitude of money laundering. The *Economist* focused on this concern, reporting an IMF estimate that "gross criminal product" is around $500 billion annually. It then concluded that: "The stock of crooked cash already invested in financial and other assets must be far larger than that. Indeed, some experts think that it is now so big that it could pose a threat to national economies and even to the stability of the international financial system" (*Economist*, 1997, p. 19).[17] Even if data on the costs and benefits of drug use to individuals and society were available and reliable, it would be difficult to take into account the costs of undermining entire civil societies (as in Colombia) and the development of international money laundering operations, when assessing the benefits and costs of prohibition.

Analysts have attempted to assess the narrower benefit-cost issue, focusing on the probable costs and benefits to consuming countries (and in particular the United States) of shifting from prohibition to a tax-and-control regime.[18] They all begin by noting that the data necessary to assess the costs and benefits of legalizing the consumption of drugs, presumably with appropriate social controls (such as exist with alcohol and cigarettes) are not available.

Attention then focuses on the costs and benefits of legalization (see

---

[17] The *Economist* further noted that the problem is especially large for some countries. It reported that estimates are that the amount of money laundered annually through Thailand is equivalent to about 15% of Thai GDP, or about $28 billion (p. 21).

[18] For a recent review of arguments in favor of shifting to a tax-and-control regime, see Wolf (1997).

Niskanen, 1992; Miron and Zwiebel, 1995). Miron and Zwiebel (1995, p. 175) provide a concise account of the generally accepted view of the negative externalities: "drug users suffer diminished health, decreased earnings and moral degradation. Similarly, ... the market in illegal drugs promotes crime, destroys inner cities, spreads AIDS, corrupts law enforcement officials and politicians, produces and exacerbates poverty and erodes the moral fabric of society."

In considering alternative policies, several questions arise. First, one must distinguish between the costs and externalities associated with using drugs per se, and the costs of prohibition. Second, one must evaluate the relevant alternative. If, for example, a lower price of drugs induced increases in consumption of drugs but reduced consumption of alcohol and cigarettes, the net costs of additional users would decline (and, by implication, the costs of an individual's addiction to drugs would be overstated if increased cigarette and alcohol consumption were the alternative).

The benefits of legalization (combined with a control program and taxation) would presumably center on reduced negative externalities of the types cited by Miron and Zwiebel. The costs would arise, it is argued, in increased drug use by addicts who were able to consume more (perhaps even begin consuming) in response to a lower price of drugs that would result from legalization.[19]

That the price of drugs would decline with legalization is generally accepted. Morgan (1991) estimated that cocaine sold for about 20 times its free market price around 1990.

On the benefit side, the argument becomes more murky. Crime would decrease if the main motives for crime are to finance drug habits (since the habits would become cheaper) but they would increase if crime is committed by people under the influence of drugs (since there would be more of them). Miron and Zwiebel (1995) believe that the weight of the evidence supports the view that crime is committed by those seeking to finance their habit.

If drug use were subject to a tax-and-control regime, the huge per unit profits to drug traffickers would diminish. That, in turn, would circumscribe the power of the drug lords, and the process of weaken-

---

[19] See Niskanen (1992) for an elaboration of this argument. Niskanen concludes that not enough evidence is available to reach a well-founded conclusion as to the benefit-cost ratio of legalization.

ing the state in drug-exporting countries would presumably cease, although it can be argued that, in some cases the damage has been done and cannot readily be reversed. Legal imports of drugs could, of course, be expected to increase. Their price would presumably be lower, as the costs of drug traffic (including risk premium) would shift downward.

There seems to be no acceptable way of assessing benefits and costs of legalizing drugs which would provide enough confidence to form the basis for a societal consensus to develop. Perhaps the best argument for legalization is the evident failure of prohibition to make significant inroads into drug use. But the greater affordability of drugs to young people who might then become addicted in increasing numbers must be recognized as a plausible offset.[20]

What does seem clear is that there is no economic basis on which to defend the demand by consuming countries that producing countries bear the cost of enforcement or make production illegal. If prohibition could be enforced in ways that reduced demand in consuming countries, it is clear that the quantity supplied would decline.

C Hazardous Substances

Most economists probably became aware of some of the issues surrounding trade in toxic wastes after Larry Summers' famous World Bank memorandum on the subject (see the *Economist* [1993, pp. 18–19] for an account). He was concerned with the possible comparative advantage of developing countries as sites for receiving toxic waste, arguing that there was lower valuation to life in poor countries, that there was less waste already there, so that in an industry with increasing costs, the costs of absorbing it would be lower, and that appreciation of the environment rises with income.

Summers' memo raised a furor, but it also pointed to an important fact: international trade in toxic waste is contentious only between industrialized and developing countries. Between industrialized countries, there is a widely accepted regime (under the Basel convention of

---

[20] Some point out that there is "glamour" associated with doing something illegal, and that ending prohibition would reduce the glamour and thus might reduce the number of new users and addicts.

1989; see United Nations Environmental Program, 1990) and the value of legal trade (i.e., the payments to those accepting toxic waste) is small relative to alcohol, tobacco, or drugs.

International trade in toxic wastes[21] became a major subject of concern in the 1980s. The 1970s had seen a spate of national legislation, controlling the disposal of industrial wastes deemed harmful to the environment. Many of these measures naturally raised the costs of waste disposal.

One response to these higher disposal costs was an increased effort to export waste materials. There quickly followed agreements among the industrialized countries, so that international shipments were subject to the same rules as disposal of domestic waste. This trade continues, does not appear to be large in dollar value[22], and apparently is not a source of contention among countries or policy-makers in developed countries (see, for example, Hilz, 1992). The OECD regularly publishes statistics on trade in toxic waste (see, for example, OECD, 1994).

However, a number of producers of industrial waste in industrialized countries apparently found mechanisms for exporting their waste to developing countries, either evading controls or sending them to places where no controls existed.[23] Issues then arose with regard to global treatment of toxic wastes. Robert Mugabe was cited as terming the trade "garbage imperialism" (cited in McKee, 1996, p. 238). Some developing countries began pressing industrial countries to extend their laws governing toxic waste disposal to cover exportation.[24] While that

---

[21] There does not seem to be any universally accepted definition of hazardous, or toxic, wastes. The *Economist* defined them as items "containing substances that require special treatment." Cited in McKee (1996, p. 238).

[22] Hilz (1992, p. 24) estimates that the cost of management of toxic waste in the United States was about $4 billion in 1989. That value has undoubtedly increased, and is doubtless matched by a similar or larger figure for the European Union. But the number suggests that the value of international trade—legal and illegal—in toxic waste is probably very small relative to trade in the other "bads" discussed here.

[23] An early instance of illegal waste exporting was to Seveso, Italy, and this led to adoption of measures by the European Parliament. Exports of waste to developing countries had, however, been taking place since the 1970s.

[24] The conclusion that it is not appropriate for the exporting country to be asked to enforce consumption prohibitions would appear as valid, on welfare grounds, for toxic waste as for drugs.

was not agreed to, a GATT Working Group on Domestically Prohibited Goods and Hazardous Substances was established (Sankey, 1989, p. 99). There were also proposals to put toxic waste management on the Uruguay Round agenda, but this was one of the issues that were not agreed to at Punte del Este.

There is little further literature in the 1990s, which suggests that the issue has died down. For the most part, it seems accepted in the literature that importing countries should regulate the treatment of imported hazardous materials in accordance with the same laws that govern the treatment of those materials when they are generated domestically (see McKee [1996] for a statement). Overall, one must conclude that both the value of trade in toxic waste, and the issues involved, are very small relative to the amount of attention they have received.

D   The Arms Trade

Efforts to enforce prohibitions on exporting countries and prohibitions against consumption are the contentious issues with regard to drugs. Whereas the schism between developed and developing countries is the focal point of policy issues with regard to the toxic waste trade, which is regulated because of environmental concerns, analysis of the weapons trade is clouded by concerns about the "wastefulness" of such expenditures by developing countries and by defense and national security issues.

For the world as a whole, arms exports are estimated to have been $49.3 billion in 1983 and $21.9 billion in 1993, and to have constituted about 0.6% of total world imports in 1993, compared with 2.7% of world imports in 1983 (U.S. Arms Control and Disarmament Agency, 1995, p. 91). By 1996, the arms trade was increasing again, with the global market estimated to be $31.8 billion, an increase of 5% over the previous year.[25] One must conjecture that almost all trade reported in official sources reflects legal trade between governments.

---

[25] These data are from a Congressional Research Service report that was quoted in the *New York Times* (1997, p. 3). The same source indicated that the three largest exporters, and their estimated shares of the market, were reported to be: United States, 35.5%; Britain, 15.1%; and Russia 14.5%.

There seems little in the literature analyzing the economic aspects of illegal arms trade. Since this is the sort with which negative externalities might be associated, the conclusion must be that either too little is known, or the trade is too small, to warrant attention.

IV Conclusions

Although the trade in "bads" can be relatively straightforwardly analyzed on welfare grounds, difficulties arise when attempting to assess the empirical importance of this trade or the underlying supply and demand determinants of trade in individual "bads." This is especially true with the largest of the bads, drugs, where the fact that the trade is illegal constitutes a major barrier to analysis of factors underlying supply and demand.

A survey of the available literature suggests that the international regimes for alcohol, tobacco, toxic waste, and weapons work reasonably well. By contrast, the apparently much larger trade in drugs obviously generates many more policy issues. Chief among these are the problems arising from insistence that exporting countries interdict exports, the emergence of large illegal cartels with consequent undermining of law and order and even of the state, and the emergence of money laundering on a large scale. Although the replacement of prohibition by a tax-and-control regime is the obvious alternative, too little is known to be able to provide a convincing case for the change.

Bibliography

Brander, J., and M.S. Taylor. 1997. "International Trade between Consumer and Conservationist Countries." Working Paper No. 6006. Cambridge, Mass.: NBER.

Dam, K.W. 1971. "The Implementation of Import Quotas: The Case of Oil." *Journal of Law and Economics* 14(1):1–60.

Economist. 1993. February 15.

Economist. 1997. July 26.

Flynn, S. 1993. "Worldwide Drug Scourge." *Brookings Review* 11(1):6–11.

Giusti, J. 1991. "The Economic and Social Significance of Narcotics." *Cepal Review* (45):137–167.

Hilz, C. 1992. *The International Toxic Waste Trade.* New York: Van Nostrand Reinhold.

McKee, D.L. 1996. "Some Reflections on the International Waste Trade and Emerging Nations." *International Journal of Social Economics* 23(4–6):235–244.

Miron, J.A., and J. Zwiebel. 1995. "The Economic Case Against Drug Prohibition." *Journal of Economic Perspectives* 9(4):175–192.

Morgan, J.P. 1991. "Prohibition is Perverse Policy: What Was True in 1933 is True Now." In: M.B. Krauss and E.P. Lazear (eds.), *Searching for Alternatives: Drug-Control Policy in the United States*. Stanford: Hoover Institution Press.

New York Times. 1997. August 16.

Niskanen, W.A. 1992. "Economists and Drug Policy." *Carnegie-Rochester Conference Series on Public Policy* 36:223–248.

OECD (Financial Action Task Force on Money Laundering). 1990. *Report*. Paris: OECD.

OECD. 1994. *Transfrontier Movements of Hazardous Wastes, 1991*. Paris: OECD.

Sankey, J. 1989. "Domestically Prohibited Goods and Hazardous Substances: A New GATT Working Group is Established." *Journal of World Trade Law* 23(6):99–108.

Stares, P.B. 1996. *Global Habit*. Washington, D.C.: Brookings Institution.

Stockholm International Peace Research Institute. 1975. *Arms Trade Registers*. Cambridge, Mass.: MIT Press.

Thoumi, F.E. 1992. "Why the Illegal Psychoactive Drugs Industry Grew in Colombia." *Journal of Interamerican Studies and World Affairs* 34(3):37–63.

Thoumi, F.E. 1993. *The Size of the Illegal Drugs Industry in Colombia*. Coral Gables, Fl.: University of Miami.

United Nations Environmental Program. 1990. *Basel Convention on the Control of Transboundary Movements of Hazardous Wastes and Their Disposal (1989)*. Nairobi, Kenya: United Nations Environmental Program, Environmental Law and Institutions Unit.

United Nations. 1995. *1994 Yearbook of International Trade Statistics*. Volume II. New York: United Nations.

United States Arms Control and Disarmament Agency. 1995. *World Military Expenditures and Arms Transfers 1993–1994*. Washington, D.C.: U.S. Government Printing Office.

Wolf, M. 1997. *Financial Times*, July 22, 29, and August 12.

Social Standards and Social Dumping

Deepak Lal

> It is no chance matter we are discussing but how one should live.
> —Plato, *Republic*

I have a tremendous sense of déjà vu about the current debate on the introduction of labor and environmental codes in the World Trade Organization (WTO). While the demand for linking trade policy to environmental standards is new, the similar demand concerning labor standards is a repetition of the events surrounding the Tokyo round of multilateral trade negotiations (1973–1979). In the Trade Act of 1974, the U.S. Congress—under pressure from labor unions—had included a provision requiring the president to raise the subject of "fair labor standards" in the GATT framework. This President Jimmy Carter duly did in October 1979 just before the end of the Tokyo Round negotiations. About the same time the European Commission suggested that "minimum labor standards" be included in the Lome convention, which provided for tariff preferences and technical and financial aid to a group of African, Caribbean, and Pacific countries. In 1980, as the multifiber agreement (MFA) regulating trade in textiles and clothing came up for renewal, organizations representing business and labor in textiles and clothing industries in America and Western Europe advanced proposals for a "social clause" to be inserted in the MFA.

I wrote a pamphlet (Lal, [1981] 1994) countering this new variant of the pauper labor argument. The new twist in the "protectionists'" case was that rather than claiming that imports from countries with low wages were inimical to the welfare of the importing countries, protection was now sought against imports produced by foreign workers who had been denied their so-called human rights, in countries without "minimum labor standards." Protection of imports from poor low-wage countries was to be instituted to promote the interests of these poor, exploited, benighted foreign workers. Fortunately, nothing came of this hypocritical drive to legislate a particular morality, in the subsequent decade. But with another Democratic president in power, and with the fear of "low-wage" imports from the developing world being fanned by the stagnation of the wages of the low-skilled in the United States and the very high unemployment rates in continental Europe—particularly France (see Goldsmith, 1994; Hindley, 1994)—protection is again being sought on the high-minded grounds of promoting the "human rights" of Third (and now also Second) World workers. *Plus ça change!*

But there are two other additions to the protectionists' armory. The first is the argument called "the race to the bottom." It is argued that with mobile capital, buying the goods produced by socially and environmentally unprotected Third World workers will lead to an erosion of the First World's labor and environmental standards, as home industries unable to compete with these "low-standard" imports locate abroad and/or use the political process to obtain a lowering of the standards in the West. To prevent this "social dumping," protection is sought, analogous to the antidumping codes which currently allow protection against purported economic dumping.

The second argument is based on what Corden (1997) has labeled "psychological spillovers." The utility of consumers in the First World is claimed to be affected by the way goods are produced or by their environmental effects in the Third World. This leads to demands for "ethical trade," as in the recent call by the U.K. Secretary of State for International Development Clare Short, and the various measures taken to label goods as ethically produced (e.g., without cruelty to animals, or destroying the rain forests, or without using child labor as certified by the Rugmark label).

On the first of these new arguments I can be brief because of two comprehensive papers surveying the analytical models and the empirical evidence concerning the "race to the bottom." Levinson (1996) surveys the empirical evidence concerning environmental regulation and industry location within the United States and internationally and finds little empirical evidence of such a race. Wilson (1996) surveys the various analytical models which have dealt with the theoretical case of a race to the bottom in environmental standards in a world with free trade and capital mobility. He finds that the case is at best mixed. There can be no race to the bottom without any domestic distortions and constraints on tax-subsidy instruments. So the relevant question is one of political economy: why governments would choose to lower standards rather than use more appropriate tax-subsidy measures? But surely, the prior question about the global harmonization of *social* standards is whether there are any such universal standards to be harmonized in the first place. We are back to ethics.

In this article I, therefore, first, summarily reiterate the detailed arguments in Lal ([1981] 1994) against attempts to include "labor standards" based on "human rights" in the WTO. Second, I discuss the question of "ethical trading" in a brief excursus through what I label the "cosmological beliefs"—as contrasted with "material beliefs"— (Lal, 1998) of the West to show that they are culturally specific. Finally, I discuss the consequences for the world economic order if the "political moralism" (Minogue, 1995) currently infecting the West turns into a new form of moral imperialism.

I   The ILO and Labor Standards

First note, that an international organization, the International Labor Organization (ILO), already exists whose "raison d'être" is to develop and promote "fair labor standards." Its success has been patchy (see ILO, 1976; Valticos, 1969). At best, it provides some "normative" pressure on countries social legislation. Even so, it is worth noting that many developing countries, e.g., India, have accepted and legislated more ILO labor standards than the United States! Thus, the ILO is the obvious forum for countries keen to promote "fair labor standards." But it is precisely the lack of teeth in the procedures for accepting the ILO labor code which has prompted the current attempt to use trade policy to legislate a particular morality based on purported universal human rights.

For despite the rhetorical resonance of universal human rights, the underlying morality is not universal. The great religions and social ethics of the East—Hinduism, Buddhism, and Confucianism—would not accept it (see Kamenka, 1978). Thus, what is being sought to be imposed on the rest of the world is a particular Western morality.

II Western Ethics and Human Rights

Even in the West, the moral theory justifying "human rights" remains elusive. They are the modern variants of "natural rights" (see Minogue, 1978, 1979). But at no time has it been generally agreed even within the Western moral tradition that there *are* any such natural rights.

A Specific and General Rights

In clarifying the issues, it is useful to make a distinction between specific and general rights. For a right is a normative resource which an individual either has or is given and which entitles him "to limit the freedom of another person" and to determine "how he should act" (Hart, [1955] 1967, p. 60). The claim that human rights exist is therefore based on the assumption that being *human* in some sense provides a moral justification for certain rights. These rights are moral or *general* rights, to be distinguished from the *specific* rights associated, for instance, with special legal or social systems or with those which arise when promises are made.

That there is nothing logically necessary about the existence of "general" rights is borne out by their repudiation by some Western moral codes, for instance, the utilitarian. As Bentham stated "right is the child of law; from real laws come real rights.... Natural rights is simply nonsense on stilts."

B Liberty as a General Right

However, many Western political and moral philosophers have accepted at least one general ("natural" or "moral" or "human") right, namely "the equal right of all men to be free" (Hart, [1955] 1967 p. 53).[1] But particularly in respect of "fair labor standards" there is a

---

[1] The most consistent attempt to work out the ethical and political implications of this general right to liberty is by Nozick (1974). By contrast, Dworkin (1977) argues against the primacy of any general right to liberty and instead seeks to put the general right of "equality of respect" as the only general moral (or human) right. Also see White (1984).

tradition, going back to Marx, which would deny that "human rights" can be restricted to the liberal notion of individualistic freedom. Instead, Marxists have identified various social and economic rights which "are, in effect, statements of desirable conditions of life for every human being" (Minogue, 1979, p. 13). It is these which form the backbone of the demand for "fair labor standards" as a matter of human rights.

C   Economic and Social Rights: Specific or General?

But can there be any such *general* (or moral) social and economic rights? Much of the confused thinking on the basis of which such general rights (often identified as "positive" freedom or liberty) are adduced is based on terminological confusion surrounding various notions of freedom (see Hart, [1955] 1967; Berlin, 1958) and, too, on a failure to distinguish between *a* right and a "morally right" action. I concentrate on the latter.

If it is granted that freedom (in its negative sense) is a *general moral right,* then its infringement must constitute an injury, which is a failure of justice and therefore demands for restitution would be just. By contrast, it maybe *morally right* (although it is not *a* right) to attempt to alleviate poverty, but failure to do so would merely be a failure to do what is good or best because the consequences would be best; it would not be a failure to render what is due as in the case of *a right* to poverty alleviation. Most of the demands for minimum labor standards not only assert that they are morally good but also raise questions of justice and rights. These are claimed, moreover, to be not merely specific rights which can arise in a host of different ways within a specific legal or social system; they are claimed to be general rights, on a par with "liberty." Why?

As this "rights chatter" is peculiarly American it is best to quote an American liberal psychologist who states: "It is legitimate and fruitful to regard instinctoid basic needs and the metaneeds as rights as well as needs. This follows immediately upon granting that human beings have a right to be human in the sense that cats have a right to be cats. In order to be fully human, these need and metaneed gratifications are necessary and, therefore, can be considered to be natural rights" (Maslow, 1970, p. xiii).

But the obvious retort is that "if being human is a fact, no rights can be inferred from it. It may, of course, be necessary that certain conditions must be met before we can fully *function* as human beings. But, again, no question of rights would arise. The function of a lawn mower is to mow lawns, but a broken-down lawn mower cannot be said to have a right to be repaired in order to become, fully and truly, a lawn mower" (Streeten, 1981, p. 367).

I take it, therefore, that no *general* welfare-promoting economic or social rights can be deduced from the general right to liberty. This does not mean that in particular societies or nations, some people may in fact come to possess what are demonstrably just, *specific* rights to various benefits of the welfare state. But the resulting obligations to subserve these rights would be the result of the specific restraints and guarantees built into a particular country's legislation and would only apply to its citizens. No general universal moral right could thereby be adduced to apply to all mankind.

D   Labor Standards as Derivative from "Liberty"?

But might there still be a case that at least some of the minimum labor standards could still be derived from the basic and general moral right of liberty. Edgren (1979) has suggested that from the large number of ILO conventions, four types of minimum labor standards could be identified as being based on human rights: those concerning freedom of association, safety and health, restriction of the use of child labor, and discrimination in employment. These are—along with restrictions on trade in goods produced by convict labor—the most likely set of standards that would be incorporated in a WTO code. On the last, prison labor, little needs to be said, as Art. XX of GATT already permitted trade restrictions against goods produced with convict labor. I briefly examine the other areas in turn.

1   Freedom of Association

Prima facie it might appear that the right to freedom of association and corresponding trade union rights could be derived from the general right to liberty. But this is only because of the ambiguity of the phrase "freedom of association." Defined to cover merely associations which do not in anyway infringe upon the rights and liberties of others, such a right can clearly be derived from the general right to liberty. On the other hand, no similar rights can be advanced in favor of a free association of individuals which constitutes a rampaging mob because its *intent* (most often) is to infringe someone else's liberty. Freedom of association cannot, therefore, be a general right, even though in many specific circumstances a right to particular kinds of freedom of association can be derived from the general right to liberty.

This means that what are often called political rights (e.g., one man, one vote) are not consequent upon the general moral right to liberty. Thus, various forms of authoritarian government are compatible with promoting the "negative" general right to liberty of a state's citizens.[2]

If no general and unqualified basic right to free association can thus be derived from the general right to liberty, it will hardly come as a surprise that so-called trade union rights, too, cannot be inferred to be general or human rights. The existing trade union "rights" are specific rights which were granted to workers during the historical evolution of Western economies. There is no logical connection between these specific rights and the general moral right to liberty.

2   Health and Safety

Similar considerations apply to health and safety standards viewed as universal human rights. For individuals, in both developed and developing countries, a large part of life consists of taking various actions in the face of all sorts of risk and uncertainty. Although, as a part of the general process of raising living standards, it may be feasible to reduce certain kinds of risk (essentially by enabling various forms of social insurance) no *general* right to such insurance can be adduced. The provision of such insurance requires resources which "belong" to par-

---

[2] Thus Berlin ([1958] 1967) notes: "Liberty in this (negative) sense is not incompatible with some kinds of autocracy, or at any rate with the absence of self-government.... there is no necessary connection between individual liberty and democratic rule. The answer to the question 'who governs me?' is logically distinct from the question 'how far does government interfere with me?'" (pp. 147–148).

ticular people. These individuals maybe willing to transfer some of their resources to provide such insurance, thereby creating specific rights for all workers facing these risks. But there would clearly be no general "right" to social insurance which the latter could demand on the grounds of human rights.

In societies so poor that they are unable to meet even the so-called basic needs of a minimum amount of food, clothing and shelter for their citizens, the legislation of health and safety standards, which have a demonstrable opportunity cost, could easily be at the expense of providing these very essentials of life. It would be hard to justify that a starving man should be prevented from voluntarily taking a job which workers in more advanced countries would consider unsafe or unhealthy when it is his only chance of avoiding starvation.

3   Child Labor

Granted that, as autonomous moral beings, children cannot be owned by their parents, they clearly must have some general rights (*if* these exist) akin to those of adults. It is, however, widely recognized in most societies that children do not become full moral beings at the moment of birth. The purpose of various initiation ceremonies as rites of passage in traditional cultures, as well as the conferring of various specific political and legal rights (and corresponding obligations) on children at the age of majority, signifies the link between the ability to make rational moral *choices* and being a fully fledged moral *person*.[3]

Before this adult status is achieved there are, it could be argued, particular rights that children have to parental "care" which are counterbalanced (if only partially) by the extent of the partial ownership rights that parents have in their children (reflected in such notions as the right of parents to, at least some degree, of obedience from their children).

A good analogy for the resulting relationship between parents and their children would be that the former are trustees of the incipient rights which the latter will acquire as full adults. From this position of trusteeship would flow both the obligations for parental care and children's obedience. Furthermore, given the resulting partial owner-

---

[3] It is implied by the logic of the language of morals that the most basic moral categories which people apply, like "ought," must imply "can."

ship of their children, the parents would have some coercive rights (for instance, to force them, against their infantile wills, to go to school or learn the piano or eat spinach). But these coercive rights cannot be absolute in any sense. Parents clearly would not have the right to sell their children into slavery. Even an incipient moral being would presumably have the right not to be extinguished as a moral being, which slavery would entail.

But what of parents sending their children to work in varying circumstances? Clearly, again, no general prohibition against such work would seem to flow from either the trusteeship role of the parents and the general rights (current or incipient) of the children. A parent who trains his child to be a carpenter at an early age and allows the fruits of the child's labor to be sold cannot be said to have infringed any of the child's general rights (including those which are incipient and of which he is a trustee). The same argument would seem to hold for restrictions on other forms of child labor. Although certain types of child labor may not be morally right, it is unclear how such work would infringe any general right (actual or incipient) of the child.

4   Discrimination in Employment

A prohibition of discrimination on grounds of race or creed can more readily be derived from notions of a general right to liberty. As the arguments against discrimination which would flow from such a general right are fairly obvious, I will not labor the point.

Thus, even within the existing Western ethical framework, apart from the standards against discrimination (and slave labor), none of the other labor standards can be adduced as being, or being derivable from, general human rights. Even if the latter exist, and many within the Western philosophical tradition would deny that they do, they would not cover the panoply of so-called economic and social rights which form the ILO code of minimum labor standards. If anything they represent either specific rights created by particular legal or social systems or they represent a logical (and terminological) confusion between what "is right" and what is "a right." Finally, even though I have argued for the existence of at least the general moral (human) right to liberty, it must be remembered that it only follows from the corpus of *Western* moral and political philosophy and even there, this notion of so-called negative freedom is of fairly recent origin (see Berlin, [1958] 1967). To try to force this Western morality on the rest of the world through punitive trade policy would be unjustified moral imperialism.

III   Labor Standards to Raise Living Standards[4]

For many, however, the argument in favor of linking trade policy with labor standards will not be the rarefied one about human rights, but the more practical one that labor standards can improve the standard of living of workers, both in developed and developing countries. I consider each in turn.

A   Developed Countries

In developed countries, improved labor standards (e.g., safety and health regulations and various trade union "rights") resulting from social legislation can be looked upon as shifting their comparative advantage away from sectors upon which such legislation particularly impinges—relative to their competitors. Any resulting reduction in national income is the "price" paid, as it were, for the improved social conditions of the groups affected.

If in addition, a tariff to impede the entry of goods from countries without similar legislation is imposed, it will inflict further costs in terms of higher prices on users of these goods in the home country, as well as on those associated with the ensuing prevention of the flow of resources out of these "inefficient" industries into those which are more efficient. And if the "protection" of these high "social standards" industries is brought about not by instituting a domestic tariff, but through raising the costs of production equivalently in the foreign countries through the international adoption of minimum labor stan-

---

[4] A recent taxonomic analysis of labor standards and trade is provided by Brown, Deardoff, and Stern (1996). They conclude that "the case for international harmonization of labour standards is rather weak.... it is likely that international harmonization of labour standards will have unintended adverse consequences for the very people they are intended to protect" (p. 272).

dards, it would still lead to the costs associated with the higher prices paid by domestic users of the product.

B   Developing Countries

Those motivated by notions of cosmopolitan welfare, however, might still argue that these losses to advanced-country consumers flowing from the international adoption of minimum labor standards would be counterbalanced by the resulting gains in the standard of living of poor countries' workers. At its most naïve, this argument, though, is based on a *non sequitur*. For although it may be true that there is a high *correlation* between observable high living standards and the existence of various aspects of the welfare state in many OECD countries, this does not mean either that the latter *cause* the former or that the latter *component* of possibly higher living standards can be acquired without costs.

This view is implicit in an ILO analysis of the likely impact of the ILO's standards concerning trade union "rights" and economic development (Claire, 1977). The demand for labor depends, in large part, on the availability of the cooperant factors of production, and, too, on the wage rate. For any given level of the former, the demand for labor will be greater, the lower the wage rate. In many developing countries the level of the available cooperant factors of production is insufficient to generate sufficient demand for the labor which would be supplied by their burgeoning labor forces at what might be considered by Westerners to be a "fair" wage. Any attempt by various combinations of labor or trade unions to raise the wages of their members must reduce the overall demand for labor, thus implying that the rise is at the expense of other workers who would henceforth be unemployed or underemployed. While the "standard of living" of the "labor aristocracy" which had found jobs in the high-wage unionized sector would no doubt be greater, it would be achieved at the expense of its numerically preponderant but unfortunate fellow workers who had not succeeded in gaining entry into this select group.

Any argument that the imposition of fair labor standards (including any notion of a global minimum wage) is in the interests of raising the standards of living of the bulk of the labor force in developing countries is thus unlikely to be valid.

IV   Ethical Trade and Western Cosmologies

It is particularly ironical that the West should have launched its moral
crusade in the name of human rights in order to promote "ethical
trade" and prevent "social dumping" at a time when many in the West
are questioning its ethical moorings—succinctly expressed by the title
of Bork's (1996) recent book, *Slouching towards Gomorrah*. How can
one reconcile this perceived moral decay at home in the West with its
resurgent moralism abroad, and what will be its consequences? An
answer to this question is relevant for the subject at hand because
despite the rational arguments against the modern variants of the pauper labor argument, the notion of "social dumping" is increasingly
resonant because of the "psychological spillovers" from the West's
desire to see its mores adopted globally.

First, note that Western cosmological beliefs, to the extent they are
coherent and commonly shared, are still deeply rooted in Christianity,
particularly its theological formalization in St. Augustine's *The City of
God* ([427] 1984). There are a number of distinctive features about
Christianity which it shares with its Semitic cousin, Islam, but not
entirely with its parent, Judaism, and which are not to be found in any
of the other great Eurasian civilizational religions, past or present. The
most important is its universality. Neither the Jews nor the Hindus or
the Sinitic civilizations had religions claiming to be universal. You
could not choose to be a Hindu, Chinese, or Jew, you were born as
one. This also meant that unlike Christianity and Islam these religions
did not proselytize. Third, only the Semitic religions, being mono-
theistic, have also been egalitarian. The others have believed in *Homo
Hierarchicus*.[5] An ethic which claims to be universal and egalitarian
and proselytizes for converts is a continuing Christian legacy even in
secular Western minds, and is the basis for the moral crusade of
"ethical trading."

It would take us too far afield to substantiate this argument in
any detail, but since Augustine's *The City of God*, the West has been
haunted by its cosmology. As I have argued elsewhere (see Lal, 1998),
from the Enlightenment to Marxism to Freudianism to Ecofundamentalism, Augustine's vision of the "heavenly city" has had a tenacious

---

[5] The title of the famous book about the Hindu caste system by Dumont (1970).

hold on the Western mind. The same narrative with a Garden of Eden, a fall leading to original sin and a Day of Judgment for the elect and hell for the damned keeps recurring. Thus the Philosophes replaced the Garden of Eden with classical Greece and Rome, and God became an abstract cause—the Divine Watchmaker. The Christian centuries were the fall, and the Christian revelations a fraud as God expressed His purpose through His laws recorded in the "great book of nature." The enlightened were the elect and the Christian paradise was replaced by posterity (see Becker, 1932). By this updating of the Christian narrative the 18th-century philosophers of the Enlightenment thought they had been able to salvage a basis for morality and social order in the world of the Divine Watchmaker. But once, as a result of Darwin, He was seen to be blind, He was dead, as Nietzsche proclaimed from the housetops at the end of the 19th century, and the moral foundations of the West were thereafter in ruins.

The subsequent attempts to found a morality based on reason are open to Nietzsche's fatal objection in his aphorism about utilitarianism: "moral sensibilities are nowadays at such cross purposes that to one man a morality is proved by its utility, while to another its utility refutes it" (Nietzsche, [1881] 1982, p. 220).[6] Nietzsche's greatness lies in clearly seeing the moral abyss that the death of its God had created for the West. Kant's attempt to ground a rational morality on his principle of universalizability—harking back to the Biblical injunction "therefore all things whatsoever ye do would that men should do to you, do even so to them"—founders on Hegel's two objections: it is merely a principle of logical consistency without any specific moral content, and worse it is as a result powerless to prevent any immoral conduct that takes our fancy. The subsequent ink spilt by moral philosophers has merely clothed their particular prejudices in rational form.

The death of the Christian God did not, however, end variations on the theme of Augustine's *The City of God*. It was to go through two further mutations in the form of Marxism and Freudianism, and a more recent and bizarre mutation in the form of Ecofundamentalism. As both Marxism and Ecofundamentalism provide the ballast for ethical

---

[6] A point only reiterated by reading the contributions in the edited volume by Sen and Williams (1982).

trading, it is worth noting their secular transformations of Augustine's "heavenly city."[7]

Marxism, like the old faith, looks to the past and the future. There is a Garden of Eden—before "property" relations corrupted "natural man." Then the fall as "commodification" leads to class societies and a continuing but impersonal conflict of material forces, which leads in turn to the Day of Judgment with the revolution and the millennial paradise of Communism. This movement towards earthly salvation being mediated not, as the Enlightenment sages had claimed, through enlightenment and the preaching of good will, but by the inexorable forces of historical materialism. Another secular "city of God" has been created.

Ecofundamentalism is the latest of these secular mutations of Augustine's *The City of God* (Lal, 1995). It carries the Christian notion of *contemptus mundi* to its logical conclusion. Humankind is evil and only by living in harmony with a deified nature can it be saved.

The environmental movement (at least in its "deep" version) is now a secular religion in many parts of the West. The historian of the ecological movement, Anna Bramwell, notes that in the past, Western man was

able to see the earth as man's unique domain precisely because of God's existence.... When science took over the role of religion in the nineteenth century, the belief that God made the world with a purpose in which man was paramount declined. But if there was no purpose, how was man to live on the earth? The hedonistic answer, to enjoy it as long as possible, was not acceptable. If Man had become God, then he had become the shepherd of the earth, the guardian, responsible for the *oekonomie* of the earth. (Bramwell, 1989, p. 23)

The spiritual and moral void created by the death of God is, thus, increasingly being filled in the secular Western world by the worship of nature. In a final irony, those haunted natural spirits which the medieval Church sought to exorcise so that the West could conquer its forests (see Southern, 1970) are now being glorified and being placed above man. The surrealist and antihuman nature of this contrast between ecomorality and what mankind has sought through its reli-

---

[7] That Freudianism follows the same narrative is argued by Gellner (1993) and Webster (1995).

gions in the past is perfectly captured by Douglas and Wildavsky (1983), who write: "the sacred places of the world are crowded with pilgrims and worshippers. Mecca is crowded, Jerusalem is crowded. In most religions, people occupy the foreground of the thinking. The Sierra Nevada are vacant places, loved explicitly because they are vacant. So the environment has come to take first place" (p. 125). The guilt evinced against sinning against God has been replaced by that of sinning against Nature. Saving Spaceship Earth has replaced the saving of souls!

But why should the rest of the world subscribe to this continuing Augustinian narrative cloaked in different secular guises?

The second point to be made is that the "political moralism" underlying the West's current global moral crusade is also the result of its Christian heritage. The Reformation is the hinge. It shattered the ideological unity of Western Christendom. It also brought to an end the commonly accepted view from Aristotle to Aquinas that there was general agreement within communities about the ends of the good society which politics was concerned with establishing (see McClelland, 1996). There was now radical disagreement among communities about the ends of life, with Catholics and Protestants, hitherto parts of the same Western Christian community willing to send each other to the stake for heresy. The ensuing bloody internecine ideological conflicts within Western civilization over the succeeding centuries have no parallel in the histories of other non-Semitic Eurasian civilizations. It also gives the lie to any claim of universality for a particular Western cosmological belief, as each one has been contested—often with blood—by a countervailing belief within the same corpus of Western thought.

The Peace of Westphalia which brought a truce in Christianity's internecine wars of religion, also legitimized the nation-state, as the main actor on the international stage. The purpose of the current "political moralism" is to replace the nationally sovereign state by an emerging international moral order (see Minogue, 1995, ch. 13). This is an ancient Christian project as Oakeshott (1993) noted in his famous distinction between the state viewed as a civil or enterprise association. Oakeshott argues that the view of the state as a civil association goes back to ancient Greece. The state is seen as the custodian of laws which do not seek to impose any preferred pattern of ends (including abstractions such as the general [social] welfare, or fundamental rights), but which merely facilitate individuals to pursue their own ends. This view has been challenged by the rival conception of the state as an enterprise association—a view which has its roots in the Judeo–Christian tradition. The state is now seen as the manager of an enterprise seeking to use the law for its own substantive purposes, and in particular for the legislation of morality. The classical liberalism of Smith and Hume entails the former, while the major secular embodiment of society viewed as an enterprise association is socialism, with its moral aim of using the state to equalize people.

Oakeshott identifies three versions of the collectivist morality such an enterprise association has since sought to enforce. Since the truce declared in the 18th century in the European wars of religion, the major substantive purposes sought by states seen as enterprise associations are "nation-building" and "the promotion of some form of egalitarianism." These correspond to what Oakeshott calls the *productivist* and *distributivist* versions of the modern embodiments of the enterprise association, whose *religious* version was epitomized by Calvinist Geneva, and in our own times is provided by Khomeni's Iran. Each of these collective forms conjures up some notion of perfection, believed to be "the common good."

The origins of the current "political moralism," Minogue (1995) claims, lies in the broadened suffrage in 19th-century Europe, so that "welfare came to be as interesting to rulers as war had always been. . . . [They were both interesting] politically because they constituted a reason for exercising dazzling powers of government and administration" (p. 114). This is the distributivist enterprise association of Oakeshott. "The substance of political moralism is in the detailed moral attitudes it inculcates" (Minogue, 1995). But the morality is a specifically Western Christian offshoot, as I have tried to show, and "ethical trading" whose opposite is "social dumping" is only one of its many contemporary hydra-headed manifestations. But why should the rest of the world worship the Christian God, clothed in whatever secular clothes current fashion dictates?

Therein lie the seeds of the impending "clash of civilizations" hypothesized by Huntington (1993). But this maybe too apocalyptic. For the West's ethical crisis noted by Nietzsche has not ended. As MacIntyre (1990) has powerfully argued, the West's current cosmological beliefs, particularly in its most advanced outpost the United States, are incoherent.

The Western notion of self, he argues, has three contradictory elements. The *first*, derives from the Enlightenment and views it as being able to stand apart from the social influences which undoubtedly mold him or her, and allows individuals to mold themselves in accordance with their own true preferences. The *second* component of the Western self concerns the evaluation by others of oneself. Here the standards are increasingly those of acquisitive and competitive success, in a bureaucratized and individualist market economy. The *third* element of the Western self derives from its remaining religious and moral norms, and is open to various "invocations of values as various as those which inform the public rhetoric of politics on the one hand and the success of *Habits of the Heart* on the other" (MacIntyre, 1990, p. 492). This aspect of the self harks back to the Christian conception of the soul, and its transcendental salvation.

These three elements comprising the Western conception of self are not only mutually incompatible they are incommensurable, and lead to incoherence as there are no shared standards by which the inevitable conflicts between them can be resolved.

So rights-based claims, utility-based claims, contractarian claims, and claims based upon this or that ideal conception of the good will be advanced in different contexts, with relatively little discomfort at the incoherence involved. For unacknowledged incoherence is the hallmark of this contemporary developing American self, a self whose public voice oscillates between phases not merely of toleration, but admiration for ruthlessly self-serving behavior and phases of high moral dudgeon and indignation at exactly the same behavior. (MacIntyre, 1990, p. 492)

This incoherence explains the oscillations in the debates on social standards and why I will not be surprised in another 15 years—if I am still around—to write yet another paper on the theme. For given this incoherence and the clearly irrational nature of the demands for ethical trading—even within its own cosmology—the Rest will be right to reject this current attempt at moral imperialism.

There is a long-standing argument in development studies whether modernization requires Westernization. As the examples of Japan (see Waswo, 1996; Eisenstadt, 1996) and increasingly China and India show, the Rest can adopt the instrumental rationality underlying the market institutions and technological marvels underlying the "European Miracle" without giving up their souls. As the epigraph from Plato asserts, the most important concern of different cultures is how their constituents should live. This relates to both their material and cosmological beliefs. While the West has clearly established its superiority in the former sphere—of which free trade untrammeled by moral concerns is a cornerstone—there are grave doubts about the viability of its beliefs in the latter sphere. So I would expect the Rest to fiercely resist the pressures for legislating universal social standards. As these do not make much sense even within the West's own cosmology, perhaps part of its fractured self will call a halt to the "political moralism" of its other part, and avoid the "clash of civilizations," which is by no means inevitable and would be yet another disaster visited upon the world because of the culture-specific, proselytizing, universal, and egalitarian ethic of what remains, at heart, Western Christendom.

Bibliography

St. Augustine. [427] 1984. *The City of God*. London: Penguin Classics.

Becker, C.L. 1932. *The Heavenly City of the Eighteenth Century Philosophers*. New Haven: Yale University Press.

Bellah, R.N., R. Madsen, W.M. Sullivan, A. Swidler, and S.M. Tipton. 1986. *Habits of the Heart*. Perennial, NY: Harper and Row.

Berlin, I. [1958] 1967. "Two Concepts of Liberty." In: A. Quinton (ed.), *Political Philosophy*, pp. 141–152. Oxford: Oxford University Press.

Bork, R.H. 1996. *Slouching Towards Gomorrah: Modern Liberalism and American Decline*. New York: Harper Collins.

Bramwell, A. 1989. *Ecology in the 20th Century: A History*. New Haven: Yale University Press.

Brown, D.K., A.V. Deardoff, and R.M. Stern. 1996. "International Labour Standards and Trade: A Theoretical Analysis." In: J.N. Bhagwati and R.E. Hudec (eds.), *Fair Trade and Harmonization*. Volume 1, pp. 227–280. Cambridge, Mass.: MIT Press.

Claire, G. 1977. *Freedom of Association and Economic Development*. Geneva: ILO.

Corden, W.M. 1997. *Trade Policy and Economic Welfare*. Second Edition. Oxford: Clarendon Press.

Douglas, M., and A. Wildavsky. 1983. *Risk and Culture*. Berkeley: University of California Press.

Dumont, L. 1970. *Homo Hierarchicus*. London: Weidenfeld and Nicholson.

Dworkin, R. 1977. *Taking Rights Seriously*. London: Duckworth.

Edgren, G. 1979. "Fair Labour Standards and Trade Liberalisation." *International Labour Review* 118(Sept./Oct).

Eisenstadt, S.N. 1996. *Japanese Civilization: A Comparative View*. Chicago: Chicago University Press.

Gellner, E. 1993. *The Psychoanalytic Movement: The Cunning of Unreason*. Evanston: Northwestern University Press.

Goldsmith, J. 1994. *The Trap*. London: Macmillan.

Hart, H.L.A. [1955] 1967. "Are There Any Natural Rights?" In: A. Quinton (ed.), *Political Philosophy*, pp. 53–66. Oxford: Oxford University Press.

Hindley, B. 1994. "The Goldsmith Fallacy." Rochester Paper No. 3. London: Trade Policy Unit, Centre for Policy Studies.

Huntington, S.P. 1993. "The Clash of Civilizations." *Foreign Affairs* 72:3.

ILO (International Labor Organization). 1976. *The Impact of International Labour Conventions and Recommendations*. Geneva: ILO.

Kamenka, E. 1978. "Introduction." In: E. Kamenka and A.E. Tay (eds.), *Human Rights*, pp. 1–12. London: Edward Arnold.

Lal, D. [1981] 1994. *Resurrection of the Pauper-Labour Argument*. In: *Against Dirigisme*, pp. 159–183. San Francisco: ICS Press.

Lal, D. 1995. "Eco-Fundamentalism." *International Affairs* 71(July).

Lal, D. 1998. *Unintended Consequences: The Impact of Factor Endowments, Culture and Politics on Long Run Economic Performance*. Cambridge, Mass.: MIT Press.

Levinson, A. 1996. "Environmental Regulations and Industry Location: International and Domestic Evidence." In: J.N. Bhagwati and R.E. Hudec (eds.), *Fair Trade and Harmonization*. Volume 1, pp. 329–356. Cambridge, Mass.: MIT Press.

MacIntyre, A. 1990. "Individual and Social Morality in Japan and the United States: Rival Conceptions of the Self." *Philosophy East and West* 40(4):489–497.

Maslow, A. 1970. *Motivation and Personality*. Second Edition. New York: Harper and Row.

McClelland, J.S. 1996. *A History of Western Political Thought*. London: Routledge.

Minogue, K. 1978. "Natural Rights, Ideology and the Game of Life." In: E. Kamenka and A.E. Tay (eds.), *Human Rights*, pp. 13–35. London: Edward Arnold.

Minogue, K. 1979. "The History of the Idea of Human Rights." In: W. Laquer and R. Rubin (eds.), *The Human Rights Reader*, pp. 3–17. New York: New American Library.

Minogue, K. 1995. *Politics*. Oxford: Oxford University Press.

Nietzsche, F. [1881] 1982. *Daybreak: Thoughts on the Prejudices of Morality*. Cambridge: Cambridge University Press.

Nozick, R. 1974. *Anarchy, State and Utopia*. Oxford: Basil Blackwell.

Oakeshott, M. 1993. *Morality and Politics in Modern Europe*. New Haven: Yale University Press.

Plato. 1973. "The Republic." In: *The Collected Dialogues of Plato*. Princeton: Princeton University Press.

Sen, A.K., and B. Williams. 1982. *Utilitarianism and Beyond*. Cambridge: Cambridge University Press.

Southern, R.W. 1970. *Western Society and the Church in the Middle Ages*. London: Penguin.

Streeten, P. 1981. *Development Perspectives.* London: Macmillan.

Valticos, N. 1969. "Fifty Years of Standard-Setting Activities by the International Labour Organization." *International Labour Review* 100(Sept.):201–237.

Waswo, A. 1996. *Modern Japanese Society: 1868–1994.* Oxford: Oxford University Press.

Webster, R. 1995. *Why Freud Was Wrong.* London: Harper Collins.

White, A.R. 1984. *Rights.* Oxford: Clarendon Press.

Wilson, J.D. 1996. "Capital Mobility and Environmental Standards: Is There a Theoretical Basis for a Race to the Bottom?" In: J.N. Bhagwati and R.E. Hudec (eds.), *Fair Trade and Harmonization.* Volume 1, pp. 393–427. Cambridge, Mass.: MIT Press.

About the Authors

DAVID M. ANDERSON teaches in the Department of Philosophy and at the Graduate School of Political Management, both of The George Washington University. He is also a Senior Research Associate at the Institute for Communitarian Policy Studies. He received a M.B.A. from George Washington University (Philosophy) and a Ph.D. from the University of Michigan (Philosophy). Professor Anderson has published articles on topics concerning Rawlsian liberalism, feminism, and communitarianism. He has also taught at the University of Cincinnati, the College of Charleston, and Trident Technical College.

CHONIRA E. ATURUPANE is a Ph.D. candidate in Economics at Stanford University. She received her undergraduate degree from Smith College (Economics) and her master's from Stanford University (Economics).

BRUCE L. BENSON is DeVoe Moore Professor and Distinguished Research Professor in Economics at Florida State University, attended the University of Montana, where he earned a B.A. (Economics) and M.A. (Economics) before doing additional graduate studies at Texas A&M University and earning a Ph.D. (Economics). Professor Benson taught at Pennsylvania State University and Montana State University before joining the faculty at Florida State University in 1985. He is the author of more than 120 scholarly articles on spatial price theory, public sector decision-making, crime and illicit drug policy, and comparative legal institutions. His most recent books are *To Serve and Protect: Privatization and Community in Criminal Justice* (1998), *The Economic Anatomy of a Drug War: Criminal Justice in the Commons* (coauthored with David W. Rasmussen, 1994), and *The Enterprise of Law: Justice Without the State* (1990).

PETER J. BOETTKE is Associate Professor of Economics and Finance, School of Business, Manhattan College, Riverdale, New York. Boettke has held faculty positions at New York University (1990–97) and Oakland University (1988–90), and visiting professorships at George Mason University, and Central European University. He has been a National Fellow at the Hoover Institution on War, Revolution and Peace at Stanford University (1992/93), and has been a visiting scholar at the Academy of Sciences in Moscow. He is the author of *The Political Economy of Soviet Socialism: The Formative Years, 1918–1928* (1990), and *Why Perestroika Failed: The Politics and Economics of Socialist Transformation* (1993). He is also the editor of *The Collapse of Development Planning* (1994) and *The Elgar Companion to Austrian Economics* (1994).

DANIEL KIWIT received his *Diplom* in Economics from the University of Freiburg in 1993. Since 1993, Kiwit has been a research fellow at the Institutional Economics Unit at the Max-Planck-Institute for Research into Economic Systems in Jena, Germany.

ANNE O. KRUEGER is the Herald L. and Caroline L. Ritch Professor of Humanities and Sciences, Director of the Center for Research on Economic Development and Policy Reform, and a Senior Fellow at the Hoover Institution at Stanford University. Prior to this, she was Arts and Sciences Professor of Economics at Duke University, Vice President of the Economics and Research Division at the World Bank, and earlier, Professor of Economics at the University of Minnesota. Professor Krueger is also immediate Past President of the American Economic Association. She specializes in international economics and economic development. Her recent books include *Trade Policies and Developing Nations* (1995), *American Trade Policy: A Tragedy in the Making* (1995), *The Political Economy of Policy Reform in Developing Countries* (1993), *Economics Policies at Cross-Purposes: The United States and Developing Countries* (1993), *Economic Policy Reform in Developing Countries* (1992), *and Swimming Against the Tide: Turkish Trade Reform in the 1980s* (coauthored with Okan H. Aktan, 1992).

DEEPAK LAL is James S. Coleman Professor of International Development Studies at the University of California, Los Angeles, and Professor Emeritus of Political Economy at University College London.

He has advised many governments and international agencies, and has published widely on problems of economic development. His books include *The Poverty of Development Economics; The Repressed Economy; The Political Economy of Poverty, Equity, and Growth* (coauthored with H. Myint), and most recently his Ohlin lectures, *Unintended Consequences* (1998).

GARY B. MADISON is Emeritus Professor of Philosophy at McMaster University, Canada, and has taught at the Université de Paris and the University of Toronto (Graduate Faculty). He has edited three collections of philosophical essays and is the author of several books on political theory and contemporary European philosophy, including *The Hermeneutics of Postmodernity: Figures and Themes* (1989) and *The Political Economy of Civil Society and Human Rights* (1998). He has written extensively on issues relating to economic methodology, globalization, and civil society, and is a founding member and Past President of The Canadian Society for Hermeneutics and Postmodern Thought.

DENNIS C. MUELLER is Professor of Economics at the University of Vienna. His main research interests are in public choice and industrial economics. He is the author of many articles and several books; among them being *Public Choice II* (1989), *Profits in the Long Run* (1986), and *Constitutional Democracy* (1996). Professor Mueller is a Past President of the Public Choice Society, the Southern Economic Association, the Industrial Organization Society and the European Association for Research in Industrial Economics.

MARK V. PAULY currently holds the positions of the Vice Dean of the Wharton Doctoral Programs, Bendheim Professor, and Chair of the Department of Health Care Systems. He is Professor of Health Care Systems, Insurance and Risk Management, and Public Policy and Management at the Wharton School, and Professor of Economics at the School of Arts and Sciences at the University of Pennsylvania. Prior to joining Pennsylvania's faculty, he was a visiting research fellow at the International Institute of Management in Berlin, Germany, and Professor of Economics at Northwestern University. He received his Ph.D. in Economics from the University of Virginia in 1967. He served as Executive Director of the Leonard Davis Institute of Health Economics (LDI) from 1984–1989 and 1989–1995 as LDI's Director of Research. Professor Pauly has made significant contributions to the fields of medical economics and health incurance. Among his books are *Health Benefits at Work: An Economic and Political Analysis of Employment-Related Health Insurance* (1997), *Doctors and Their Workshops* (1980), and *Medical Care at Public Expense* (1971).

ALAN PEACOCK graduated from the University of St. Andrews in 1947, becoming, successively, Reader in Public Finance at the London School of Economics (1951–1956), Professor of Economics at the Universities of Edinburgh (1956–1962); York (1962–1978, where he founded the Economics Department); Buckingham (1978–1984); Heriot-Watt (1984 to date); Vice-Chancellor (President) of Britain's only private university, Buckingham (1980–84); and Chief Economic Adviser, U.K. Departments of Industry and Trade (1973–1976). He has served on various U.K. Government and international commissions and was knighted for public service in 1987. He has published more than 30 books and over 200 professional articles mainly concerning the economics of public policy. He is an Honorary Fellow of the London School of Economics, Honorary President of the International Institute of Public Finance, and a Fellow of the British Academy. During his "official" retirement, he became joint founder and first Executive Director of The David Hume Institute, Edinburgh (1985–1990), and remains a Trustee and Economic Consultant to that Institute. His present research interests include the economics of government regulation and, unusually, the economics of the creative and performing arts.

STEFAN VOIGT received his *Diplom* in Economics from the University of Freiburg in 1988 and his doctorate at the same university in 1992. He was a research assistant at the University of Mannheim in 1989/90 and the University of Freiburg from 1990 to 1994. Since 1994, Dr. Voigt has been a research fellow at the Institutional Economics Unit at the Max-Planck-Institute for Research into Economic Systems in Jena, Germany. His research interests are: constitutional economics, especially the possibility of positive constitutional economics. His books are: *Die Welthandelsordnung zwischen Konflikt und Stabilität: Konfliktpotentiale und Konfliktlösungsmechanismen* (1992), *Europa reformieren: Ökonomen und Juristen zur zukünftigen Verfaßtheit Europas* (edited together with Manfred Streit, 1996), and *Explaining Constitu-*

tional Change: Towards a Positive Economic Theory of Constitutions (in print).

EDWIN G. WEST received his Ph.D. in Economics from the University of London. Now Professor Emeritus at Carleton University, Ottawa, Canada, he is the author of over a dozen books and approximately one hundred articles in scholarly journals. His book *Education and the State* was first published in 1965 and the latest (3rd) edition was published in 1994. Professor West is also author of *Adam Smith: The Man and His Works* (1977), and of *Education and the Industrial Revolution* (1975). His main areas of interest include public finance, the economics of education, public choice, and the history of economic thought. Among his latest writings are *Adam Smith and Modern Economics: From Market Behaviour to Public Choice* (1990) and *Adam Smith into the Twenty-First Century* (1996).

Springer
and the
environment

At Springer we firmly believe that an international science publisher has a special obligation to the environment, and our corporate policies consistently reflect this conviction.
We also expect our business partners – paper mills, printers, packaging manufacturers, etc. – to commit themselves to using materials and production processes that do not harm the environment. The paper in this book is made from low- or no-chlorine pulp and is acid free, in conformance with international standards for paper permanency.

 Springer